SEVEN DAYS OF FREEDOM

NOEL BARBER

SEVEN DAYS OF FREEDOM

FREEDOM

The Hungarian Uprising 1956

STEIN AND DAY/*Publishers*/New York

First published in the United States of America in 1974
Copyright © 1974 by Noel Barber
Library of Congress Catalog Card No. 74–78536
All rights reserved
Printed in the United States of America
Stein and Day/*Publishers*/Scarborough House,
Briarcliff Manor, N. Y. 10510
ISBN 0–8128–1730–3

FOR
Lisa and Jack Anderson
WITH LOVE

Contents

Appendices

Illustrations

Thanks are due to Associated Press for 1*a*, 1*b*, 1*c*, 5*a*, 8. The remainder were either taken by the author or are in his possession.

Maps

Preface

So many people in so many countries helped me with the research for this book that it seems invidious to name only a few, and I must beg the forgiveness of those I have omitted, particularly the scores of men and women who contributed perhaps one fleeting memory, disposed of in a single paragraph, yet none the less extremely important in the task of covering the bare bones of my story with flesh and blood.

For the 'bones' I searched far and wide, starting with the files of the United Nations, and I owe a great debt to George Ivan Smith of the U.N. in London and William C. Powell in New York, who provided me with fascinating unpublished documents, rivalling those of Columbia University, whose two-year research project on the uprising has resulted in a staggering amount of information freely made available to writers.

I also owe a great debt to Leo Cherne, the dynamic Executive Director of the Research Institute of America Inc. (who was in Budapest during the revolution) for his valued help in New York, and to the Hon. John Richardson, jr, Assistant Secretary of State, for his help when I visited him in Washington. John Dunning, assistant to the President of Radio Free Europe, helped me in New York to put the controversial role of this organisation into proper perspective. The Council on Foreign Relations Inc. in New York made available to me its vast library of clippings. I was also helped by the International Association for Cultural Freedom in Paris.

Among the Hungarians to whom I owe a great debt I must mention Tibor Meray, a close friend of Nagy's, with whom I spent many delightful hours in Paris, and who was unsparing with his help; Anna Kethly, the veteran Socialist whom I visited in Brussels; Jozsef Kovago, the Mayor of Budapest during the uprising, who now lives in America, and who allowed me to take to England documents very precious to him; and finally Bela Szasz, who lives in London, and whose advice I have sought time and again.

Sir Leslie Fry, who was British Minister in Budapest in 1956 and has had a long and distinguished career in the Foreign Office, was most helpful when I was in Budapest, and my thanks also go to 'Ham' Whyte of the Foreign Office, who is currently stationed in America, but was in Vienna during the uprising, where he was partly concerned with helping refugees.

Two ladies whose help I badly needed proved rather elusive. Joan Fish, the splendid British Consul in Budapest in 1956, at first seemed untraceable, but I remembered that she was of Cornish origin. By telephoning everyone in Cornwall called Fish it was finally possible to speak to her mother, who told me that her daughter was married to an American and living near Nashville, Tennessee, where she invited me to stay with her.

Dora Scarlett, the British Communist who was in Budapest in 1956, also seemed to have vanished without trace. I advertised for her whereabouts in the *Daily Telegraph*, and received several letters. The first I opened was from Dame Rebecca West, and so I traced Dora to south-east India where she now runs, with very little money, a desperately needed clinic.

I would like to take this opportunity to thank the many publishers who have given me permission to quote extracts from books concerned with the revolution, and finally to two old friends – Donald Dinsley for his indefatigable help in research, and George Greenfield, who first suggested that I write this book.

London, 1974   N.B.

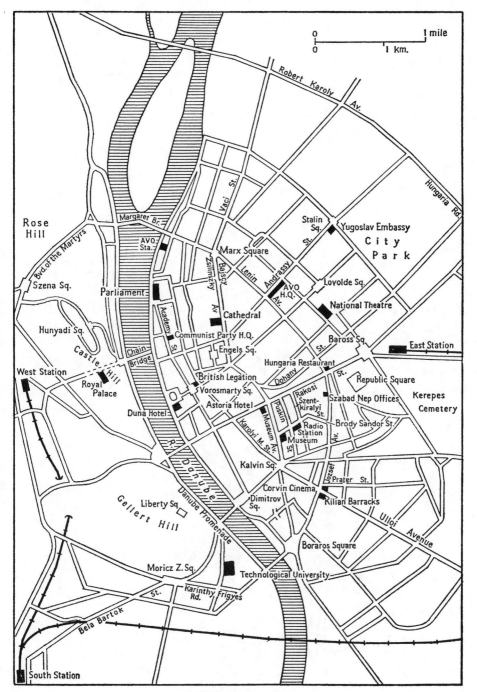

Budapest, 1956
Many street-names have changed

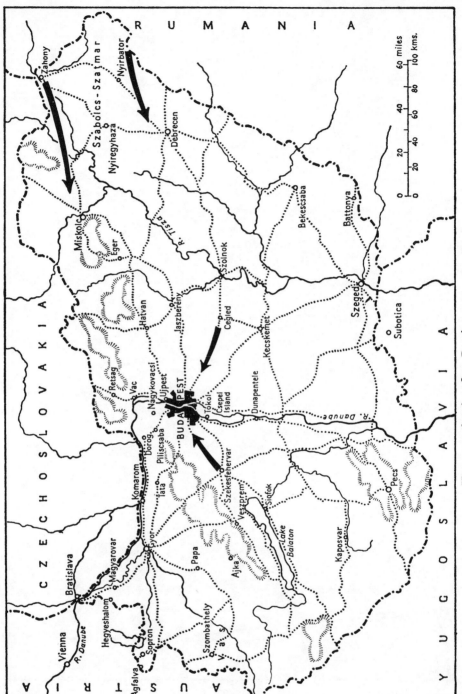

Hungary, showing first Russian troop-movements

'If ten or so Hungarian writers had been shot at the right moment, the revolution would never have occurred.'
NIKITA KHRUSHCHEV

PART I

The Road to Freedom

I

The Opening Shots

Tuesday, 23 October 1956

It was dark and it was cold. Above the chanting teenagers the old-fashioned gas lamps on their ornate iron poles cast pools of light on the upturned faces, small islands in a sea of darkness.

The crowd filled the cobbled street, focusing on the old wooden main gates of the baroque radio station, protecting the wide stone portico over the entrance. Pushing, shouting, cursing, a group of youngsters backed an old car time after time against the gates, but though they creaked and the wood splintered the gates held. From one corner another group hurled bricks and stones against the lighted first-floor windows, behind which 500 men and women waited on the rooftops. Above the secret police were hiding, armed with guns, hoses and tear gas.

There was a warning volley of blanks from an automatic rifle, and for a moment the crowd, which had assembled without thought of violence, was silenced. Then, excited perhaps by the flashes of gunfire, a policeman on the roof hurled a canister of tear gas into the crowd.

It hit a teenager, exploding in his face. Anna Gabor, a twenty-two-year-old secretary standing nearby, remembered later, 'One minute there was a face, the next minute none. But the most terrible thing was the crowd was so dense that the body without a head remained standing for what seemed like minutes.'

That was the moment – 8.30 on the evening of Tuesday, 23 October – when a day of peaceful demonstrations erupted into a bloody, hopeless fight for freedom that would echo round the world: the Hungarian revolution of 1956.

For perhaps a minute the crowd teetered on the edge of panic.

There were many women present, and as more shots rang out from the rooftops and the first bodies fell twisted into grotesque attitudes some of the women tried to run. 'None of us could believe our eyes,' Anna Gabor recalls. 'We couldn't connect the dead bodies with the rifle shots.'

The shrieks of fear gave way to a sullen muttering against the secret police until the street was alive with one cry, 'Death to the Avo!'[1] The crowd could just make out the Avos on the rooftops or leaning out of upper windows, guns pointed to the street, safe against an unarmed crowd that could only hurl bricks in impotent rage. 'I will always remember one split second,' Anna continues. 'The sight of two Avos at a window pointing downwards and laughing.'

Then, rammed again and again by the car, the ancient wooden doors finally fell. George Kovacs, a radio reporter, was inside a glass conservatory at the far end of the courtyard. Normally used as a waiting-room for distinguished broadcasters, it was affectionately known to the radio staff as 'the pagoda', and Kovacs suddenly saw 'a huge tide of human beings clamber over the smashed doors. I ran through the back door of the pagoda into the studios behind.' The Avo, who had been in a state of readiness for several hours, attacked with fixed bayonets in their traditional wedge-shaped formation. It was still only 8.45. The moment was later described laconically in the United Nations Special Report on Hungary: 'AVH men rushed from the entrance and began shooting in all directions.'

The more courageous in the crowd ran towards the gates to drag away the dead and succour the wounded. Suddenly the crack of bullets was replaced by the sound of ambulance bells. Bearing Red Cross markings, two white vehicles stopped at the corner of Museum Avenue, and the crowd, still numbed by shock, parted to allow them into the street, to approach the doors and collect the wounded.

---

[1] Avo was the tagline for the merciless Hungarian secret police. It was at first an arm of the state police. In 1946 it was detached, placed under the Ministry of the Interior, and called the Allamvedelmi Osztaly, or Avo. In 1949 it became a special department answerable only to the top leaders, under the name of Allamvedelmi Hivatal, or AVH. But the old name still stuck. The AVH were distinguishable by the blue lapels on their uniforms.

The first ambulance vanished through the portico. The second swerved into one of the broken doors. White-clad figures scrambled out – and started to unload sub-machine-guns and cases of ammunition. Anna Gabor caught a glimpse of Avo uniform trousers beneath a white coat. The crowd surged towards them and followed them into the courtyard. The Avos inside opened fire again and two bodies fell near an ambulance. The white-clad figures managed to escape into the building. The students retreated, but not before they had grabbed the sub-machine-guns which the Avos had dropped in their flight.

So the first arms of the Hungarian revolution passed into the hands of the freedom fighters. Soon they were to have more. A detachment from a mechanised army division arrived in three trucks from its headquarters in Piliscsaba, west of Budapest. It moved into position inside the museum gardens, but in no time the men were fraternising with the insurgents. They were followed by two Hungarian armoured cars which clattered to a halt near the main gates. An old man in a cloth cap jumped on one armoured car, shouting the first lines of a famous Hungarian poem, 'Shoot not, my son, for I shall also be in the crowd.' The soldiers hesitated, looked at their officer, who shrugged, then the troops jumped off and joined the crowd. One officer shouted through a hand megaphone, 'We will never fire on Hungarians!'

He had barely finished speaking when there was a murderous burst of fire from the building. The officer was killed instantly, together with several members of the crowd.

The radio station, to which the vast crowd now laid siege, was no ordinary building. Its main entrance lay in the narrow, cobbled Brody Sandor Street; its tall buildings made it seem even narrower. The station filled an entire block, running back from Brody Sandor Street between two parallel roads, Puskin and Szentkiralyi streets, with a garage entrance in Krudy Street at the rear, and the National Museum, with its gardens, on the west side. Housing every department from studios to technical offices, it was an overcrowded, antiquated jumble of buildings which had mushroomed round the central office, a rococo four-storey house of grey stone, with its arched portico over the massive oak front gates. Cherubs smiled benignly from the top of each supporting column and the roof of the portico formed a narrow balcony hedged by a stone balustrade, backed by french windows leading to first-floor offices.

The action against the radio station had begun without thought of bloodshed. Spurred on by discontented writers, encouraged by Gomulka's victory in Poland on 19 October, 5000 students meeting at the Technological University during the night had drafted a 16-point memorandum demanding reforms.[1] They asked the Communist-controlled Radio Budapest to broadcast it. When their demands were refused, thousands of demonstrators descended on Brody Sandor Street, shouting and singing patriotic songs. There was no organised plan. People at one end of the street hardly knew what those at the other were doing – until the firing started.

Now five Avos sprinted on to the balcony dragging fire hoses which they trained on the crowd, and Major-General Hegyi, the elderly, grey-haired chief of the Hungarian Army's training section, arrived in a Zis car, to try to restore order. He was allowed through the gates and appeared on the portico balcony. Hegyi was no diehard Stalinist and the crowd were prepared to give him a hearing. Using a megaphone, he appealed, 'Please disperse and return to your homes.'

For a moment he had the sympathy of the crowd, horrified by the slaughter. But then, unwisely, Hegyi turned to officers near him and announced that he would take command, and immediately ordered the officers to deploy their men to break up the crowd. Lieutenant-Colonel Solymosy, commanding officer of the 1st Motorised Regiment, seized the megaphone and shouted, 'I reserve for myself the right to command.' His soldiers cheered him, scrambled from their vehicles and joined the civilians, handing out the few weapons they could spare. Other officers refused to order their men to attack, and Hegyi was forced to retreat into the radio building, from where he was spirited out by way of the garage at the rear. From there the old soldier set off on foot to report to the Communist Party headquarters.

Inside the studios George Kovacs, following standard orders for an emergency, switched on a programme of light music. Then he telephoned a friend. 'I'm sorry I won't be able to keep our appointment,' he said.

[1] For the text of the memorandum, see Appendix 1.

'Why not?' asked the friend.

'Because', said Kovacs dramatically, 'the revolution has started.'

'What the hell are you talking about?' asked the friend, who lived only fifteen miles outside Budapest.

The insurgents now needed more weapons quickly. One of the students went to Csepel, the big industrial complex on an island south of Budapest, to tell the workers what had happened. Another, Lazlo Beke of the Technological University, gathered together nearly fifty of his fellow students and led them to the police headquarters in Vigyazo Ferenc Street, two miles away.

Beke had a particular reason for hating the Avo. A newly married man of twenty-four, he was studying at the Technological University after finishing his military service. He and his wife Eva, who was expecting a baby, were already in disgrace for visiting the British Legation in Liberty Square to learn a smattering of English, and watch British films. The Avo stopped them as they were leaving the Legation one night. Two days later the head of the university told them that their scholarship money had been stopped. Then their identity cards were confiscated; without them it was impossible to get work.

Seeing 'mute approval' on the faces of the guards at police headquarters, Beke made for the command room, where he demanded, 'In the name of the Students' Revolutionary Council, surrender your arms!' He was, as he later remembered, 'astonished at my own loud tones'. The officer in charge had about two hundred policemen in the building and the youngsters were unarmed. 'My heart pounded as I gazed at him, then at my student friends around me. We were defenceless. The next move was up to him.'

The police officer stepped up to the youngsters and saluted.

'All right, boys,' he said, and Beke was so overwhelmed that he rushed up and embraced him.

Not far from the radio station, a tussle of a different nature – between man and metal – was taking place in Stalin Square, a large open space dominated by a fifty-foot bronze statue of the one-time Soviet leader that dwarfed even the trees of the nearby City Park. Thousands of people had marched towards the hated

emblem, including Thomas Szabo, a boy of fifteen, his friend
Feri and two girl friends, all vaguely looking for adventure. They
were crossing Margaret Bridge when Szabo heard someone cry,
'Let's break up the Stalin Statue!'

Thomas Szabo, tall, dark-haired with a cheerful boyish grin,
had joined the revolution almost by chance, for the Szabo family
had only just been allowed to return to Budapest after three
years of exile in the country. Mr Szabo, a singer on the radio,
never discovered the reason for the exile. To Thomas, parted
from his schoolfriends, it had been misery, and the entire family
'had been filled with an intense longing for Budapest with its
yellow trams, for the thick traffic of the capital and its great
dusty buildings'.

Earlier in the day Thomas had been walking down Museum
Avenue with his father when a girl thrust a leaflet into his father's
hands. Thomas asked to see it, and read for the first time about
the student demands. Without hesitation he decided to join the
movement. It was his mother's birthday the following day, and
telling his father that he wanted to buy her some flowers he set
off. He never did buy the flowers. Instead he made his way to
join his friends.

It was not, he discovered, easy to reach Stalin Square. When
he did it was full, but all attempts to dislodge the statue had
failed. Men had tied ropes to trucks and tried to pull it down,
but each time the ropes snapped. The trucks were still there, but
as Thomas watched suddenly the crowd was silent. A young man
came forward with a blowtorch and, training it on the limbs of
the giant, effectively managed to crack the left leg.'

Every eye, it seemed to Thomas, was fixed on the harsh, hissing
blue flame. Then some truck drivers managed to find steel cables,
and tied them round Stalin's neck. The cables tautened, took the
strain as the truck slowly moved, and held. With a mighty crash
the bronze head fell on the pink marble pedestal of the
statue.

A youngster ran forward, fished in his pocket for something,
set light to it, and tossed it through the neck into the hollow head.
Others followed him. Thomas asked a workman what they were
burning. The man took a small booklet from his pocket. 'That's

what they're burning,' he said, throwing his Party card into the flames.

Finally the headless statue was toppled from its pink pedestal and only the boots remained. Men and women tried to cut off pieces of the statute as souvenirs. The head of the dictator – emblem of all the hatred bottled up for years – was loaded on a truck and dumped near Parliament Square. A youngster found a street sign in a nearby road that was under repair, and tied it round the head.

It read, 'Dead End'.

News travels fast in a crisis and half Budapest was suddenly chanting, 'To the radio station!' Thomas Szabo and his friend Feri were burning their student cards at about 9.30 p.m. when a truck filled with students came to a stop near them and someone shouted, 'Everybody to the radio station. The secret police are killing defenceless people.'

As he clambered aboard, Szabo shouted to Feri to look after the girls, but as Feri jumped on the truck he retorted that they could look after themselves.

Not far from them a British woman stood in the midst of a vast crowd in Parliament Square. Dora Scarlett was a staunch member of the British Communist Party who had arrived in Budapest some years previously to work in the English section of the Hungarian state radio. Short, stocky and prematurely white-haired, she was in her forties and immensely capable. As soon as she heard the rumour, she phoned the radio station from a side street, and was told, 'The main entrance is being besieged.' As she hurried past Vorosmarty Square she heard the sound of firing – 'a brief, sharp volley'. Walking down Vaci Street, she heard a second volley, and by the time she reached Museum Avenue she was confronted with truckloads of youngsters. At the corner of Brody Sandor Street an overturned van was burning fiercely. Someone told her that it was an Avo van. Two more burning vans greeted her in the street itself as she forced her way through the squelching mud caused by the hoses, her eyes smarting from the last wisps of tear gas.

Several trucks packed with Hungarian regular troops were parked at the corner, where the Museum Gardens were railed off.

There was no tension between them and the youngsters who laughed and joked with them. By the main doors Dora Scarlett saw the two Hungarian armoured cars that had arrived earlier. 'On one of them civilians had climbed and were sitting there, and on the other stood a soldier with a tommy gun.' Over the portico she could see several young men talking into microphones, but the din was so great she could not make out the words. In front of her several civilians and regular troops – but no Avos – had linked arms to keep back the crowds who were demanding to know if there were still any secret police in the building.

In fact there were. As the first freedom fighters broke in, some members of the radio staff fled to the back of the building, many to escape through the garage, but Miss Valeria Benke, the director of the radio, and senior officers had remained. Only when bricks were hurled through Miss Benke's window, did she and her colleagues move to a room at the back. But soon the entire first floor was under siege. About forty members of the staff fled to the comparative safety of the women's washroom. All but two were women and none knew of a rumour that the Avos had killed sixteen members of a student delegation. The insurgents were combing the building for Avo men.

Suddenly three Avos shattered the lock of the cloakroom door with a burst of machine-gun fire, injuring four of the women; then the Avos, evidently frightened, ran into their midst. They demanded from the screaming women clothes to help them escape; one brandished a machine gun threateningly. The two men working for the radio started taking off their trousers and shirts, while two Avos hurriedly undressed. The third signalled to a woman to take off her dress and long overcoat, and was putting them over his tunic when four tousle-headed, grimy youngsters with tommy-guns burst through the door.

According to Dora's flat-mate, who was in the cloakroom, the boys searched everyone for weapons, then ordered the Avo men to remain. Dora heard later that they were executed.

It was Hungary's first manifestation of freedom after eleven years of oppressive Communist rule.

Soon more insurgents were gathering arms. Thomas Szabo and Feri went with a section of the crowd to a barracks in Szentkiralyi

Street, only to find the gates securely locked. Someone shouted 'Break them down!' Several boys started pushing with their shoulders when 'a harsh voice' from an upstairs window shouted, 'If you try to break down the door I'll fire on you.' As Szabo and the others hesitated, 'the ground floor windows were flung open and soldiers began to pass guns out to us through the bars.'

Thomas received a tommy-gun which he hugged close to his chest. 'I had never had an object like this in my hands before, and I hadn't any idea how it worked.' Szabo noticed that 'Feri was in the same boat. He was holding his gun fearfully as if he was expecting it to go off.'

A man with a scar on his face led them back to a building opposite the radio station and asked them, 'Is there anyone here who doesn't know how to use these firearms?' A dozen hands shot up, and Scarface gave them their first lesson in the use of automatic weapons.

Szabo and Feri were among the first to enter the radio building, where they found the studios wrecked, the furniture smashed and the floors littered with paper. But this was only part of the headquarters, which honeycombed its way into adjacent buildings, some still in the hands of the Avo reinforcements who had entered through the garage. Another contingent of Avos was firing from two workmen's huts on a building-site nearby. Thus the crowd was caught in a crossfire.

Not all the Avos opened fire, according to George Urban, author of *The Nineteen Days*. When an officer ordered his men to fire into the crowd and they refused, 'he mowed down his own men. The officer was seized and beaten to death by the insurgents.'

In a last desperate effort to prevent more bloodshed, four hundred men of a special shock detachment of the civil police were rushed in trucks from their barracks in Mosonyi Street. For years they had been kept in reserve for precisely this kind of emergency. But the major in charge sized up the situation immediately and before a shot was fired called to the insurgents through a loud hailer that his men would retire from the area if they were allowed to do so unmolested. They marched away to the cheers of the crowd.

The uprising was now spreading over large areas of the city.

Students ran to a barracks in Hungaria Road where arms were passed to them over the wall; trucks sped to the offices of the Union Gas Carbide Company, which made arms, and received more supplies. Others went again to Csepel Island.

By the time Dora Scarlett left the radio station and walked down the shop-lined Rakosi Street insurgents were attacking the Party newspaper *Szabad Nep* which had its offices just behind the National Theatre. The flames of two blazing cars lit the street so Dora Scarlett could plainly see the newspaper staff at the windows, 'throwing down leaflets hurriedly printed to affirm their solidarity with the insurgents'. Newspapermen placed two pictures of national heroes in a large first-floor window. Between them they draped the Hungarian tricolour. From another window men dropped portraits of Stalin and Marxist text-books which were hurled into the blazing cars.

Here she heard that Csepel had come out on strike – a move which would affect the whole country, for Csepel was a gigantic industrial complex, based on the thirty-mile-long island where the Danube divided into two branches. In the past Csepel Island had contained little more than a lazy, peaceful village, but at the turn of the century the Csepel Iron and Steel Works had been founded there. The Communists had transformed the island (of which only the northern tip was part of the city of Budapest) into a forest of chimneys. Thirty thousand people worked there; the strike would bring the whole country to a standstill.

Revolutions rarely follow a pattern. The Hungarians in 1956 had no centralised authority, no headquarters, no spokesmen in the way the Continental Congress was the spokesmen for the 'rebels' in the American Revolution, or the Duma in the Russian Revolution of 1917. Nor was the revolution planned, in the way that Lenin planned his 1917 coup or Franco his 1936 military revolt.

Neither was the revolution sparked off by discontented workers, for those who had lost everything were too demoralised to rise against the government. As with the slaves throughout the ages, their entire life was bound up in the day-to-day struggle to survive.

The first to rebel – the writers – were for the most part

privileged Communists, well paid, but suffering from frustration and at times guilt for having in some measure aided the Stalinist regime. The writers, being the most articulate, had only been putting into words the inchoate thoughts and aspirations of every patriotic Hungarian, whose dream was expressed in one word: freedom. Then they were joined by another privileged class – the students, who were infuriated by the brutality of the secret police, the forced regimentation and the need for unquestioning obedience to Stalinism. All that was required to urge them into action was a spark – this was supplied by the Polish rising against the Soviet Union in mid-October.

At first, all the students and writers asked was the right to broadcast their manifesto. Had this been given them the revolution might never have happened. The will of one woman, however, had barred their way earlier in the evening.

The director of Radio Budapest, Miss Valeria Benke, was watching the crowds through the net curtains of her first-floor office before the shooting started. A woman in her forties, plainly dressed with straight, dark, 'no nonsense' hair and spurning all cosmetics, she was an ex-Minister of Education and a member of the Central Committee. Her office was handsomely furnished with an antique desk and, on the wall above, the large framed 'standard issue' photographs of Lenin and Stalin that graced every important functionary's office in Hungary. The huge room, once the salon of a beautiful flat, was, by the arrangement of the furniture, divided into two sections, the second part having a long conference table complete with blotting-pads, paper and pencils, and surrounded by about two dozen chairs.

The room was crowded. George Kovacs, who had worked for five years in one of the overseas sections, and who had never before ventured into Benke's office, followed the stream of people flocking to see the director. As he entered, the crowd outside shouted, 'The radio belongs to the people!' Kovacs heard Miss Benke sneer to those near her, 'But *they* are not the people'. Angrily Kovacs, who remembers Benke 'not as a woman, but as a statue representing the Party', muttered, 'Then who are the people? Benke with her large villa and her Zis car?'

Like a flash an Avo man was at his side demanding to know what he had said. Fortunately for Kovacs, Miss Benke shouted for silence at that moment. The menace of the crowd had increased so much that she finally agreed to receive a delegation of twenty-five people. But when Kovacs offered to go down, open the doors, and escort the delegation through the portico and up the stairs, Benke was horrified.

'You must be a fool,' she told him. 'Once you open those doors the whole street will come in.'

Finally Kovacs walked on to the balcony, but as the net curtains were drawn back and he emerged through the tall, old-fashioned french windows he was greeted with catcalls and jeers. For several minutes he could not make himself heard. Miss Benke, he announced, would receive a delegation. But when he had to admit that there was no way in the jeers started again.

The students lost no time. Without much difficulty they clambered on to the roofs of radio cars in the streets; willing hands hoisted them up the outside walls, where they could clutch cherubs or griffins until they reached the balcony. Miraculously no one was hurt, and finally a dishevelled group of youngsters assembled on the balcony, dusting their trousers, straightening their hair. The window leading into Miss Benke's office was open and they trooped in, with, as Kovacs remembers, 'a quaint mixture of bravado and apprehension, not unlike schoolboys confronting their headmaster'.[1]

Seated at the head of the long table, Miss Benke surveyed the group and asked coldly, 'Well, what do you want with the radio?'

Inevitably the delegation, drawn from so many different groups, fidgeted until one boy blurted out, 'We want the radio to belong to the people,' adding aggressively, 'and what's more, we refuse to leave here until we obtain satisfaction.'

Sarcastically Valeria Benke asked him what he meant by the phrase 'belong to the people'. How could the people run it? Where were the technicians? Where would they find the announcers? Scornfully she told him not to be a fool. The radio was for experts, not schoolboys.

At this point Miss Benke left the conference table to telephone from her desk. She must have been afraid that the crowd would burst in, for Kovacs heard her order the manager of the main

[1] An almost complete record of this meeting was published in *Nepszabadsag* in January 1957.

transmitting station at Lakihegy, ten miles or so outside Budapest, 'If you hear any unusual voices or programmes, cut off all
transmissions.' She returned to the table angrily and told the
deputation to adjourn for the moment.

Significantly, none of the delegation was allowed to leave.
After an hour, Lazlo Beke 'began to worry about our friends [who]
were to have been out in ten minutes'. Beke and several others
near the entrance began to bang on the gates, crying, 'We want
our students freed.'

Without warning, several things happened in swift succession.
Shortly after seven o'clock a truckload of Avo reinforcements,
carrying rifles with fixed bayonets, tore up Museum Avenue and
came to a halt at the corner of Brody Sandor Street. They were
seen only by the fringe of the crowd before vanishing in a matter
of seconds – tumbling out of the truck and racing into the garage
entrance at the rear – an entrance overlooked, incidentally,
by the insurgents.

Soon another kind of vehicle arrived, this time a mobile radio
truck with a crew of five technicians guarded by a policeman.
A woman announcer in a burgundy-coloured coat climbed on
the roof and shouted through her microphone for silence. Valeria
Benke, she said, had agreed to the students' demands to broadcast their manifesto. The announcer would make the broadcast
now, in full view of the crowd.

A cheer rolled like a wave along the street, followed by an
almost uncanny silence as the announcer, with professional calm
and poise, opened with the routine Radio Budapest station
identification call. After telling listeners to stand by for 'an
important announcement', she started to read the manifesto
slowly and carefully.

Her slowness was her undoing. Had she rattled through the
manifesto, Valeria Benke's duplicity might not immediately have
been discovered; but people looking down on the crowds from
flats high above could not hear, and hurried inside to switch on
their sets, only to find that Radio Budapest was transmitting
nothing more revolutionary than gipsy music. The entire operation was an elaborate hoax – which was why the student delegation had not been allowed to return to the street.

From every window overlooking the street shouts of derision

drowned the voice of the woman announcer. One man climbed on the van and tore the microphone from her hand. When he tugged at the wire, in theory plugged in to the transmitter, it came away in his hands.

Infuriated, those nearest clambered on to the car as the hoaxers escaped into the radio station, and it was at this moment that they started to batter down the doors.

Now the shooting had started and, drunk with the heady wine of a brief success, the first freedom fighters could only see one thing: at last men, boys and girls who loved their country had won a precious right to speak their mind openly, uninhibited by *esengofrasz* ('bell fever'), the first intimation of a midnight visit by the Avo. In the first flush of power they could not see that the only fragile hope of success lay in containing the fighting, having made their protest, in the hope that Russia would grant some concessions in preference to staging a demonstration of military power. They were on moderately friendly terms with the Russian troops; they had forgotten the implacable masters of the Kremlin.

For Thomas Szabo, who spent the rest of the night lying on a piano, his last thoughts as he drifted into uneasy sleep were that he must let his parents know that he was safe. However, he reflected, 'At the moment I just have not the time. Later, after the victory – for we shall win.'

After the students finally captured the radio station around 3 a.m. – but not the wavelength for there was a duplicate transmitter in the Ministry of the Interior – Lazlo Beke had a similar twinge of conscience about Eva, his pregnant wife. 'I had to get home,' he decided, 'if only for a few minutes to see if she was safe.'

Eva was sitting by the radio in their tiny room and she hardly recognised her husband, with his tommy-gun slung on a leather strap and four grenades dangling from his belt. He was 'covered from head to foot in dust and cement, the grime of battle, the grease of arms and machinery'.

About the same time Dora Scarlett was leaving the *Szabad Nep* building, and walking down Mayakovsky Street in the direction of her home. For the first time she realised that she was 'dog tired. Up to this moment I had not noticed it, borne up by the excitement around me. But I had been out for twelve hours without once stopping to rest or having a bite to eat.'

Thankfully she tumbled into bed soon after 3 a.m. At 5 she was awakened by a sinister noise. It was the grinding roar of Russian tanks passing along Bajaz Street, outside her bedroom window.

2

The Corridors of Power

Dusk to dawn, Tuesday–Wednesday, 23–4 October

While fighting raged in the streets, a struggle of a different kind was taking place in the Communist Party headquarters in Academy Street. It was not a struggle between individuals jockeying for position, but a last-ditch stand by a diehard Moscow-backed Stalinist determined to hold on to power which the revolution threatened to erode.

Erno Gero was the First Secretary of the Hungarian Communist Party, a post carrying more authority than the Premier. Brilliant, ascetic, humourless, he had made a name for himself during the Spanish Civil War by dominating the purge in Catalonia, a role that came easily to a Moscow agent whose primary function was that of executioner. His role in Spain was highly sinister, and after the collapse of the Republican regime he made his way to Russia and became a Soviet citizen. A chain-smoking fanatic who worked sixteen hours a day, his life was dominated by an incurable stomach disease, and increasing eye trouble that forced him to change his spectacles regularly. The Hungarian writer Pal Ignotus saw him as 'a soulless Stalinist technocrat, a cross between an inquisitor and a computer'.

By Tuesday evening Party headquarters resembled an armed camp preparing to withstand a siege. Gun-toting Avos scurried along the normally calm passages as Gero waited with mounting anger for the man he believed to be responsible for the chaos now tearing the city apart. He had summoned Imre Nagy,[1] who had been premier of Hungary in 1953 – until Khrushchev dismissed him for being too liberal.

[1] Pronounced Imreh Nodge.

Nagy presented a potent danger, for though he had no office he was far and away the most popular man in Hungary. Earlier in the evening he had, against his will, been persuaded to make a short speech from the balcony of Parliament Building, and when Gero heard of it he sent for him.

Accompanied by his son-in-law, Ferenc Janosi, and two colleagues, Nagy walked the short distance to Academy Street. At the entrance two armed Avo officers stepped on either side of Nagy to form an unobtrusive bodyguard as he mounted the red-carpeted stairway leading to Gero's private office.

The Avos did not molest the visitors, but Janosi felt 'they were obviously there to see we did not escape'. When Nagy sat down to await Gero's summons, the guards stood at his side. Leslie Bain, an American journalist, witnessed the scene, but when Nagy heard him ask Janosi for permission to talk to Nagy the ex-premier 'looked up and shook his head'. Janosi then whispered to Bain that though Nagy was not under arrest he was not allowed to talk to anyone.

Finally Nagy was called into Gero's office. Gero was sitting at his plain, large desk, with book-lined walls behind. In front of the desk were two leather armchairs and a large leather sofa, but Gero did not ask Nagy to sit down. It was a confrontation between the two men of utterly different characters. Nagy had the burly frame of a farmer. He sported a pair of flowing moustaches, and at times affected *pince nez*. In direct contrast to the cold clipped voice of Gero, he still spoke with the rich, rolling country accent of Kaposvar where he had been born fifty-seven years previously. He was a man who enjoyed the good things of life. He loved the arts, painting, music, the opera, the theatre, as well as pastries and tea at Gerbaud's, the smartest coffee-shop in Budapest. He was an enthusiastic follower of Hungary's famous Honved football team.

The two men had one thing in common: both were dedicated Communists of forty years standing, both trained in Moscow. But there the resemblance ended, for whereas Gero ruled with the tyranny of a machine taking no account of human beings Nagy was a man of the people who believed that Communism should mean more bread for the worker, more land for the peasant. While Gero was the most hated man in the country, Nagy was idolised by almost all of Hungary's ten million people who saw in him their only hope of deliverance from the mailed fist of the Party, with its nationwide spy apparatus, its 'norm' system of factory production, its collectivisation of farm land.

With unconcealed hostility Gero launched into a violent tirade against Nagy. 'You instigated the riots,' he cried. 'Now you can stew in your own juice.'

Nagy was equally angry. For months he had been trying to warn the Party leaders of the dangerous current of unrest. It was not his fault, he said, if the Party refused to heed his advice. 'And', he added, 'I have instigated nothing, and you know it.' In fact, though Nagy's followers were demanding his return to power, Nagy had taken no part either in the meetings during the previous night or in the demonstrations earlier in the day.

'You have no position, no authority,' said Gero, 'so how did you dare to go to Parliament and incite the crowds by speaking from the balcony?'

It was useless for Nagy to insist that he had never wanted to go to Parliament. He had spent the afternoon quietly at his home with close friends like Geza Losonczy, Miklos Vasarhelyi of *Szabad Nep*, Miklos Gimes and Janosi, his son-in-law; but later in the evening, when nearly a quarter of a million people assembled in the vast square facing Parliament Building, all of them chanting 'We want Nagy!' his friends had persuaded him, very much against his will, to go to Parliament and address the crowd. There had been no incitement. In fact the short speech had no effect on events, but this was not Gero's view.

'Well,' he asked scornfully, 'if you are such a good Party member, why *did* you go to Parliament Square?'

Nagy could make no reply. All he said was, 'Everything that is happening now could have been prevented if you had handled the situation better during the day.'

Nagy was right. Their meeting was in fact the culmination of a disastrous Tuesday for Gero, who had only returned from a 'state' visit to Tito in Belgrade that very morning, to be greeted by students demanding the right to stage a peaceful demonstration in sympathy with the Poles and to publicise the manifesto they had drawn up during the night.

None of the student demands advocated a return to Western-style democracy, for few if any Hungarians thought of changing the devil they knew for one they did not. Rather, as good Marxists, the students and writers were eager to show that in Hungary the Government was perverting true Marxism.

Their demands had of course been sparked off by events in Poland, for when Gomulka openly attacked Stalinist policies in the first half of October the Hungarians saw a miracle unfold: Khrushchev flew into the Polish capital, ordered the Soviet tanks to withdraw, and accepted Gomulka. The lesson was there for every Hungarian to see.

No sooner had Gero in the morning driven from the station to his office at Party headquarters than he was met by delegations from the Writers' Union, the Petofi Debating Circle, the Technological University and the senior staff of *Szabad Nep*, the Party newspaper. The scene was one of total confusion, and Balazs Nagy (no relation to Imre), the secretary of the Petofi Circle, remembers the chaos: 'Nearly all the leaders of the Party were gathered together. in a turmoil of confusion, fear and hesitation. The members of the delegations were making the Party leaders responsible in advance for any events that might take place. They themselves had not the slightest idea of the best attitude to adopt.' Balazs Nagy watched as Antal Apro, a member of the Central Committee, 'lifted his hands to heaven, almost in tears'. At one point 'Gero left the meeting in exasperation, while the others, pale and restless, hesitated'.

When a delegation of students confronted Andras Hegedus, the Prime Minister, Gyula Hay, the Hungarian dramatist who was in the delegation, remembers how Hegedus looked at the manifesto 'with a disdainful air', then turned to the youngsters and made an astonishing remark. 'You have no right to declare your sympathies with Poland,' he said, 'because the Central Committee has not yet come to a decision on the subject.'

Marton Horvath, director of the editorial committee of *Szabad Nep*, told Gero bluntly, 'The demands of the masses must be given more consideration.'

Gero replied, 'You've lost your heads. We have all the means we need to control troublemakers.' The first step, he said, was simple. The demonstration would be forbidden. 'And,' he added, 'if there is no demonstration, there can't be any trouble.'

Horvath pointed out that by now – nearly midday – students were already milling around in their thousands in the centre of Budapest, waiting for the signal to start. It might be too late to ban the march. And what, he asked, would happen if they ignored the ban?

Jozsef Revai, one-time director of Cultural Affairs, shouted, 'We would fire on them.' Within the hour Radio Budapest interrupted its programme of gipsy music to read a communiqué by Lazlo Piros, an ex-butcher now Minister of the Interior: 'In order to assure public order, the Minister of the Interior has forbidden any public meetings or demonstrations until further notice.'

It was too late. The crowds were already gathering, and increased because many with no intention of marching became so incensed with the government order that they joined in. With one stroke Piros had transformed a quiet march in support of the Polish nation into a demonstration of bitter antagonism to the Government.

Now Gero was beginning to panic. He must have realised that Piros had blundered. At 2.35 p.m. – barely half an hour before the march was officially due to begin – Radio Budapest announced that Piros had lifted the ban. For the people of Hungary it was a stupendous victory. They had proved that 'a bunch of schoolkids', as one observer described them, could challenge the might of a Communist oligarchy, and win.

Inevitably the demonstrators – though still with no thought of violence – grew bolder. Soon the more courageous started cutting the hated Communist hammer and sheaf of wheat out of the centre of the Hungarian tricolour. Others tore down the red stars from prominent buildings. Red, white and green rosettes appeared in buttonholes, even on the occasional soldier's cap. Students duplicated thousands of copies of the manifesto on ancient machines and pasted them up in every street; and once the manifesto *did* become public the excitement spread like an epidemic. Dora Scarlett, mingling with the crowds, felt 'neither before nor since have I seen Budapest so happy'. A man standing next to her, 'his face aglow', said to her, 'We haven't had such a day for eight years.'

A sense of exhilaration dusted the streets of the capital, as though a city which for centuries had boasted proudly of its patriotism had suddenly awakened from a nightmare. People long cowed by the fear of spies among friends stopped whispering. 'The most exciting sound I heard that day', Anna Gabor remembered, 'was the sound of laughter – people laughing aloud in the streets.'

Even then the situation might have been saved had not Gero decided to broadcast to the nation at 8 p.m. To Hungarians hoping for even the smallest promise of reform, the speech was a disaster. Nagy's friend, Tibor Meray observed that 'this speech is generally regarded as the fuse that set off the explosion. Gero's words, demonstrating the speaker's harsh inhumanity, his servility towards – and respect for – the Soviet Union, his lack of comprehension, and his aggressiveness, would have exasperated the most patient leaders. And the demonstrators before the Radio Building were not very patient.'

With his very first words Gero made it clear that he was totally against compromise. 'We condemn those who seek to instil in our youth the poison of chauvinism and to take advantage of democratic liberties that our state guarantees to the workers to organise a national demonstration,' he said.

But it was not only *what* Gero said; it was the way he said it that angered people. He peppered his speech with menacing references to 'national subversion', 'hostile elements', and 'provocation'. His 'obstinate rejection of the overtures from the young demonstrators revolted them', Meray said. He had learned no lesson from the day's events.

It was a speech of unutterable folly; in imagining that a public scolding would calm the rising tempers, he must have been entirely ignorant of the hatred which had been simmering for nearly ten years. As Tito, so recently his host, said scathingly, 'In such a critical moment, when all was in turmoil, he dared to fling the term "mob" at people among whom a large number, perhaps even the majority, consisted of Communists and youth.'

Now, it was too late. As Gero sat facing Nagy, he realised that, with blood flowing in the streets, he must take a humiliating step if he wished to restore order – and retain power. He must make an accommodation with Nagy, his bitterest enemy, for he needed him as a shield.

Around midnight Gero told Nagy, 'The Politbureau is meeting in a few minutes. I am inviting you to attend the meeting,' adding coldly, 'as a guest.'

Nagy's friends were brusquely banished to wait in a small office.

Gero was about to move into the imposing panelled council chamber on the second floor when a breathless middle-aged man, with a row of medals on his Russian-style tunic, stumbled through the door. Major-General Hegyi was on the verge of collapse. He had run most of the way from the radio station to make his report.

It was brief. The radio building, he announced, was on the point of being occupied.

Gero now had to face up to the bitter truth. The Army had betrayed him. Some police had betrayed him. Even some of the Avos had betrayed him. A decade of painstaking, intensive Communist indoctrination had not been able to buy him an evening of loyalty. When the meeting started, it was, according to Tibor Meray, 'stormy and dramatic and extremely confused'. The hard-line Stalinists insisted that the revolt must be crushed without mercy. Jozsef Revai, who had spent part of the evening in the offices of *Szabad Nep*, before being spirited out to save him from a lynching, demanded 'repeatedly and dementedly' that troops should open fire on the insurgents.

Not until the discussions had dragged on for four hours did Gero finally decide that Nagy was, as Tibor Meray put it, 'the wisp of straw by which they hoped to be saved'. Yet, when there was still a possibility of preventing further bloodshed – by reaching a formula for modest reform similar to that achieved in Poland – Gero lost his nerve. At one moment – the exact time will never be known – he gave instructions to telephone the Kremlin. A direct line to Moscow was connected in a private office on the 'K'[1] circuit which could not be tapped. Gero had decided to hedge his bet and call in Russian troops.

He knew that logistically there were no problems. Two Soviet

---

[1] Kozvetlen, or 'direct'.

tank units – the 2nd and 17th Mechanised Divisions – were stationed at Cegled and Szekesfehervar, each about forty miles from Budapest, while if reserves were needed from Russia floating pontoon bridges had already been assembled at Zahony on the Russian–Hungarian border.

Who made the fateful call will never be known, though two members of the Politbureau have laid claim to that doubtful honour. Gyorgy Marosan, a hard-line Stalinist, boasted (later) that he had called Moscow; but Marosan was little more than a functionary, kept in office as a useful puppet, so if he did make the call it must have been on the direct orders of Gero.

Hegedus has also been 'credited' with making the call. In fact he more or less admitted to it that very evening, when the Central Committee called a recess.

It so happened that Zoltan Zelk, the poet, arrived at Party headquarters with a deputation of writers and saw Hegedus, who said to him, at the very moment the insurgents were attacking the radio station, that unless the 'Fascist' uprising was suppressed by the morning Soviet help would be called in. 'Hegedus said all this', Zelk remembered later, 'with a broad smile on his face, like someone who had thought out a devilish plan.' Zelk was firmly convinced that the move to call in Soviet troops 'was already decided'. As General Bela Kiraly, of the Hungarian Army, later told the United Nations, 'Gero had obviously acted out of panic'.

Certainly Nagy knew nothing of the calls to the Soviet Union. He was in an unenviable position, attending the Central Committee deliberations as an outsider without any voice in its decisions, or any right to speak, as Zoltan Zelk discovered when he asked Hegedus if he could meet Nagy and was told brusquely that he was 'not available'.

Zelk pictured the confusion with his discerning eye. He caught a glimpse of Revai 'who emerged from the meeting for a second with frightened face'. He saw Janosi, Nagy's son-in-law, 'hanging about lonely and haggard in the waiting-room, panic stricken about his fate'.

In the early hours of Wednesday, Gero finally agreed to a reconstruction of the Government. He would remain as Party First Secretary, which meant he would still wield absolute power. Nagy was appointed Prime Minister, and Hegedus was demoted to First Deputy Premier and assistant to Nagy. Only two of Nagy's followers were given responsible Party posts, Ferenc Donath and Geza Losonczy, who were both made members of the Central Committee. Among the first decisions was a proclamation of martial law. The question of troops was never mentioned.

For Gero this was a great victory – or so he imagined. He was offering Nagy as a dummy to the crowds, while making certain that he would be effectively hemmed in by hard-line Stalinists. Yet Gero needed one more safeguard to ensure his power. For the time being he must keep the new Prime Minister out of touch with his followers. Gero sent for the Avo commander in the building and told him that on no account must Nagy be allowed to leave Party headquarters, not even to go to the Prime Minister's office in Parliament House, where the business of government was normally carried on.

So the man saddled with the task of bringing peace out of bloodshed, of keeping a balance of friendship with the Soviet leaders in the Kremlin, started his second term as Prime Minister of Hungary a prisoner with his phone tapped, his letters intercepted, his person guarded by Avo sub-machine-guns.

Gero snatched an hour's sleep on a camp bed in Party headquarters, presumably content with the manner in which he had handled the political crisis. But there was one thing he had not reckoned with. In the Kremlin, Khrushchev, no doubt displeased at the way in which Party control was disintegrating in Hungary, had despatched two high-powered officials to Budapest. Their orders were clear – though Gero did not know them.

3

The Battle Is Joined

Wednesday, 24 October

In the heyday of Budapest there was a saying, 'Vienna is the city to live in, Prague the city to see, but Budapest is the place to have a good time in.' One of Europe's fairest capitals, graced by the curving sweep of the 'blue' Danube, that separated the two sections, Pest, the business and shopping district on the east bank, from Buda, the hilly residential area. Budapest was a city not only of beautiful spires, rococo buildings and green, open parks, but of wit and charm.

Pal Ignotus, the Hungarian writer, found it 'a corrupt and happy-go-lucky society, vulgar in some respects, sophisticated, often astoundingly naïve'. The Hungarian-born writer George Mikes felt that 'life was full of breathless interest and excitement and was lived by us mostly in the cafés, which ... were fortresses of bourgeois culture. Lack of money was regarded as charming and bohemian and not to be confused with poverty and other proletarian vices.'

This was the city into which, before dawn of Wednesday, 24 October, there clattered the first Russian tanks summoned by Gero. They came from Szekesfehervar, about forty miles southwest of the capital, and were first sighted in the Moricz Zsigmond Square in Buda. After stopping there for a short while they crossed the Danube by the Margaret Bridge into Pest. Some remained on guard duty at the bridge. Others patrolled the embankment. From the east, another unit advanced directly into Pest from Cegled, also about forty miles from the capital.

But there had been far more sinister troop movements during the two previous days. On the Sunday and Monday – 21 and 22

October – all Soviet officers in neighbouring Romania who spoke Hungarian or German were recalled from leave, and Hungarian police reported that Russian forces from Romania entered Hungary at 1 a.m. on 24 October.[1]

At Zahony, on the Russian–Hungarian frontier, floating bridges had been assembled, and it was over these that Soviet tanks rumbled across the river frontier and moved towards the town of Miskolc, north-east of Budapest. Other Russian tanks, probably from Romania, made for Debrecen, due east of the capital.

All the military planning for these complicated troop movements must have been taken before Gero and Hegedus returned from their visit to Tito. Hegedus might boast that he had called in Russian troops, but in fact the Russians seem to have made independent preparations at the time of the Warsaw uprising. Nevertheless they were no doubt delighted when the Hungarian leaders 'invited' them to help, for this bolstered the figment of legality.

The sudden appearance of foreign armour changed the character of the uprising. The squat outlines of Russian tanks, their guns silhouetted against first light, the rumbling of their motors, the grating of their treads clattering on the cobbled streets, turned bitterness against the Government (and the Avo) into a blinding desire to rid Hungary of the Russians. The insurgents in Budapest were not rising merely because the Poles had successfully fought Stalinism; this was no echo of Warsaw, it was a revolution fostered in Hungary's particular brand of national pride and set against a background of tortured history.

Since the days of the Magyars, who founded Hungary at the end of the ninth century, freedom, with one solitary interlude, had eluded the Hungarians. After years of Turkish domination, the country became part of the Austro-Hungarian Empire, ruled from Vienna. Time and again Hungary fought for freedom. At times the cherished dream seemed tantalisingly close, but not until 1918, when the Hapsburg Empire was erased from the map, did she achieve her independence.

It was short-lived. After fighting with Germany in the Second

[1] Some wounded Russian troops treated in a Budapest hospital had Romanian money in their pockets.

World War, Hungary was 'liberated' by Soviet Russia, and it was then that the tragedy of her recent history was born.

Stalin appointed Matyas Rakosi as master of Hungary after the German defeat, and for a decade Rakosi ruled Hungary with a savagery surpassed only by Stalin himself. He wielded immense power through the secret police who on his orders arrested and tortured tens of thousands of innocent Hungarians. The bald little man, who thought of himself as 'Stalin's Hungarian disciple', was called 'Arsehole' behind his back. Life under the dictatorship of Russia's proconsul was a grey existence of fear.

When Khrushchev came to power in 1953, he realised that the Hungarian economy was grinding to a halt owing to Rakosi's insane policy of over-industrialising an agricultural nation. He abruptly dismissed Rakosi from the premiership, though he retained his position as First Secretary of the Party. Imre Nagy was appointed premier.

Within a few months in 1953 the face of Hungary changed. Independent shopkeepers hounded out of business took down their shutters. A man could read a book by a Western author without fear of arrest. The legendary beautiful women of Budapest started using cosmetics again. Beauty parlours reopened. Night clubs like the 'River Room' offered American jazz until the small hours. Simple chores such as repairing a broken radio which had previously taken months now took a matter of hours because the Hungarian artisans were back at work. Nagy's regime was new and exhilarating and as different from the recent past as Nagy was different from Rakosi.

But the irony was that Nagy was too popular for the Kremlin leaders, and after twenty months of plotting against him Rakosi persuaded them to dismiss him on the grounds of 'deviationism'. Rakosi, the housebroken Communist warhorse, was reinstated.

Because of Nagy's popularity, he had to be silenced, so Rakosi excluded him from the Central Committee, stripped him of all his political offices and, when Nagy refused to make the customary confession of error, expelled him from the Party.

Nevertheless Rakosi's stupidity backfired, for even he, with a muzzled press, could not hide the fact that under Nagy the Hungarian people had enjoyed a brief escape from oppression.

By persecuting a man who had proved that Communism was not necessarily synonymous with dictatorship, Rakosi turned Nagy into a hero.

Nagy, instead of sinking into oblivion, became the chief topic of conversation among disillusioned intellectuals, particularly writers and journalists gathering at his home in Orso Street. All Nagy wanted was to change Communism from the quagmire of dictatorship into which it had sunk to the pure form of Marx and Lenin. Many of Nagy's 'disciples' had been exiled or jailed, like Geza Losonczy, who had been removed from a government post on Rakosi's orders and thrown into prison for no reason. Among Nagy's visitors were two of *Szabad Nep*'s most brilliant journalists, Miklos Vasarhelyi, who had been threatened with arrest for meeting Losonczy, and Tibor Meray, who had been summarily dismissed from the Party newspaper.

Gradually the Communist writers, who had been pampered by Party chiefs and had previously turned a blind eye to arbitrary injustice, became stricken with remorse as they realised that Rakosi was little more than a criminal. As Tamas Aczel and Tibor Meray, both young, both brilliant, both Communists, later wrote in *The Revolt of the Mind*, 'Now the writers wriggled desperately in the throes of a deadly shame.... They were ashamed of their privileges, of having accepted and enjoyed advantages that millions had to go without, and of the price they had paid for those privileges.'

Their anger and shame erupted in the autumn of 1955, when fifty-nine prominent figures in the arts signed a manifesto protesting at 'administrative methods' employed against intellectuals. Rakosi bided his time until he could arrest them; but he waited too long, for within three months the Soviet empire – and indeed the whole world – was stunned by the most traumatic turning-point in the history of Communism.

Stalin, for decades pictured as the wise and fatherly leader, was unmasked as the greatest monster of our time by his former lieutenant Nikita Khrushchev. In his famous six-hour speech at the Twentieth Party Congress in February 1956, Khrushchev denounced the Stalin personality cult and enumerated the horrors for which Stalin had been responsible.

In Hungary Rakosi failed to realise that this was the end of the personality cult, the beginning of a new liberalised form of Communism (in theory, anyway), even when in June the Petofi Circle, a debating society attracting intellectuals from the broadest spectrum of Hungarian life, held an open meeting to discuss 'Questions of Information and Press'. Over 6000 people queued in the rain to enter the Officers' Club, or listen until 4 a.m. to speeches relayed into nearby streets.

The climax came in the early hours of the morning when a bespectacled man with thick black hair walked to the rostrum. He was the final speaker. Geza Losonczy was an intimate friend of Nagy's and had been falsely imprisoned for years. The son of a Protestant pastor, he had none of the strident rhetoric of the Communist orator, but he spoke in a quiet, almost gentle voice that was far more effective.

Point by point, he described what he called 'The Nagy Affair'. It was, he said, impossible to speak of democracy within the Party while Nagy was not given the opportunity to defend his policies. As Tibor Meray remembers, 'At the mention of Nagy's name, the entire audience rose and began chanting for his return.'

Hurriedly Rakosi convened a meeting of the Central Committee. The ·Petofi Circle was dissolved and several members expelled from the Party, while Rakosi drew up a list of 400 people to be arrested. Nagy's name headed the list, though he had not been at the meeting.

It was Rakosi's final blunder, for in Moscow Khrushchev, committed to a policy of rapprochement, was horrified when he heard of it, and within two days had dismissed Rakosi. Rakosi flew to refuge and obscurity in Russia, never to return.

At this moment in time Russia and Hungary faced their greatest opportunity to work together. Had Nagy been allowed to return to office, the Hungarian revolution might never have happened; but instead Khrushchev appointed Rakosi's hench-man Erno Gero as First Secretary, so that within a few days all Budapest was saying bitterly, 'In place of a bald Rakosi, we've got a thin one.'

Early in October Nagy wrote to Gero demanding readmittance to the Communist Party which he had served loyally for forty years. His request was granted on 13 October, and the next morning Gero and his prime minister, Hegedus, cheerfully set off on their visit to Tito. Gero could not have had the faintest premonition of the disaster that would await him on his return.

Five days later came Warsaw. When Gomulka demanded an end to Stalinist policies in Poland and the Communist government faced a crisis, his opponents called in Soviet help. Russian tanks rumbled into Warsaw. Students and workers started to mobilise, in what, until that moment on 19 October, was an exact dress rehearsal of the Hungarian uprising. Then Khrushchev flew into Warsaw and, presumably guided by his new anti-Stalinist policies, backed down. The tanks left.

To the Hungarians, now involved in a deadly revolution, there seemed to be no reason why history should not repeat itself – particularly history that was less than a week old.

Joan Fish, the British consul in Budapest,[1] heard the first gunfire during the night. With her access to diplomatic knowledge, she had half expected it. A dynamic, dark-haired woman in her thirties who spoke fluent Hungarian, she was also a brilliant horsewoman who had astonished the Hungarians earlier in the year by winning the Budapest ladies' showjumping championship.

She made for the living-room of her flat on Gellert Hill in Buda, overlooking the Danube, and decided to brew a cup of coffee before setting off early for the British Legation. Normally Miss Fish's Hungarian cook would have made the coffee, but she was away – and for an odd reason. She had been given a three-day trip to Vienna as a reward for successfully spying on the British consul.

To Joan Fish it was a huge joke; as she remembers, 'I knew she was spying on me. She knew I knew, and I knew she knew I knew. But, to keep everybody happy, I felt unimportant "evidence" around to make her seem useful to the Hungarian secret police.'

The Consul's flat was also bugged, but that did not worry her either, even though the location of the microphones were constantly changed, for she had trained her dog Kislany – a chestnut-

---

[1] Now married to an American, Charles Hunt, and living in Waco-Lynville, Tennessee.

coloured Hungarian Vizla hunting dog – to sniff out unerringly the position of any hidden microphone.

Joan Fish had no trouble reaching the imposing, square, granite building of the British Legation, with its Union Jack jutting out on a pole above the large wooden doors that were pad-locked each night. The Legation was just off Vorosmarty Square, near the Danube, and was already alive with Hungarian secretaries brandishing copies of the students' manifesto. A few minutes later from an upstairs window she watched the arrival of the British Minister, Mr Leslie Fry.

Mr Fry, who lived in Buda, was sitting upright in the back seat of his old-fashioned square-shaped Austin Princess. From the car mast the Union Jack fluttered proudly, and behind the Minister was an unrequested escort – a Soviet tank. Mr Fry, who combined a sense of dignity proper to his station with a wry sense of humour, stepped out of his car, gave the curtest of nods in the direction of the unseen tank crew, and walked into the Legation to begin the day's work.

To Jozsef Kovago, who had been the first post-war Mayor of Budapest in 1945, the sound of gunfire broke up a party given by friends to celebrate his sudden release from jail after seven years of Avo torture. Kovago had been jailed first by the Gestapo for his work with the Hungarian resistance, and later by the Avo, for a reason he never discovered.

The party had been a success. One of the main toasts of the evening had been made to a man whose identity was a mystery. He was an anonymous benefactor who had sent Kovago's wife Lonci regular sums of money while Kovago was in jail, cut off from all news of her and their baby daughter.

Around midnight Kovago and Lonci set off for home by tram. 'There was a contagious excitement in the air and we could hear shots,' he remembers. 'We saw people running down the streets.' Finally the tramdriver, frightened by the shooting, decided he could go no further. The Kovagos started walking towards the heart of the city, with the shots very close. Lonci was frightened – not for herself but for her husband – thinking that the Avo might pick him up again. However, they reached the safety of their flat and within a few minutes Kovago was fast asleep.

He was wakened by a sharp, curious noise. 'It sounded as though somebody had dropped a glass and stepped on it near my bed.' Half asleep he jumped up, telling his wife that someone in the street below had knocked over a dustbin. Then, before turning out the light, he carefully picked up a bullet and put it in the ashtray near his bed. It had been fired (as he discovered later) by an Avo from a room on the other side of the street.

Before falling asleep again, he thought to himself, 'This shot was almost like a message, warning me that great things were in the offing, and that I could not hesitate to take my part and do my duty.'

Mark Molnar, tall, dark, good looking, every inch the career army officer (which he had been until 1946), was thrust into the revolution almost against his will. Coming from a family that had once been well-to-do, Captain Molnar had resigned his commission when ordered to join the Party. After that life had been tough – he had been forced to take a succession of menial jobs ranging from swineherd to plumber's mate, until now he was earning good money as a coalman.

The previous night he had taken a girlfriend to dinner at the Hungaria restaurant – the Maxime's of Budapest – and because of traffic disruption spent the night with his girlfriend in her small flat. Early in the morning he went out to buy her some bread from the bakery in Semmerweis Street; he did not see her again for two weeks.

Molnar – something of a cynic and bitterly anti-Communist – had been unperturbed by the night's gunfire, thinking, 'If the Commies want to kill each other, that's fine by me.' But now, with the flat loaf of hot bread under his arm, he stared in disbelief.

In the middle of the road stood an anti-tank gun. Though Russian and Hungarian uniforms were similar, his expertise as a career officer made him realise instantly that this was a Russian gun – and if there was one thing he hated more than Communists it was the Russians who had been his prison guards for five years.

Not far from the bakery a group of youngsters stood uncertainly. Two carried rifles, one some hand grenades, the others pistols. Something in the ramrod-straight bearing of the soldier-turned-coalman prompted one of them to ask if he could help. Molnar explained that he had been in the Army. The boys clustered round. They wanted, they said, to capture the Russian anti-tank gun.

'You must be crazy,' Molnar exploded. 'You probably don't even know how to use your weapons.'

And yet – crazy or not – Molnar was seething with anger at the thought of Russian troops in Budapest. The gun at the end of the street, he noticed, was manned by half a dozen soldiers, but they seemed isolated.

'Anyone know how to handle grenades?' he asked.

They had only the vaguest idea, so he gave the two brightest boys a ten-minute lesson on the art of grenade-throwing. Then he explained his plan of action. When they were ready, those with guns would shoot – and keep shooting. Those with grenades would hold their action in the hope of capturing the gun intact. Then everyone would shout and scream and run as though they were crazy. 'The Russians will either shoot back and kill us all,' he added, 'or they'll panic and run.'

Whooping and shooting into the air, for all the world like Red Indians in a Western, they surged forward with Molnar at the head. Undecided (and probably at that time under orders not to provoke Hungarians) the Russians hesitated. It was fatal. As the boys ran forward the Russians suddenly found the bullets flying round their heads. They bolted up a side street. Two who attempted to return were shot. The boys trundled the precious gun into the courtyard of a block of flats and Molnar, after congratulating them, prepared to return to his girl-friend.

The boys, he remembered, looked stupefied. They didn't know how to use the gun, they said. They had also captured some strange-looking machine pistols. They needed help, instruction, a leader. They would never have taken the gun without him. They clustered around him, and Molnar noticed that the group now numbered more than twenty.

That was the moment when 'Molnar's men' were formed. By nightfall, 300 freedom fighters had flocked to Mark's 'colours'. They remained with him, as a disciplined body, split into companies and platoons, ranging over the city in search of Russians, until the moment came when Mark Molnar was appointed aide-de-camp to the greatest resistance hero thrown up by the revolution.

Lazlo Beke's first thought when he heard that Russian tanks had been sighted was to make sure Eva was safe, so that when he visited her in future she would be 'free from house guards and prying eyes'. In the cold early morning Eva packed a small bag, put on her shabby raincoat, then the young couple left behind everything else they owned in their first home. A truck gave them a lift to the Technological University's student home in Buda, a handsome building between the South Station and a large park bearing the spectacular name 'The Field of Blood'.

Once she was safely installed, Lazlo set off, his belt with its grenades over his brown suit, for the Technological University, where already hundreds of its five thousand students were turning the building into a battle headquarters. It was ideally placed in a 'V' of land between Bela Bartok Street and Karinthy Frigyes Road – controlling the only major streets leading to the river bridges in that area which any tanks would have to cross to reach Pest. It backed on to a favourite bathing *plage* on the Danube, still decorated with a few coloured umbrellas, tables and chairs.

There were nearly two hundred classrooms on the ground floor of the old-fashioned building with its twin towers, and these 'were quickly turned into machine-gun distribution rooms, ammunition rooms, committee rooms, Red Cross and hospital rooms – even a flag and ribbon room', for only by the tricolour ribbons could people distinguish friend from foe.

Lazlo's first battle was not against the Russians, but against the even more hated enemy, the Avo. Operating from their head-quarters at 60, Andrassy Street in Pest, the 30,000 Avos, supported by countless thousands of part-time informers, had influenced the lives of almost every one of Hungary's ten million people. At the peak of their power in 1956 nearly 200,000 political prisoners had been shut up in prisons or concentration camps. The Avo's personal files included a million names of 'suspicious characters'. Letters from abroad seized by the Avos filled four large rooms.

So did tape recordings of phone calls, seemingly harmless remarks made by people in every stratum of society from high government officials to the humblest workers.

Here the black, curtained Poboda cars of the Avo had brought prisoners, usually at night, often never to be seen again. The cars did not pull up at the main entrance, but round the corner in Csengery Street, driving into a courtyard, innocent enough in appearance from the outside, but sinister once the gates had shut. Along one end the Avo had built a brick wall twenty feet high, unbroken by a single window. In another corner was a tall skeleton tower, manned day and night by machine-gunners.

Outwardly, Andrassy Street was a normal, busy street thronged with people going about their business, and the entrance to number 60 had the appearance of any well-to-do, solidly established business office. Hundreds of people a day passed it without so much as a second glance – unless it were to admire the red geraniums in window-boxes flanking the entrance. But behind the door lurked a secret world of dank cells equipped with instruments of torture ranging from nail presses, whips, limb crushers, to twin baths (where prisoners would be first immersed in icy water, then in boiling water). There were long dark passages containing tiny damp 'punishment cells' where an obdurate prisoner would be left for days unable either to lie down or stand upright. Here Geza Losonczy had been tortured. Here Bela Szasz, a close friend of Nagy's, had nearly starved to death in a windowless room with one electric bulb that glowed day and night 'throwing its beam straight into the eyes of the prisoner'.

And it was above these cells, where human beings could be forgotten for months, that Vladimir Farkhas, one of the most sadistic torturers, personally distributed gold watches and ordered champagne for 'deserving' Avos, and when everyone was drunk once had Cardinal Mindszenty brought up from his cell. He offered the old man a glass of champagne, and when the Cardinal refused Farkhas threw the contents in his face.

By the fifties the Avo headquarters extended the entire length of Andrassy Street. At one corner was a room which Bela Szasz found more sinister than the punishment cell, for it was gay with chintz curtains through which the sunlight filtered on a summer's day. Tables and chairs were placed on a carpeted floor, and a counter was filled with a mouthwatering assortment of cakes and pastries, coffee and free cigarettes.

This was the 'back-to-normal room' where semi-starved prisoners who had finally signed their spurious confessions under torture were fattened up for their public appearance at staged show trials.

In 1956 the Avos were not only the most ruthless, but among the most privileged people in the country. They were handsomely paid with pension rights (plus lavish bonuses for extra arrests or confessions) and were given rent-free flats or villas, shopped at their own subsidised stores which stocked Western goods at cut prices. They even had their own luxuriously equipped holiday village on Lake Balaton.

Peter Fryer, an ardent member of the British Communist Party who was in Hungary during the revolution, felt sickened enough to describe the Avos as 'the oppressors of a whole people ... moulded and trained on the approved Stalinist pattern, completely lacking in either political understanding or common humanity, guilty of the most unspeakable crimes'.

No wonder the United Nations felt that 'to participants in the uprising, the AVH had become a symbol of the rule by terror which they were struggling to end'.

With five other students Lazlo Beke drove in an ancient American jeep towards the sound of machine-gun fire. Clearly it was coming from an Avo station in Buda, a grey building just off the Boulevard of the Martyrs which linked the Margaret Bridge and Szena Square. A small park leading down from Rose Hill, one of Buda's many garden suburbs, lapped the western edge of the road where students had already set up machine-gun posts behind trees and benches. As Beke rattled towards the park he saw an ominous sign – Hungarian flags taken from doors and windows to cover the corpses of insurgents already killed. He had almost reached Szena Square when he saw two youngsters, taking cover behind a truck, stand up; a murderous burst of machine-gun fire killed them instantly. Two more with Red Cross arm bands ran forward with stretchers. They, too, were cut down.

As Beke reached the square facing the Avo station 'a scene of horrible ruin met our eyes. A Hungarian tank had

ploughed into a large gaping hole in the pavement. The whole
square was a mass of wreckage. The café on the corner was a
shambles, chairs littered all over the street, and bodies strewn
here and there.'

With a group of students he darted across the square to join
men firing from behind the wrecked tank. Their target was the
wooden gate guarding the Avo building. It gave way in a flurry
of splintered wood and the building was defenceless. A Hungarian
armoured car appeared. All who could scrambled on it, drove
straight to the shattered gate and a Hungarian soldier shouted,
'We will give you two minutes to come out before we start shelling
the building.'

Within sixty seconds the first of sixty-eight terrified Avo men
emerged, filing behind a major pushing a girl of five or six in
front of him and shouting, 'I won't harm her if you don't shoot.'
Shots from inside the building told their own grim story – the
final moments of those Avo men who preferred suicide to a
possible lynching.

In a brief moment of uncanny silence, the morning air
sharpened by the reek of cordite, both sides faced each other:
the young and the old, the amateurs and the professionals of
death, with a pawn in the shape of a child. It was broken by the
lonely crack of a single shot. Someone had aimed for the Avo
major's feet in order not to harm the girl. The major crumpled to
his knees. The girl scampered away, never to be seen again, and
then as Beke remembered, 'Ten years of oppression and visions
of tens of thousands of tortured and murdered Hungarians came
to the minds of the students as they saw the miserable AVH
major fall.' The manner in which he had shielded behind the
skirts of a girl seemed symptomatic of everything the secret police
stood for.

The enraged youngsters dragged the major over to a tree in
the park; they tied his ankles and strapped him to a low branch
so that he dangled two or three feet from the ground. As he
kicked to try to free himself a small fortune in Hungarian paper
money spilled from his pockets, 'more money than a worker could
have saved in years'.

The other Avo men were lined up at pistol-point to watch,
as students gathered a pile of autumn leaves, twigs, fallen

branches, waste paper, every single piece of the major's money, then lit the fire under his feet.

As the flames burned his uniform, crept upwards, and finally licked his face and singed his hair, the Avo major screamed his last words – 'Long live world Communism!'

Around 9 a.m. two Soviet tanks near Marx Square opened fire without provocation, killing two civilians. A tank near the Western Station killed an unarmed soldier talking to a civilian, and fired again, wounding a boy who ran to the soldier's assistance. When another Russian tank opened fire for no apparent reason near the People's Park, a mile or so further along Ulloi Avenue, resistance fighters led by a young army lieutenant called Decsi disabled it with petrol bombs. One group of fighters installed themselves in the East Station. Horvath Square was barricaded with burned-out cars. Other large forces barricaded Szena Square. Some insurgents occupied district police stations, usually without difficulty. Centres of resistance were springing up all over the city.

Thomas Szabo was awakened in his 'bed' on the piano by a shout, 'Everyone to the Corvin Cinema!' and when another boy asked for time to go home and tell his parents he was safe Scarface cried, 'Anyone who isn't going immediately to the Corvin must give up his gun.'

Szabo walked out into the street, into the cold autumn air, vaguely expecting to find the street empty after the previous night's unreal dream. Instead, 'we had the feeling that nobody in the city had been to bed'. Knots of men and women talked at every corner. One group with buckets of whitewash was painting 'General Strike!' or 'Russians go home!' on every available wall. The streets behind the radio station were littered with the skeletons of burned cars; the old-fashioned yellow tramcars were overturned, the tram lines had been torn up, the overhead electric cables hung like festoons. In one street Szabo saw boys prising paving-stones out of the road with picks and axes, as he set off down Museum Avenue, across Kalvin Square, and along Ulloi Avenue until he reached the cinema at the corner of Jozsef Avenue.

The cinema – one of the largest in Budapest – occupied the ground floor of a four-storey block of flats. Over its stucco front and brown-painted entrance doors a canopy gave shelter to queues on rainy evenings. The cobbled road in front was wide enough for a double line of tram tracks. A small alley jutted out behind the cinema.

This was Corvin Passage, destined to become the most colourful base in the city for hit-and-run guerilla operations, for it fitted perfectly into a pattern of resistance quickly taking shape. Still bewildered by the twist of events, still with no plan for organised resistance, the people of Budapest instinctively made for closed-in buildings, alleyways and those blocks of flats, typical of Budapest, that faced inwards to courtyards – places where tanks could not penetrate, but from which forays could be launched into the main streets.

The Corvin Passage had two other advantages – a nearby petrol pump with sufficient fuel to make thousands of Molotov cocktails out of bottles filled with petrol, and, opposite the cinema, a large, dilapidated building sandwiched between shops and flats. This was the Kilian Barracks, a fortress with walls five feet thick and virtually impregnable.

By the time Thomas Szabo and Feri reached the Corvin Cinema, the rows of seats were almost filled. The screen had been removed and on the stage stood a captain in Hungarian Army uniform. He had taken the braid from the shoulders of his uniform and stitched it on his collar where it had always been worn in the past. Szabo noticed that all the soldiers in the crowd had torn the red stars from their caps and replaced them with tricolour rosettes.

The officer, who turned out to be a Captain Kiss, banged for silence and shouted, 'Citizens, we are now going to form the Corvin battalion. If the Soviet troops intervene, the Corvin battalion will fight them. But first we are going to sing the national anthem.'

The audience stood up, and as they started to sing the first words, 'God Bless Hungary ...', young Thomas felt the tears streaming down his face, but 'I knew that everyone was feeling exactly what I felt, that every heart was beating for the same reason.'

The new recruits were split into five companies, with Thomas in one commanded by Scarface, who now revealed his true identity: Captain Janos Kovacs of the police. He ordered Szabo to round up all the school friends who had spent the night at the radio station, and appointed him leader of the group which would be responsible to Kovacs.

No one in Szabo's group of thirty-eight was more than fifteen or sixteen years old, and they had barely taken a roster when a man in black-rimmed spectacles confronted them and announced that he was a schoolmaster. 'What class are you in, you boys?' he asked.

'Class two!' one boy answered.

In a brisk tone of authority the schoolmaster ordered every boy under sixteen to return to his home. His words were drowned in catcalls and jeers as the boys trooped to their barracks – a classroom in a three-storey school behind the cinema. They piled all the benches and desks in one corner, and most of them were soon asleep on the floor.

Erno Gero was not asleep. Though unaware that Soviet emissaries were on their way to Budapest, he must still have been concerned lest Moscow blame him for the escalation of the fighting. Street demonstrations were one thing, but a complete breakdown of authority quite another. To protect himself, he devised a scheme to denigrate Nagy in the public eye by shifting on to him the blame for calling in Soviet armour. The plan involved a carefully worked-out timetable of radio broadcasts, and Gero masterminded the operation himself, drafting the radio announcements, handing them personally one at a time to the announcers to make certain they were not inadvertently broadcast in the wrong sequence.

At 4.30 a.m. on Wednesday Radio Budapest, operating on its alternative wavelength in the Ministry of the Interior, wished its listeners a polite good morning, then plunged immediately into the business of the day, which had been tactfully ignored until now.

'Fascist reactionary elements', said the announcer, 'have launched an armed attack on our public buildings and on our armed security formations.' It was the first mention of fighting, and the announcement was, according to the radio, signed by the Council of Ministers. This was Gero's method of preparing listeners for the news yet to come, and the announcement was repeated twice during the next two hours, though with one subtle difference. The word 'Fascist' was replaced by 'counter-revolutionary'.

Gero's next step was to introduce the 'hero of the hour', Nagy; but he had to be presented in a manner leaving a bitter taste. Gero waited until 8.30 a.m. before making the radio announcement that Nagy had been elected Prime Minister, and it was done so skilfully that it all but doused the joy that should have greeted such momentous news. The announcer underscored the Central Committee's decision that Gero was irreplaceable and Hegedus indispensable.

Anna Gabor, who was having coffee and toast in her tiny flat, turned to her mother and cried, 'How can a man like Nagy work with a beast like Gero? It's an insult to Hungarians to keep Gero in office.' Lazlo Beke, sitting on a 'bed' made of boards he had scavenged, was listening on the radio he had bought by saving lunch money, and felt, 'We had faith in Nagy to this moment, and now he appeared to be nothing more than a cover-up man for the old-guard Communists.'

Gero had not finished. He decided to drive home an elementary lesson in politics. It was directed to those Hungarians who might still wonder if Nagy had been forced to compromise. Gero's aim was simple: to give Nagy's followers a shock that would turn their admiration into dismay.

Thirty minutes after the broadcast of Nagy's appointment, Budapest Radio announced that martial law had been proclaimed, with summary death penalties for troublemakers. The statement carefully stressed that the declaration was signed by 'Imre Nagy, Chairman of the Council of Ministers'.

Nagy had in fact unwillingly agreed with the majority to proclaim martial law, but it was not this that chilled the listeners, it was the cold impersonal words of the edict.

'We wanted to hear him talking to *us*,' Anna Gabor felt. 'We wanted him to ask us to help – we'd have done anything for him – but instead there was Nagy suddenly issuing orders without explanation just like any politicians who reach the top.'

Fifteen minutes later Gero delivered the *coup de grâce*. Once again Radio Budapest interrupted its programme of music for 'an important announcement'. The Government, said the radio, was unprepared for 'the dastardly armed attack of counter-revolutionary gangs during the night ... and have therefore applied for help to the Soviet formations stationed in Hungary under the terms of the Warsaw Treaty'.

The information was hardly news, but there was an interesting difference between the two broadcasts: the first made it crystal clear that Nagy was involved in the declaration of martial law; the second deliberately gave no indication of responsibility. One broadcast followed so swiftly on the heels of the other that almost every listener believed both announcements had been made by the new government, that it was Nagy who had called in the Soviet tanks.

Gero must have known full well that few, if any, of the men and women already fighting in the streets could possibly have noticed the difference. Nor would they be able to work out for themselves how Nagy, who did not become premier until dawn, could summon Soviet troops which arrived during the night.

Worse still, Nagy now received a vicious blow from an outside source in which every oppressed Hungarian had faith. Without troubling to analyse, the American Radio Free Europe accepted the Hungarian Radio announcements at their face value and broadcast the news back to millions of Hungarians furtively listening to the clandestine radio whose every word, to them, spoke truth, and which now told them that it was none other than Nagy who had requested military assistance.

When Jozsef Kovago and Lonci heard the news on Radio Free Europe, Lonci's reaction was typical of millions of Hungarians. 'Nagy is a gangster too,' she told her husband. 'I told you not to trust him.' Kovago heard a friend chime in, 'He should be hung up next to Gero.'

In many ways this broadcast by Radio Free Europe was a pivotal point in the revolution. As Leslie Bain wrote later, 'after Nagy assumed the premiership, he was violently and incessantly attacked by foreign radios, principally by Radio Free Europe and the Voice of America, as having brought in the Russians ... the effect of this calumny was tremendous and contributed most importantly to the inability of Nagy to control events.' To the vital question of whether Nagy sent for Russian troops, 'The

West hurled a deafening Yes, and a very large part of the population believed it.'

Gero must have felt highly elated at this additional bonus, for the news dumbfounded Budapest. Now Gero decided to tackle another problem – the danger of defections in the Hungarian Army. From his office Gero put a telephone call through to Major-General Toth, Commander-in-Chief. His orders were to the point. General Toth would immediately send an officer of proven loyalty to Kilian Barracks in Ulloi Avenue to stiffen the morale of any troops whose sympathies might be in doubt.

It was a telephone call whose repercussions Gero could never have imagined in his wildest dreams, for it plucked out of obscurity a man who, in Hungary's darkest hours, displayed the courage of a hero.

4

The Living Legend

Colonel Pal Maleter happened to be duty officer at the Ministry of Defence on Wednesday. A lanky thirty-six-year-old, he was six feet three inches tall, his thick black hair already flecked with grey, his grey-blue eyes set wide apart above a strong nose, a large mouth, and a stubborn chin. The son of a professor of law, he had studied at a Hungarian military academy, and during the Second World War had been parachuted behind the German lines to lead a partisan group.

Throughout the night Maleter had been inundated with demands on the telephone in his cream-coloured duty room at the Ministry of Defence. Almost all came from junior officers desperate for advice on what action to take in the face of mounting desertions. Sternly Maleter had warned each officer, 'Your only loyalties are to the Army, the country and our legal government.' And that meant Gero – like him or not.

On Wednesday morning, after a sleepless night, the Colonel was nodding on a kitchen-type chair when he was wakened by the telephone. It was Major-General Toth, his commander-in-chief.

Toth – like Gero – was worried that defections would increase, for bitterness in the Hungarian Army had been brewing for years. Soviet advisory staffs all but controlled the nine divisions totalling 250,000 Hungarians, and Toth himself was surrounded by scores of Soviet 'advisors'.

They had rigorously imposed hated restrictions on the Hungarians. In any conflict of views the Soviet political officer took precedence over the Hungarian, irrespective of rank. Soviet military manuals translated into Hungarian often imposed rules

based on old Tsarist Russian traditions alien to the Hungarians. In
the past Hungarian troops had always slept a dozen or so to a
barrack room. The Russians insisted that a full company of a
hundred and fifty men must share one dormitory – with the
sergeant's bed by the door. The Russians changed the meal
customs. Hungarian soldiers had always eaten their big hot meal
of the day in the evening. Now they were compelled to follow
the Russian pattern of eating it in the morning.

Little things irked the Hungarians, but none more than the
Soviet-style blouse. Ever since the Congress of Berlin when
Bismarck talked disparagingly about uneducated troops who wore
their shirt outside their trousers, Hungarians had laughed at
these 'backward races'. Now they had to put up with the taunts
of their friends about men 'wearing shirts outside their pants'.

When it came to arms, their ammunition was rationed as
though, in the words of one soldier, 'they were handing out sweets
to a child'. Even though Russian T34 tanks were built in Hungary under Soviet licence, the Russians never granted a licence
for one small, vital piece of mechanism, immobilising each tank
until the missing piece was supplied from the Soviet Union.

Over the years resentment had built up, and even before Gero's
phone call General Toth knew that men at Kilian Barracks were
fraternising with insurgents in the Corvin Cinema, and allowing
them into the barracks.

He ordered Maleter to proceed to Kilian Barracks in charge
of a troop of five Hungarian tanks of the Aszod Armoured
Regiment and 'break the resistance of the revolutionaries near or
in the barracks'.

The barracks was an old building of no military significance –
except one. It was not only near the Corvin Cinema and the
complex called the Korvinplatz, but was connected with many
of the buildings, now being hurriedly fortified, by a warren of
underground tunnels, which had been dug when the building was
built so the barracks would never be in danger of a total siege.

By 1956 the barracks was used mainly for Hungarian soldiers
conscripted each October, who sat for their entrance examinations
in the lofty, ornate rooms, but to Toth this posed another potential danger for at this moment the garrison consisted of nine
hundred raw recruits for the engineering corps whose loyalties

might be open to question. The C.-in-C.'s apprehensions were well founded, for at the very moment when he was giving Maleter his orders insurgents were being warmly welcomed in the barracks.

By the time Maleter's tanks were making their way along Ulloi Avenue, towards Kalvin Square, the Colonel could hear the sound of gunfire. Insurgents darting out of Corvin Passage were hurling petrol bombs at two Soviet tanks. Snipers from rooftops killed any Russian who showed his head.

'We had no choice but to welcome the Russkies with rifle shots,' said one of the defenders.[1] 'That was all we had at the time. Then more tanks rumbled down and I could see the first coming straight at us. It crawled down as far as the crossing in front of the barracks.' At this moment two men set fire to it with Molotov cocktails and those on the roof sprayed it with a hail of bullets. 'Suddenly the Russians discovered where we were shooting from and trained their main guns at us and brought down a section three storeys high. There were many casualties.'

As Maleter neared the barracks his path was partly blocked by two disabled Soviet tanks. He had no wish to become embroiled with the Russians and he ordered the patrol to halt. It was at this moment that he had his first doubts. 'I was horrified and deeply upset by what I saw,' he remembered a few days later.[2] 'It didn't seem to me that these were Fascists or counter-revolutionaries. All I saw were the bodies of kids lying in the street – and tanks being shot up by rifle fire.'

Maleter sent two of his junior officers on foot to discover exactly what was happening. According to Maleter, 'Within half an hour they were back, and the first thing they told me was that the only civilians in the barracks were students, many of them teenagers, and some policemen.' He ordered his tanks to follow him, and stopped his own tank outside the main doors of the barracks, blocking the entrance. Presumably the Russians were also not anxious to tussle with the Hungarian armour, for the remaining Soviet tanks withdrew into Ulloi Avenue and Maleter got out, stood by his tank, surveying 'a scene that might have been the end of a battle in a major war. Bodies lay all over the place, the wounded were screaming and I ordered my men to

[1] Quoted in George Urban, *The Nineteen Days* (1957).
[2] In a conversation with the author on 28 October.

improvise stretchers out of house doors and carry them inside.'

Then he went inside. No one will ever know his thoughts at this moment; there are some who felt that Maleter's military career was not entirely above reproach, and that he was something of an opportunist. None, however, denies his bravery, and his very first action inside the barracks was typical of a professional soldier. Calling an insurgent forward, he asked him if he minded being questioned.

'No, sir,' replied the man.

'There is no such thing as "sir" in the People's Army, only comrades,' Maleter retorted sharply.

The young man had an intelligent face, and Maleter asked him his name, where he worked, how he had acquired his tommy-gun and grenades. The youngster told the Colonel of Hungary's standard of living, freedom 'which existed only on paper', of a patriotism being 'perverted and emptied of all meaning'. Then the youngster fished in his pocket for his Party card and produced the students' sixteen demands scribbled on the back.

Maleter had embraced Communism many years previously, though whether he had done so to further his army career or because of deep convictions is hard to say; but now, as he later remembered, 'This was the moment I knew I would have to make a decision that would change my life. Once in the barracks, it was clear to me that those fighting for their freedom were not bandits, but loyal sons of Hungary.'

At this point the discipline of a good soldier came to the fore. The decision reached, he ordered one of the insurgents to lead him to a telephone. When he heard General Toth's voice on the other end of the line, 'I informed him that I was going over to the insurgents.'

From that moment Pal Maleter took command. The five Hungarian tanks were deployed to guard the main gates. Two anti-tank guns from the modest arsenal added to their firepower. Swiftly the one-time partisan, skilled in the art of guerilla warfare, turned the barracks and neighbouring buildings into an elaborate fortress so that in a matter of hours the insurgents were 'at home in the rabbit warren of small houses and blocks of flats. ... When faced by overwhelming force, they simply disappeared into narrow alleys and houses, only to emerge later, still fighting.'

All over Hungary the news of the struggle in Budapest spread with the speed of a forest fire. Nothing like this had happened since the historic uprising of 1848.

Nowhere was the response to danger more fervent than in the farmlands of the Great Plain. This is a vast area, covering more than half the country, of rustling maize and sunflowers and, in the autumn, carpets of peppers drying by the sides of the empty roads that seem to stretch into infinity. The horizon is broken here and there by a barefoot peasant boy tending a flock of geese, or the skeletal arm of an old well's crossbeam.

It seemed a world apart, and yet, in some miraculous fashion, everyone here seemed to know what was happening. Perhaps the peasants could read between the radio's lines and still trusted Nagy, the man who had once tried to save them. Miraculously, too, the Hungarian telephone never stopped functioning.

Everyone who could walk or ride a bicycle wanted to go to Budapest 'to save Imre Nagy'. In the straggling villages of one-storey vine-covered houses of sun-dried mud, bouquets of flowers – marigolds, geraniums and madonna lilies – were placed on the war memorial to Hungarian dead that graced the main street of almost every village, yet had to be officially ignored; while at the other end of the village the more daring spirits among the younger men climbed the angular black granite obelisk of the Soviet memorial to tear down the red star.

In the dark kitchens, smelling of cheese and spices and rough wine, black-shawled grandmothers who had never been to Budapest started packing parcels of food, while the old men hobbled to the *italbolt* – literally the 'drink shop' – to fetch a bottle of spirits for sons eager to leave for 'the war in Budapest'.

In the provincial towns, factories and bus companies handed over their vehicles. Attendants in the petrol stations filled up the tanks, and spurned payment. Near the town of Siofok on Lake Balaton peasant women gathered up the food they were selling in the market and gave it to a truck driver to help 'the fighters in Budapest'. Far to the north-east in Eger, at the foot of the Bukk Mountains, every poacher turned gamekeeper and a load of illicitly shot game was soon speeding to Pest.

Arms seemed to be spirited out of a dozen provincial arsenals. When miners from Ajka and factory workers from Veszprem drove across the Bakony Mountains and descended on the big police station at Papa, demanding arms, the police major in command said simply, 'Take whatever you require. Go and help the people of Budapest.' The local army barracks handed out more weapons. In the industrial centre of Dunapentele, once a small village before the Communists transformed it into a city of 28,000 steel, iron and chemical workers,[1] representatives from each factory formed a Workers' Revolutionary Council.

At Gyor Major Krecz, local commander of the Hungarian Army, salved any twinges of conscience by declaring that he would follow to the letter his military oath, 'Through fire and water with the people.'

In some places officers temporised in this first day of fighting. At Szolnok, a garrison town mid-way between Budapest and the Romanian frontier, the Hungarian commander confined every man to barracks 'so they would keep out of trouble'.

Shortly after noon Nagy broadcast an appeal to the nation.[2] Though only a few people had been able to catch more than a word or two the previous night, all Hungary now tuned in, everyone totally ignorant of the secret drama that lay behind the apparently uninspired speech peppered with jingoistic Communist phrases. For Imre Nagy, legal Prime Minister of Hungary, was compelled to make the broadcast under the watchful eyes of three Avos, in the studio beside him, their guns drawn. His fellow countrymen listened with mounting despair to phrases like 'hostile elements' who, said Nagy, had 'joined the ranks of peacefully demonstrating Hungarian youth'. He begged his listeners, 'to line up behind the Party', admonished those who had 'turned against the People's Democracy'.

To the listeners, fired with the promise of a new world, he made only the vaguest promises. 'I will soon announce in detail the programme of the new government which will be debated in the National Assembly which will meet soon,' he said.

---

[1] They rechristened it Stalinvaros in the process.
[2] For the full text, see Appendix III.

But there is no tomorrow in a battle, and the fighters in the streets, their friends dying by their sides, cared nothing for the National Assembly or when it would meet. To them the image of Nagy they admired had vanished, replaced by that of a doctrinaire leader who seemed out of touch with popular sentiment.

They could not know that from the early morning Nagy had demanded the right to speak on the radio. Every suggestion was brushed aside by Gero, and when Nagy persisted an angry Gero ordered the Avos to keep the Prime Minister in his office by force if necessary.

After giving Nagy time to cool off – or so he hoped – Gero reappeared brandishing a radio script which he had dictated in his office.

'Go and read this into the tape recorder,' he said.

Nagy took one look at the opening words, which contained the phrase 'rebel Fascist bandits', and threw the sheets of paper on the floor. He would never make such a speech, he declared, even if his life were forfeit. An Avo picked up the script and handed it to Gero who stormed out, again ordering the Avos to keep Nagy locked in his office.

Gero returned an hour later, more conciliatory, apparently realising that sooner or later Nagy must make some sort of speech or the public would become suspicious. He asked Nagy if he would care to make some changes. The draft script went back and forth between the two men several times, with Nagy still a prisoner.

Nagy was in a difficult position. He felt that at all costs he must talk to the nation and that therefore he would have to compromise. He spent a long time drafting changes, with one hope in the back of his mind: that, though he could say nothing, he might be able to spell out a message to the more perceptive in his audience by the very nature of his omissions. With great skill he cut out all references to the presence of Soviet troops in Hungary, hoping that people would be puzzled, that they would expect at least some kind of excuse, however feeble and contrived, if he *had* asked for the Russians to intervene. Nor did he even once mention the name of Gero, or take the opportunity of denouncing Rakosi.

He did manage, however, to wring one concession out of Gero

for agreeing to broadcast 'his' message: an amnesty for all freedom fighters who lay down their arms by 2 p.m. Finally Gero
approved the script, and Nagy was hustled off to a small studio
at the back of Party headquarters. There was only one window –
but out of it, as the technicians tested the microphone, Nagy
could see Soviet tanks guarding the street below.

When all was ready three Avos entered the room. Their task,
as charged by Gero, was to make certain that not one single word
was changed. They drew their revolvers; Nagy sat down at a
small green-baize table; the red light went on; Nagy started
to tape his speech.

Few people realised the truth, for Nagy's listeners were not
trained in the art of detecting broadcasting nuances, but Tibor
Meray noticed that 'the second part of the speech was more
ordered than the first, which sounded almost breathless'. This
was in fact because Nagy had added the amnesty message almost
at the last moment.

Dezso Kosak, of the Hungarian News Agency on Nap Hill, felt
that 'the short declaration on the radio seemed peculiar'. Kosak
had a premonition that 'there was something wrong somewhere'
so he tried to telephone Nagy on the secret 'K' line 'to inform
him about the actual situation in the country'. Kosak knew the
number of the Prime Minister's office – the 'K' line was limited to
two hundred numbers – but when he telephoned he was met
with a muttered 'wrong number'. He rang again (not knowing of
course that Nagy was not in Parliament Building) and this time
tried to leave a message about 'the desperate state of the fighting'.
A female voice on the other end of the line shouted 'Lies!' and
hung up.

Nagy's broadcast had been ineffectual enough, but it was nothing
compared with many of the naïve Radio Budapest broadcasts
during the day. Some were utterly ridiculous. In an effort to
rouse popular support against the revolution, Radio Budapest
even brought in its most famous sports commentator, Gyorgy
Szepesi, to point out that if the fighting did not cease the famous
Hungarian football team might not be able to play in the Olympic
Games at Melbourne.

'Our sports life stands on the threshold of gigantic tests,' he announced solemnly. 'Wouldn't it be a happy moment if the Hungarian flag were again hoisted on the Olympic mast at Melbourne.' On a more local, and immediate, note, Szepesi then told his listeners, 'Let us hope the revolution will end by Sunday because the people of Hungary would not like to miss the international match with Sweden.'

Szepesi was stupid enough to talk about the insurgents looting – something that never happened during the revolution – and this brought waves of anger. Placards denouncing him appeared in the streets, together with demands that he should never be allowed to broadcast again.[1]

Other radio crackpots added fuel to the fires. The hitherto unimportant National Council of Hungarian Women attacked 'the infamous counter-revolutionaries', while the equally obscure National Council of Peace described the fighters as 'bandits, thieves and bands of murderers'.

No one was more disturbed by the attitude of the radio than its staff member Dora Scarlett. 'The radio was in fact playing a strange game,' she remembered later. 'It broadcast all government announcements and proclamations and all important speeches, as it was bound to do, but it was giving an account of events which was quite at variance with that of the trade unions and the Revolutionary Councils. From the beginning it talked about the Fascist, reactionary and counter-revolutionary bands. The radio was creating anger and hostility by the whole tone of its broadcasts. More and more notices appeared on the streets saying: "The radio lies; don't listen to it." '

---

[1] Memories are short and Szepesi soon returned as Budapest's favourite sports commentator.

5

The Schoolkids' War

Wednesday, 24 October (concluded)

As the fighting spread, it was youth triumphant that remained the vital character of the revolution, as it had been from the beginning. Teenagers seemed to take an almost perverse delight in devising new weapons to combat Soviet tanks. From the overhead tram-cables they hung saucepans filled with water dangling three or four feet above the ground, which to a man inside a turret must have looked every inch a deadly anti-tank weapon. When the tank driver hesitated, insurgents from windows above hurled down petrol bombs or grenades.

In Szena Square a group of youngsters raided a nearby shop reserved for Party leaders, seizing several bales of silk. After spreading it over most of the square they poured oil on it. When Soviet tanks reached the silk, they were unable to move on the slippery surface and, their treads turning uselessly, they became stationary targets for petrol bombs. In Moricz Zsigmond Square, where some of the first tanks appeared, almost the entire surface had been doused with liquid soap. As the tanks became immobilised, daring youngsters darted forward below the arc of fire and with sticky fingers daubed jam over the tanks' glass panels. A tank driver foolish enough to switch on his wipers found it impossible to see through the smear. Across the wide boulevards, soup plates filled with soil looked like land mines.

Lazlo Beke was driving along the Boulevard of the Martyrs in Buda when he saw three Soviet tanks down a side street some distance away. Then a group of youngsters emerged from the Catholic church near Szena Square and seeing Beke begged him to hide and watch. One boy carried a long rope. 'He darted across the street with it, his friend holding the other end.' The tanks had still not turned the corner. Another boy ran into the middle of the road and fastened three bottles filled with petrol to the rope which lay on the ground. The boys then juggled the bottles back and forth until they were roughly in line with the treads of the approaching tanks. By the time the tanks turned the corner, not a Hungarian was in sight. When the first tank scooped up a bottle, three boys ran out and threw burning paper at the bottles. As they exploded, damaging the tank tracks, the boys reached the safety of the church where Beke was watching – and listening to Budapest Radio solemnly announce, 'Sorry, but the children's hour has been cancelled tonight. Don't be angry, children, that you have to go to bed without your bed-time stories.'

From the safety of the alleyway behind the church, Beke drove the boys away, but as he looked at their pink excited faces one question intrigued him. How had they learned the arts of partisan war so quickly?

One of them, with 'a schoolboy grin, impish and defiant', answered cheerfully, 'Oh! It's easy. Twice a week our masters take us into the fields and teach us things like this from the Russian classic *The Young Guardsman* by Fadeyev. They told us this would be the way we would fight the enemies from the West.'

Apart from the students at the Technological University who were fighting mostly in Buda, much of the toughest fighting on this first chaotic Wednesday took place in the heavily populated 8th and 9th districts of Pest, an area dominated by the hundred-year-old East railway station, with its huge glass-domed central hall – and a statue of Stephenson. Imposing buildings lined the boulevards, yet just behind them workers' flats separated by narrow alleys housed thousands of workers. The two suburbs formed a 'village' with a flavour of their own, as distinct as the old Les Halles in Paris or Covent Garden in London, with workers and artisans living cheek by jowl, each one with his favourite smoky Bohemian café, long a source of inspiration to Hungarian writers.

No freedom fighters wanted for food or shelter in the 8th and 9th districts. Flats were hastily turned into improvised first-aid posts. At one stage insurgents even attacked the East railway station, but were driven off by Soviet tanks; in the open the Hungarians could not hope to be a match for Russian armour.

For this reason isolated battles often took on an almost unreal quality of craziness, for guns would be blazing in one street, yet round the corner shawled women would be queueing for bread.

One extraordinary battle, involving one lone Hungarian against five Soviet tanks, lasted for two hours in a block of flats at Engels Square, near the British Legation. Here a Hungarian sniper was holed up and the Russians were determined to ferret him out after he shot dead a member of a tank crew. In the street below two tanks and a mounted gun kept up a steady but vain barrage to dislodge him. Three more Soviet tanks patrolled up and down the street. Each time the Russian firing stopped for a moment, the sudden silence was broken by the whine of a single rifle bullet from behind a shattered window.

To John MacCormac of the *New York Times*, who watched the battle, the final touch of unreality came when 'in the middle of it all a civilian calmly strolled across the line of fire with a briefcase under his arm'.

It was the same in the provinces. Fighting had broken out in most towns, and Vlado Teslic of the Yugoslav newspaper *Borba* found it so difficult driving on roads choked with truckloads of youths on their way to Budapest that he decided to try to get a meal in Szeged, a town of 136,000 people on his route from the Yugoslav frontier. The manifestations of war had been so evident on the drive that he was astonished to walk into the city's main restaurant and find that 'a band was playing and about twenty couples were dancing'.

There was little co-ordinated action; it was every man for himself. As a Hungarian professor of philosophy, unnamed as his relatives live in Hungary, told the United Nations:

It was unique in history that the Hungarian revolution had no leaders. It was not organised; it was not centrally directed. The will for freedom was the moving force in every action. At the beginning of the revolution, the leading role was played by Communists almost exclusively. Everybody helped the fighters. When standing in line for food they were given free entry. 'They are our sons!' was the slogan.

*   *   *

One of Joan Fish's first problems was to deal with stranded British businessmen. The first cry for help came from Mr James All-march, a textile merchant from Manchester – at the Hotel Astoria, which the Russians had commandeered as their head-quarters.

Four businessmen were in the Astoria, he said. They had little or no money, the hotel would not or could not cash their travellers' cheques. Worst of all, the Russian guards refused to let them leave the hotel. Every request was met with blank and stony refusals 'by bloody officers in long grey overcoats smoking cigarettes in cardboard holders'. Allmarch had been trying for twenty-four hours to telephone the British consul without success.

Joan Fish decided to go to the Astoria herself. She set off in her Land Rover, driven by the Hungarian Legation driver Receczy, who spoke Russian. At the last moment, Mr Fry, the Minister, decided to follow.

The consul arrived first and, before the Russians had time to react, the burly Receczy pushed Joan and himself through the front doors and into the lobby. Mr Fry was not so lucky. As he stepped out of his car, a Russian sentry, feet astride, barred his way by the simple process of holding his rifle horizontally across the glass door.

For fifteen minutes Receczy haggled with officers. Joan Fish could hear the occasional, 'But this is the British Minister!' And, more frequently, that well-known Russian monosyllable, *'Niet!'*

Finally Mr Fry was allowed in – and then out, with the four businessman. He drove them back to his house in Buda for a good breakfast.

By early afternoon the dominating personality of Pal Maleter in the Kilian Barracks was making itself felt. The area became a fortress in fact as well as appearance. Using Thomas Szabo's school in nearby Prater Street as headquarters, Maleter set up a Revolutionary High Command. Hastily he telephoned all his old friends in the Army, trying to enlist their support. 'I never tried to persuade anyone,' he remembered later. 'Though I had made up *my* mind, I didn't feel it right to force my opinions on others. I just asked. But I wasn't surprised at the number who decided to join us.'

Soon more than a score of officers were making their way to Prater Street School – on foot, by car, one colonel on a bicycle – and were given commands in different parts of the city – mainly at the Technological College, Fo Street, Szena Square and Baross Square, all comparatively easy to defend against an enemy with no infantry, each of them in contact with Maleter by telephone.

Employing the partisan tactics he had used in the past, Maleter sent out raiding parties to gather arms or fight the Avo, as Thomas Szabo discovered when he was suddenly told to proceed to a building in Dohany Street, near the famous Café Hungaria where Avos in a building were firing down on insurgents.

In theory Thomas and his squad could have raced to the Hungaria in a few minutes. But they had barely passed Rakosi Street, one block north of the radio station, when they came face to face with four Soviet tanks ranged by the plush Hotel Astoria at the corner of Rakosi Street, now a Russian stronghold. 'We cautiously advanced in Indian file as far as the Ady Cinema, but we were unable to fire from that position, so we tried to get past on the other side of the street.'

That was the moment the Avos spotted them. They immediately opened fire with a stream of tracer bullets. The boys dashed to safety through the broken windows of a shattered shop, clambering over the balustrade separating the windows from the pavement – all but two who had lagged behind. As they reached the shopfront, the Avo bullets hit them. One boy was killed; the other, like Szabo only fifteen, was shot in the leg. Szabo 'scuttled outside for a moment to bring him in. I lifted him in my arms and held him out to my friends inside the window.'

But, in saving the boy, Szabo could not get back in and the Avos were concentrating their fire on him. The shop windows, barely two yards distant, but which he could not enter without standing up, 'seemed quite inaccessible'. Flattening himself on the ground, he sheltered behind the body of the dead boy, shivering as he touched the corpse. 'Suddenly I noticed that he had red hair.' It was a boy with whom he had shared guard duty in the night.

The Russian tanks were pounding the area, and as Szabo lay there paralysed with fear for what seemed hours – it was in fact only a matter of minutes – all he could repeat to himself was a cry from a boy's heart, 'I don't want to die, I want to go home.'

Without warning, without any explanation, the firing stopped. In the curious way that battles throughout the revolution would erupt with uncontrolled ferocity and then unaccountably be broken off as abruptly as they had started, the street was suddenly quiet. Szabo tried to crawl back, 'but I could not manage it; my legs were numb'. Two boys dragged him to safety and massaged his legs back to life.

Szabo escaped just in time, for almost immediately the Russian tanks opened fire again, this time not in the direction of Dohany Street, but down Museum Avenue. Unknown to Szabo, Mark Molnar and his men had decided to launch an all-out attack on the Astoria.

Molnar had prepared his plans carefully. Each night he sent his troops home, meeting different battalions at different places each morning. His headquarters was in a cellar at 92 Rakosi Street – 'I'll never forget that address!' – which he shared with the concierge, an old friend called Furst, with whom he had once for five months shared a prison cell. There had been a third man in the cell and Furst knew where to find him. He worked in one of the big arms factories at Csepel, and when Molnar outlined his plans for attacking the Astoria Furst said, 'Without some sort of artillery you won't stand a chance. Leave it to me.'

During the night two trucks arrived from Csepel, loaded with arms – including two field guns. Molnar knew just where to hide them. He climbed aboard the truck carrying the guns and drove down nearby Puskin Street which he had already reconnoitred. One building, with a courtyard, ran right through the block, opening on to the parallel Museum Avenue – directly opposite the Astoria. During the night they trundled the guns from one street to another, and now, unaware of Szabo's predicament, Molnar opened fire.

With the first shots, half of the first-floor wall collapsed. Two of his machine-guns backed up the field guns, spraying the windows, every exit, any man who moved. When the Soviet tanks – at first caught by surprise – swivelled and opened fire with their heavier guns, Molnar's 'infantry' went in, darting under the arc of fire with their grenades.

There was one tragedy. Among Molnar's best fighters was a girl in her twenties who had been a tram conductor – she kept her grenades in the large pouch worn by all Budapest conductors for their tickets and money. She tossed three grenades. Each one missed the target. 'Then she must have got mad,' Molnar remembers. 'A Russian officer appeared in a turret for a moment. She ran forward, clawed her way on to the tank, but to make sure she waited until she had almost reached the turret before she blew up the tank – and herself.'

Endre Martin of the Associated Press, who watched the battle from the windows of the British Legation, found later that every window in the Astoria Hotel had been broken and all the glass shattered on 'the shiny passenger cars with foreign number plates'. The hotel walls were pockmarked with shellfire. A small fire was burning in one wing.

Szabo left the dead and the wounded boy in the care of civilians before returning to the Corvin Cinema to report to Colonel Maleter.

On the other side of the Danube, Beke was making his first contact with Maleter's command. The Technological University had been turned into a fortress by now. In the famous 'Room Seven', known to thousands of students of organic chemistry, forty boys and three young professors had 'formed a human conveyor belt to pass rifles, machine-guns and hundreds of boxes of ammunition which had arrived from Csepel Island'. As Beke watched, a blond young man ran up the stairs shouting, 'I'm from the Kilian Barracks. I'd like to see some of the student leaders here.' Beke introduced himself and two other members of the Revolutionary Council.

'My father wants to send two officers here to help you to fight the Russians,' the boy explained, at which one student asked, 'But who are you? And who's this father of yours?'

'Colonel Maleter,' the blond boy replied. 'That's who my father is. I'm Peter Maleter.'

Within hours two officers arrived in Buda, setting up their headquarters in the barracks behind the ornate thirteenth-century Royal Palace on Castle Hill, north of the Technological University, and backing on to the Danube. Beke was sent to be interviewed by one of the officers for a very good reason. He was the only member of the students' Revolutionary Council who had served as an officer in the Hungarian Army, and so was the logical choice as link man between the University and the Buda branch of Maleter's command. In addition Beke nursed a hope that he might be able to get a radio transmitter, for communications were the students' biggest problem. 'We were already using boys not yet in their teens to run messages.'

The officer wasted no time, and Beke never forgot his opening words. 'The most faithful allies of the Army,' he told Beke, 'are the students and the workers in the city and the peasants in the country. We must link these forces so we can hit harder at the Soviets, and we must always know what the left hand is doing when we strike with the right.'

Beke was promised his radio transmitter with which to keep Central Command in Pest fully informed about all fighting in Buda. He was also ordered to establish contact with the Students' Freedom Movement in Gyor. 'Despite splendid patriotism,' the officer told him, 'there is no real co-ordination between universities and colleges.'

Beke, driven by the faithful Feri, set off for Pest to pick up the transmitter. Driving across the Chain Bridge, they had just reached Vigado Square, near the Duna Hotel, when Fero stopped. At the corner of the square, on the Danube Promenade, in summer the mecca of Budapest sunbathers, the bodies of twelve youngsters hung limply from trees and lamposts. The Avo, Beke discovered later, had executed them in revenge for pulling down a sculptured Soviet plane from the top of a nearby Liberation monument. As Feri drove away, the radio in their armoured car announced, 'Revolutionary gangs have been largely liquidated.'

If the youngsters fighting in the streets learned their partisan techniques from Soviet books, the workers of Hungary could also thank the Soviet-controlled press for their ability to organise their first general strike. There had been no major strike in Hungary for twenty-five years, but every worker knew just what to do, thanks to the lengthy and enthusiastic accounts of strikes in Britain, France and Italy that appeared regularly in *Szabad Nep*.

The call for a general strike was obeyed with alacrity by workers who now saw an opportunity of fulfilling what had been in the past a cherished right. In factory after factory the workers downed tools. Urgently Radio Budapest, in a special appeal to the country's 800,000 card-carrying members of the Party, cried, 'Communists! Militants! In these grave hours when fighting is in progress ... all members of the Party have the duty to protect peace and order. You must convince the waverers, stop all disorder.'

The message fell on deaf ears, for if the students and writers had rebelled against frustration the workers were even more bitter because of the ever-widening gulf between promises and the harsh facts of reality. 'Under Communism, we should have had a share in governing Hungary,' said one worker from the Red Star Tractor works, 'but instead we're the poorest people in the country. We're just regarded as factory fodder. Rakosi never kept a single promise to the workers.'

The decision to strike was followed swiftly by the formation of Workers' Councils which were touched with the same mark of irony so evident throughout the revolution. For, though the radio appealed to the workers not to join the councils, the workers were in fact only doing what the Bolsheviks had done in 1917. Despairing of their central government, the Hungarian councils – in other words the Soviets – were trying to overrule the National Assembly, in other words the Duma of 1917.

The first council in Budapest was formed at the Incandescent Lamp factory. Soon Workers' Councils were springing up all over Hungary and taking on the role of a national liberation movement.

Late on Wednesday morning – the exact time has never been established – the revolution received a tremendous fillip. On the direct orders of the chief of the Budapest Police Force, thirty-six-year-old Colonel Sandor Kopacsi, the entire force went over to the insurgents. The police in many stations had already helped the freedom fighters, and others had tried to remain in the background as much as possible, but this official decision was a very different matter.

Kopacsi, the son of factory-workers in northern Hungary, had

made his own way to the top, and his first instincts, as a good
policeman, had been to uphold the law at all costs. Indeed the
previous evening he had fired over the heads of a crowd below
his office windows, believing the radio's denunciations against
'Fascists' and 'bourgeois reactionaries'. But when Kopacsi interviewed a few people who had been arrested he had been
astonished to find nothing more menacing than young, enthusiastic Communists.

Kopacsi himself was a frustrated Communist, an admirer of
Nagy, who saw the role of the police in normal times as very
different from that of the Avo. 'People are afraid of so many
things,' he was fond of telling his men. 'It's our job to protect
them and above all not to make them afraid.' His attitude was
shared by his force, which was not concerned with making political arrests and hated the Avo which, as Ferenc Vali felt, 'displayed
a haughty, condescending or violently critical attitude towards
its step-brother'.

Sometime during the Wednesday morning Kopacsi made his
way to Parliament Building to seek an interview with Nagy. He
was surprised to learn that the Prime Minister was not in his
office and had not been there since his appointment. He immediately went to Party headquarters and demanded to see
Nagy.

Armed Avo guards told him it was impossible. When he argued,
he was threatened. Kopasci was a personal friend of the Premier's
and the incident disturbed him. Deeply suspicious – though for
the moment he kept his suspicions to himself – Kopacsi returned
to police headquarters behind Parliament Building, a grim
fifteen-storey building of white stone topped by a radio mast and
fronted by green lawns.

He made some enquiries, and discovered that Nagy was not
as free to act as a prime minister should be. Geza Losonczy told
him on the telephone of the events of the previous evening, and
also expressed fears for Nagy's safety, though, as he stressed,
nothing could be proved for the simple reason that nobody could
make contact with the Prime Minister.

Within the hour Kopacsi decided to throw in his lot with the
insurgents. He issued orders for the police to provide the revolu-

tion with weapons. The order was immediately flashed to every major police station in Hungary.

The reaction from Party headquarters was dramatic. Gero telephoned Kopacsi and ordered him to rescind it. Otherwise, Gero threatened, he would send in the Avo to arrest Kopacsi. Since his huge headquarters was admirably guarded by members of his own loyal force, Kopacsi answered the First Secretary laconically, 'Then come and get me.'

Now Kopacsi took another unprecedented step. He dismissed his Soviet advisor who, according to Ferenc Vali, 'had been seen on the night of 23–4 October sitting frightened at his desk repeatedly muttering, "*Grazhdanskaya voyna!*" (civil war).'

From that moment police headquarters in Budapest became one of the key nerve centres of the revolution. Now one more task faced the courageous police chief: to discover, if possible, what was happening to Nagy, and if necessary to rescue him. It was a task that would take him two days.

By the nature of things, the news that Kopacsi had pledged his support to the insurgents became common gossip once the decision had been flashed over the police radio and the first arms distributed. That afternoon an even more momentous decision was taken; but this time, tragically, it was kept secret, on orders from the Kremlin.

Around 2 o'clock two armoured cars, sandwiched between two Soviet tanks, appeared in Academy Street and stopped outside Party headquarters. Half a dozen Russian troops leapt from the tanks and stood guard with tommy-guns as the doors of the armoured cars were opened. From the first one stepped a short Armenian with a hooked nose. It was Anastas Mikoyan. From the second, a tall, thin, man clambered out with difficulty. It was Mikhail Suslov, a Russian. They were both Soviet Deputy Premiers. They had been driven from the airport after flying into Budapest at Khrushchev's bidding.

The two men were strangely contrasted, not only in height and looks, but in political ideologies. Suslov was a diehard Stalinist who (aided by Molotov) had bitterly opposed Khrushchev's fawning overtures (and public apology) to Tito. Mikoyan, on the other hand, genuinely admired Nagy, the true Communist. Suslov had on several occasions made no bones about his admiration for Rakosi.

Now, however, their differing lines of political thought were welded by white-hot anger against none other than Gero. Without any pretence of diplomatic niceties, the two men went straight to Gero's office in Party headquarters, and though we shall probably never know the details of their fateful meeting we do have a general account of what transpired. All agree with the summing-up of Tibor Meray, who wrote that 'the accusations ... literally poured out. Gero had shown himself to be a poor politician; he had not instituted the changes demanded by the spirit of the Twentieth Congress. In spite of Soviet advice, he had not called on Comrade Nagy. His unfortunate speech over the radio had only aroused the people.'

According to other sources Mikoyan accused Gero of having 'stampeded' Moscow into sending Russian troops by his 'exaggerated and distorted' picture of the fighting, while Suslov bluntly 'suggested' that Gero should resign. When Gero protested, reminding Suslov that Khrushchev himself had said he was needed to hold the Party together, Mikoyan retorted, 'The Party has already fallen apart, thanks to your incredible blunders.'

After an hour of wrangling, Gero was finally advised to resign; but then an extraordinary thing happened. It was decided that to maintain some outward semblance of Party unity the dismissal of Gero would for the time being be kept secret. He was told that he would not be allowed to make any speeches, nor must he attend any public meetings or discussions. His successor as First Party Secretary would be Janos Kadar and, though Kadar would in the future be the Party spokesman, no announcement of any changes would be made.

It was an extraordinary blunder by the Russians and it is hard to understand how two men who had survived for forty years in the Kremlin political jungle could not read more clearly the outward signs – that Gero had supplanted Rakosi as the most hated man in the country. Possibly the truth never seeped through the thick walls of Party headquarters whose only real contact with the stirring events came from Budapest Radio; but had the dismissal of Gero been made public at once everything might have changed.

Mikoyan and Suslov now made another blunder, when they went to discuss a course of action with Nagy. Nagy had met them before, and both men told him they were aghast at the carnage they had seen while driving in from the airport, and both insisted that the simplest, the most direct course of action would be to crush the 'counter-revolutionaries' with brute force. 'The quicker the better,' said Mikoyan.

Nagy was horrified – and said so. For two hours he begged them to let him have an opportunity of proving that he could stop the fighting. Obviously Mikoyan and Suslov would have been delighted had he been able to do this, but to every argument put forward by Nagy there was one stumbling-block: Nagy insisted that to win the support of the people he must first wipe out Gero's smear campaign labelling him as the man who called in Russian troops. To achieve this, he told Mikoyan and Suslov, all he had to do was to broadcast to the nation. 'I have no wish to blame Comrade Gero or anyone else for the decision,' he said, 'but I have the right to tell the nation that I had nothing to do with it. After that they will do anything I ask of them.'

The Russians flatly refused. Possibly they were hedging their bet, or perhaps they considered, as Suslov put it, that 'The imperialists have already profited too much from the blunders in Hungary.'

So the two Kremlin experts, in the course of one afternoon, committed two blunders of the first magnitude. Had Nagy been allowed to restore his popularity, he might well have been able to persuade the freedom fighters to trust him to achieve at least some of their aims without spilling more blood, as Gomulka had done in Poland; and the Soviet Union would have been spared the opprobium of world opinion for the course of action on which it later decided.

That evening the two visitors from the Kremlin had a cold supper in Party headquarters, and then retired to spend the night in a large office furnished with two camp beds and a small portable radio. There were no curtains. Below them they could hear the tanks as they manœuvred, the spatter of machine-gun fire and the heavier thud of cannon; the darkness was split sporadically by the light of fires. On the radio Janos Kadar was making his first speech as Party spokesman, lacing it with laudatory praise for our 'Soviet brothers' who were so gallantly helping Hungary to defend herself against counter-revolutionaries 'backed by imperialist forces'.

One wonders if Mikoyan and Suslov, both battle-scarred revolutionaries in their youth, listened to the radio that evening, and if so whether they saw the irony. Not by the wildest stretch of the imagination could anyone say that Soviet Russia was helping in a fight against the agents of imperialism. In fact the opposite was the case: Russian imperialists were at this very moment attempting to crush Hungarian Soviets.

6

The Slaughter of the Innocents

Thursday and Friday, 25–6 October

By Thursday morning the city was calmer. When the Polish writer Marian Bieliciki reached Budapest, she discovered 'Long walls of empty factories. Little houses in front of which a few people hover, ready to hide. Something uncanny in the air. Is it horror, fear, hatred, or despair? From windows and balconies heavy wet flags are drooping, white-green-red, and also black colours of mourning. The symbol of freedom and the symbol of death, the price of mourning.'[1]

The battle was by no means over, but exhaustion was taking its toll. Some insurgents were running out of ammunition, others quietly disposed of their arms and took advantage of the amnesty that had twice been extended. The Government even urged workers on the 6.30 a.m. news to return to their factories, so that 'life might resume its normal course'.

This was not remotely possible, for none of the original demands had been met and the presence of Gero still infuriated most Hungarians. Still, as Dora Scarlett found, 'it was possible to walk through a large part of the city, avoiding the main streets which were being cleared by the Soviet tanks'.

Eva, the pregnant young wife of Lazlo Beke, found much the same thing when, somewhat unwisely, she left the sanctuary of the students' hostel. Lazlo had not returned to see her in the night so, depressed and anxious, she felt the need for a breath of air. She decided to cross the Danube to Pest. Anna Gabor, the young secretary who had watched the attack on the radio station, also felt that 'I had to get out, do something, see what was happening'.

[1] In the Polish newspaper *Po Prostu*.

Many people walked the streets out of curiosity, for overnight the face of Budapest had changed. Along most avenues where tanks had operated, holes gaped in the grey buildings; ceilings seemed to hang crazily in mid-air, supported by invisible threads. People had to pick their way across debris, torn-up roadways, past the carcases of tanks – and past corpses too.

The paths of the three women all led towards Parliament Square where a crowd was converging in a peaceful unarmed demonstration, quite unlike any other in the revolution. The fact was that the marchers were led by Russian soldiers, their tanks bedecked with Hungarian flags. It seemed incredible, but there were smiling Russians helping eager Hungarian youngsters to scramble on their tanks.

It had started in a curious way at 8.30 a.m., when fewer than a thousand men and women assembled near the shattered and shelled Hotel Astoria. The Russian tanks of the previous day had returned, but their crews stood idly by, for the crowd consisted mainly of middle-aged people with their children. They were certainly not insurgents and none was armed. Waving Hungarian flags they set off for Parliament Square in the hope of seeing Nagy (unaware that he was still captive in Party headquarters).

A quarter of a mile along Tanacs Street three Soviet tanks near the Budapest Cathedral opened fire. No one was hurt. Half the people darted into side streets, the rest ran back towards the Astoria Hotel, where the first group of Russian tanks did not seem disposed to interfere with the demonstrators. Indeed, some Russian crewmen were talking to Hungarians who had gathered there at the sound of shooting. The demonstrators joined them and asked in halting Russian (which all schoolchildren were compelled to learn) why some Russians fired on unarmed demonstrators, while others refrained. To the astonishment of the Hungarians, several Russians agreed that their comrades had been wrong.

'We stood there for the best part of an hour talking and arguing,' Anna remembers. 'It was crazy really when you come to think of it – the Russians had been sent to kill us if necessary, but we were all talking like old friends.'

The upshot was extraordinary. Dora Scarlett was turning the

corner of Sziv Street into Lovolde Square when she saw that 'a tank had stopped and the crew got out and asked for an interpreter. They were given a Hungarian flag and put it up. As soon as someone was found who could talk to them, the crew asked what they should do.'

Jozsef Kovago the ex-Mayor of Budapest was also there, and watched a 'little old lady' go into action when another tank made a threatening gesture by training its guns on some teenagers. She walked straight up to the tank and exclaimed indignantly, 'We don't want to occupy your country, so why do you take ours?'

As Kovago watched and listened, the Russian suddenly declared, 'I refuse to shoot on women and children.' He offered his tank 'to take them anywhere they wanted to go'. As the teenagers gleefully clambered aboard, one cried with a laugh, 'Good Russki! Show us how good a cabbie you are!' The Russian laughed back, and Dora Scarlett heard someone cry, 'Go with us to Parliament Building – there's going to be a big demonstration there!'

All accounts agree with the United Nations report that this is just what happened. 'After about an hour's discussion the crew of a Soviet tank said they felt that the demands of the demonstrators were justified and that they should go to the Parliament Building together.'

Excited Hungarians clambered aboard three tanks, planting the national colours in the turrets. A burly crew-cropped Russian 'with an engaging, cheerful grin' lifted Anna bodily on to the leading tank and told her to show him the way. More than a score of others managed to get free rides.

The tanks set off, the Hungarian flags flying. The leading tank had to cross one end of Lovolde Square where, as Dora could see, other 'Soviet tanks squatted in front of the Commandatura, their guns pointing directly across its route. I was afraid it would be challenged, but it trundled on its way unmolested.'

At least 20,000 people were assembling in Parliament Square when the column of Soviet tanks appeared and stopped in one corner. Though all demonstrations were still banned – nobody seemed concerned until an Avo officer with a loudspeaker ordered the crowd to disperse. The crowd yelled back, 'Pig!' 'Assassins!' and 'Down with the Avo!'

On the other side of the square, directly opposite Parliament Building, stood the Ministry of Agriculture, a neo-classic building 200 years old, which had first been used as a barracks during the reign of the Empress Maria Theresa. Unknown to the crowd, a detachment of Avos had been stationed on the roof to control the square.

Without warning they opened fire. The order may have been given by jittery officers – no one will ever know – but in seconds the dead and wounded littered the square. Men, women and children fell where they stood. Those on the edge of the crowd escaped into nearby side streets. Others forced open the doors of Parliament Building and took refuge inside. But most could not escape from the square in time.

Another burst of machine-gun fire sprayed the crowd – and this time three Russians fell mortally wounded, and the scene erupted from massacre into ugly revenge. No doubt the Russians thought they had been led by smiles into a deadly ambush. They obeyed the first instinct of soldiers and opened fire, mainly at the rooftops, but also into the crowd.

To Eva it seemed (as she sobbed to her husband that evening) as if 'our whole nation is being massacred. No one could realise what was happening; it was cold murder. Bits and pieces of people were all over the square. A woman standing next to me saw both her children mowed down. They were a girl about nine, and a boy about eleven.'

The United Nations said between 300 and 800 people were killed. A member of the British Legation counted twelve truck-loads of corpses being removed from the square later in the day. Dora Scarlett remembered, 'It will never be known exactly how many died because the bodies were dumped in the Danube.'

It was the bloodiest outrage of the revolution. The fury of Hungary against the Avos became more intensified than ever.

The event stung even Mikoyan and Suslov into action. Within half an hour of the slaughter – just before lunch on this terrible Thursday – Radio Budapest announced that Gero had been dismissed.

Blood had wiped out one error – the decision not to announce immediately the dismissal of Gero – but Mikoyan and Suslov were still in Party headquarters, still in control. Nagy's every step was watched by the Avo, and only a few intimates were able to see him before Gero's dismissal was made public. When a delegation of six workers finally received permission to see the Prime Minister, it was only after the Avo took extraordinary precautions.

The men represented workers who had taken over the Red Spark printing plant, on which they had run off tens of thousands of copies of the various manifestoes. Nagy's behaviour had been so out of character that they had begun to wonder if he had ever been permitted to read one. They decided to present the sixteen-point declaration to him in person and walked boldly into the main hall of Party headquarters. They were taken down two flights of stairs to a cellar where they received a preliminary interrogation at the hands of the Avo. They produced their identity cards, and gave them all the required information.

After a few minutes the prime minister came down to the cellar. A dozen Avos brandishing sub-machine-guns hustled him to a table where he sat down facing the deputation, the machine-gunners ranged behind him. The leader of the deputation read out the manifesto; Nagy replied to each point, assuring the workers they were all part of his programme. But when one delegate asked the Premier if he could fix a date for the withdrawal of Russian troops Nagy 'showed signs of losing patience'. It was naïve to ask for a date, he replied, adding, 'The withdrawal of a large number of troops isn't a simple matter.' The delegation persisted. Would he disband the Avo? And when? Testily the Prime Minister replied that reorganisation of the Avo was part of his programme, 'but you must have faith in me. I'm just as much a good Hungarian as you are.' According to witnesses who later testified to the United Nations, 'At this and other points in his speech, Mr Nagy implied doubt as to whether what he said was really what was in his mind.'

In fact Nagy must have almost reached the end of his mental and physical endurance. The Avo was swarming in every corridor of Party headquarters. He was still virtually a prisoner. To make matters worse, Losonczy – a wise counsellor as well as a true friend – had urged him to purge the Government of pro-Stalinist elements, and when Nagy (knowing it was impossible while

Mikoyan and Suslov remained in Budapest) refused Losonczy stalked angrily out of Party headquarters.

On Friday Mikoyan and Suslov were driven to the airport in tanks. Nagy must surely have breathed a sigh of relief at their departure, particularly as Gero and Hegedus also took advantage of an offer by Mikoyan to send them in tanks to the airport. Gero, it was rumoured, flew to Bratislava, Czechoslovakia, and Radio Budapest, which had so recently obeyed his every command, commented gleefully, 'The news of Gero's departure has been hailed by the people with unreserved joy. Workers embraced and kissed each other. Cheers echo everywhere.'

Another man who breathed a sigh of relief was Colonel Sandor Kopacsi. The Budapest police commissioner, who harboured doubts about Nagy's liberty of action, had not been idle. The Avo was not alone in having a spy network, and though Kopacsi could boast of only a handful of special agents, used mainly to watch the activities of the Avo, they did include a girl chosen for her apparently impeccable pro-Communist and even pro-Avo credentials. Quietly she was infiltrated into Party headquarters, where she had soon been able to confirm Kopacsi's worst fears. Yet while the Russians remained with Gero in Academy Street Kopacsi had to nurse the revelation in secret.

Now they had left, Kopacsi debated on a course of action. Though the power of the Avo might have waned with the departure of Gero, Kopacsi knew they were fighting for survival, and to launch an attack on Party headquarters was unthinkable – quite apart from the fact that he would receive no thanks from Nagy for such an attack on the power structure. Finally he decided on a compromise – and fortunately it worked. 'Once I was completely certain that the Prime Minister was in the hands of the secret police,' he recalled later,[1] 'I immediately ordered a shock detachment of my own police force to stand by. Then I sent my personal representative – alone, to avoid attracting too much attention – to see senior Avo officers.'

Kopacsi's envoy told the Avo that in the national interest the Prime Minister 'must have full freedom of movement and action'.

[1] In an interview on 1 November in *Magyar Vilag*.

At first the Avo demurred, but the climate had changed. Janos Kadar, who had replaced Gero, was sitting on the fence, and the Avo could expect little backing from him. Sensing this, Kopacsi issued the ultimatum he had been holding back, but hoped never to use.

'If the security police does not comply with my request,' he told the Avo, 'I will order armed units of the Budapest civil police to use force to set him at liberty.' And, as Kopasci added laconically to the Hungarian reporter interviewing him, 'The Avo gave way.'

Nagy was free – but he still had to contend with jealous, pro-Moscow members of the cabinet, together with another factor – provincial leaders who wanted the fighting to be stepped up. But Nagy knew that every effort must now be directed to one objective – a ceasefire that would lead to political talks.

When Nagy walked the short distance across the square from Party headquarters to Parliament Building, his stride seemed jaunty, and but for the unexpected he might well have gained forty-eight hours of precious time in which to prove his theories. However, another senseless massacre of the innocents kindled anew the flames of revolt, this time not in Budapest, but far to the north in a sleepy little farming town barely ten miles from Austria.

Its name was Magyarovar.

Around lunchtime on Friday, several hundred unarmed youths, women and children, led by students from the local agricultural college, marched in a peaceful demonstration to the 'village' green of Magyarovar, a small town that had escaped bloodshed. At the same time the author was driving in his hired car towards the frontier and stopped for a few minutes in the town.[1] Children playing in the main street waved to him. Knots of old women huddled for shade in doorways.

From behind the main street he could hear hundreds of voices chanting patriotic songs as the students led the way to the green, ringed with beautiful trees and facing the town hall. The

[1] At this time, the author was chief correspondent of the London *Daily Mail*, and flew to Vienna, then drove during the night of 24–5 October to Budapest.

demonstrators wanted nothing more than to present the student demands to their local mayor. Directly in front of the town hall two semi-circular trenches had been built, one at each corner; in each one a small group of Avos in uniform manned a machine-gun. But no one was worried; this was a peaceful demonstration. The crowd began to chant for the mayor to make an appearance. Someone started yet another song.

The author was talking to the villagers when the air exploded with machine-gun fire. He saw the flutter of a black cloud of frightened rooks, then heard screams, followed by the thud of bursting grenades. He drove quickly to the village green. There, in front of him, scores of men, women and children lay dying. They had still been singing when the Avo machine-guns opened fire. As the first bodies fell, the stupefied survivors flattened themselves. Three Avos climbed out of the trenches and hurled hand grenades. When the people jumped up to run they were in turn machine-gunned.

To the Englishman standing there, it seemed that half the screaming people were women and children. A mother, holding her baby in her arms, as though to protect it, lay mercifully dead. Behind them was a teenage boy. An explosion had blown off one leg and ripped away most of his clothing. He was trying to wriggle to the edge of the field, dragging one stump after him. Near him a man lay shot in the stomach; he was still alive, muttering incomprehensibly. His entrails were hanging out. There seemed to be legs and arms everywhere. In all 82 innocent people had been murdered; another 200 were hurt, many of them maimed for life.

In one corner of the village green the Avos picked up their machine-gun and carried it towards the town hall. Within a few minutes ambulances from Gyor reached the field and took the wounded to the village hospital. First-aid workers piled up grisly mounds of severed limbs. Then they carried the dead to the local church, laying them out in rows in the crypt. Soon the first jeeps arrived, crowded with insurgents who ranged up in front of the town hall where the Avos had taken refuge. All but two of the Avos were shot. The last two, who had pressed the triggers, were lynched by the crowd.

*   *   *

News of the latest massacre by the Avo, barely twenty-four hours after the tragedy in Parliament Square, had the effect of switching the fury of the insurgents in Budapest from the Russians back to the secret police. All over the city the pursuit of the Avo quickened. They were, as Dora Scarlett found, 'hunted down like animals, hung on trees, or just beaten to death by passers-by'. The rage of the insurgents was intensified when they found pay slips in Avo pockets showing that officers were earning 9000 forints a month – eleven times the wage of an unskilled worker. When an Avo was killed, the pay slip was pinned to his body. Any money in his pockets was usually burned. Their Poboda cars were set on fire. Nobody exulted when an Avo died a gruesome death. A knot of people near an upturned Avo car and a body hanging from the lamp-post just stood there; words were not necessary.

Some Avos managed to dispose of their uniforms and steal civilian clothes. The wounded crawled into attics or cellars to recuperate or die, often to the terror of the woman left alone in the house. One described the dread that thousands of lonely women must have experienced: [1]

We were sheltering in our cellar with other tenants. We had been there for hours while outside the insurgents were hunting down the Avo. The cellar door was gone, and the steps up to the street open but unlit. We huddled there, listening to the horrors from outside. We heard footsteps running, pausing, out of sight upstairs – a man's exhausted, panting breath. The firing got nearer. The man's breath quickened, he began to take painful steps down the dark stairs towards the cellar, slowly, gasping. His feet came into sight, his legs. They were the uniform of the Avo. We sat paralysed with fear. All we could hear was his gasping breath, the shots outside – his *fear*. For what seemed ages we were frozen, wondering if he would come further down, see us, kill us – or we would have to kill him somehow. The shots outside moved away. His gasping slowed. Slowly, step by step, his feet began to climb the steps again, slowly, cautiously, until they

[1] Told to the author by a woman who cannot be identified as her relatives are still in Budapest.

were out of sight. We heard him move carefully out of our way. Only then could we breathe again.

On many occasions the Avos won lonely battles, as Katica Ormrazny, an eighteen-year-old factory worker, discovered. Katica joined the freedom fighters with one of her brothers Sonar, who asked her to go home and get a bag of food and some sheets to be used as bandages. 'Leave your gun here,' Sonar suggested, 'and tell mum and dad not to worry – everything will be all right.'

When Katica walked into the courtyard round which their block of flats was built, it was empty but for the naked body of a man suspended by tied wrists to a spike in the wall above his head. He had been shot in the chest. His army uniform lay in a heap at his feet. It was Katica's eldest brother Janos, a private in the Army.

As she stood there, an old woman known to all the flat dwellers as 'Granny' Zeruichcicz, came out of a door, white and trembling. 'I saw it,' she said. 'The Avo made us stand here while they brought your brother out of your flat. They told us he was a traitor who had killed an Avo and now we should see a traitor die. Before he died, he shouted "Long live Hungary!"'

Some Avo officers escaped simply by sitting out the revolution; Major Lazlo Szabo of the Avo was duty officer at the Ministry of the Interior in Budapest the night the revolution broke out and remained inside with his colleagues until Soviet troops transferred them to a Russian camp. 'We had one hour to get ready,' Szabo remembered later.[1] 'We packed our things, locked the vaults. The Soviets lined our route to a camp in the country with tanks and trucks.'

When Lazlo Beke and three friends heard that Colonel Erwin Revesz of the Avo was hiding in his villa in the Roszadomb suburb of Buda, they decided to ferret him out. The villa seemed deserted, some of the blinds were drawn, the windows locked. Two boys smashed in the back door and walked into the main living-room, filled with antique furniture and good paintings,

---

[1] Szabo defected to the American Embassy in London on 18 October 1965 after serving 20 years in the Hungarian police, mostly in the Avo. He later testified before a Central Intelligence Agency subcommittee in Washington in March 1966.

and with a picture window overlooking the Danube.

To their astonishment a quiet, middle-aged woman stood calmly in the centre of the room, 'surveying this group of un-shaven, grimy intruders on the privacy of her mansion'. One boy asked if she were Mrs Revesz.

'I am,' she replied calmly. 'What do you want?'

'Your husband,' said Beke. 'Who else is in the house?'

'No one except one of my servants,' she replied. 'He's in the other room – through that door.'

The boys headed for the door. As they were almost through, 'a sudden hiss and whirr of an electric motor made us turn'. The colonel's wife was standing close to the mantelpiece and the entire section was revolving. Before anyone could drag her off, she vanished. To Beke, it was 'as though we were watching a scene from an old film'. They searched for hours, vainly trying to find a hidden knob or switch. They made for the cellar, only to be confronted by a thick wall of reinforced concrete. Beke heard later that many Avo and Party leaders had houses linked by a network of secret escape tunnels. The Avo colonel was never captured.

One Avo even penetrated into Kilian Barracks. Thomas Szabo was near the main gates when a civilian who wanted to join the insurgents was being questioned by sentries. Something seemed to be amiss and, as Thomas watched, the man turned round and their eyes met. It was an Avo man who had once interrogated Szabo. As Thomas shouted, 'Don't let him go!' the man fired. Thomas's reply was instinctive, though to this day he cannot remember bringing his gun into action. 'I heard a burst of machine-gun fire and the man fell on his face.' His first reaction was that Captain Kovacs would be furious with him, his second that 'I didn't want the man to die.'

That was not the end of the affair. Kovacs arrived, searched the dead man's pockets, took out a piece of paper, barked out an order, 'Everyone to the gymnasium!' When they were all present, Kovacs announced gravely, 'Comrades, we have a traitor among us. I have just learned this from this paper found on the man you shot.'

As he read out the name, there was a scuffle at the back of the room. Kovacs shouted for silence. Still the fighting went on. Only when Kovacs fired two shots into the air did the brawl stop. By the door lay a mutilated corpse.

'You shouldn't have done that,' said Kovacs, 'even if he deserved it.'

Some insurgents searching for Avos found themselves involved in a happier task – freeing political prisoners. Thousands still languished in jails or camps all over Hungary. Before the end of the first week at least 5500 were freed, a figure that probably does not include many liberated from small country prisons. Nearly 600 who had been sentenced to ten years' forced labour were freed from the infamous Dorog mines. None had been told the length of their sentences. None had been allowed food parcels or visitors.

In the Marko Street prison in Budapest insurgents found a hundred lost souls who had been taken prisoner by the Russians during the last days of the Second World War. After the war, as the climate thawed, the Russians freed them, gave them new clothes, money, and put them on a comfortable train for home. It does not take much imagination to conjure up the thoughts of these men as the train reached the frontier – and expected freedom.

Instead, the moment they crossed into Hungary, the Avo arrested every man. Without any trial they were clapped into gaol, and remained there until 1956. They were arrested for one simple 'crime'; Rakosi, who was in the process of painting a glowing picture of Hungary's benevolent Russian neighbour (to replace the grim, wartime memories of looting and rape[1]) did not dare to allow malcontents into Hungary to spread stories about conditions in the Soviet Union.

Another 450 men were freed from the notorious Gyustofoghaz prison in Budapest on Friday. They still wore their pyjama-like striped jackets and trousers. Peter Fryer, the British Communist, saw them emerge. 'Some of them were raving mad,' he remem-

[1] Because of the conduct of Russians the word 'rape' was forbidden in Hungarian literature, and when a deputation of writers protested to Rakosi he replied, 'What is there to write about? In Hungary there are, let's say, 3000 villages. Supposing the Russians violated, say, three women in every village. Nine thousand in all. Is that so much? You writers have no idea of the law of large numbers.'

bered, 'and had to be restrained and taken into gentler custody.'
Fryer made an inspection of the prison, and in one cell he
found, on the grimy wall, a poem scratched by a prisoner. It had
a Latin title, 'Pro Libertate'.

The most dramatic mass escape took place at the fortress
prison of Vac, a town thirty miles or so north of Budapest. Vac
had one of the worst reputations in Hungary. Bela Szasz and
Anna Kethly all but died in its dank, slimy, airless cells. Pal
Ignotus, who spent years in Vac, described it as follows: 'A society
of frieze-dressed cripples, caricatures of the social values which had
dwindled and collapsed before and during our imprisonment.
We dragged ourselves along in our sweat-soaked ill-fitting uniforms, with our bristly, emaciated faces, often trembling in the
hope of an extra dixie-full of foul food.'

For days the prisoners at Vac had been in a turmoil of sus-
pense after hearing a strange cry of hope from the outside world.
One wall of the prison was lapped by the Danube and a man –
never identified, but presumably in a rowboat under the walls –
had shouted several days previously, 'Don't worry! You'll be
free soon!'

Almost immediately the routine of the prison changed. The
guards were doubled. Nests of machine-guns sprouted from the
roof above the exercise yard. Then, to the astonishment of the
prisoners, many of the Avos discarded their uniforms, and
swarmed through the corridors in civilian clothes. One prisoner
remembered later that they all seemed 'jittery'.

One wall of the prison faced on to a street and prisoners could
hear the sounds of patriotic songs. They could not see the street,
but they could see a square of sky above the street level, and in
a prison alive with rumour only one moment of truth was needed
to cause a revolt. It came when, for a few seconds, some of the
ten men in a small cell saw something they had never seen before.
A procession must have been passing by, for suddenly they had
a glimpse of Hungarian flags held aloft – all with holes in the
centre where the Russian emblem had been cut out.

All thoughts of torture, the threat of the rubber truncheon,
starvation diet, punishment cells, vanished in that moment. From
that one cell men shouted to the next. Like a roar the tidings
passed along the corridor of the main block. The Avo guards

blustered, threatened, loosed off a few rounds of ammunition, all to no avail. As the shouting and disorder increased, the Avos tried to pacify the men, even offering them cigarettes if they would keep quiet. Men who would sacrifice a day's rations for one cigarette threw them back in the faces of their guards.

How the first prisoners escaped from a cell is not known for certain. One account has it that men armed with a broken table forced open one of the old locks. Another says that when an Avo came to the barred door with cigarettes a hand gripped his throat and someone grabbed his revolver and shot off the lock. Soon every cell door was open, and a thousand prisoners swept in a flood of tattered, filthy, vermin-ridden humanity towards the main gates. From the roof machine-gun fire spattered them, but they pressed on. A 'trusty' found the keys in the governor's office. A few minutes later the gates opened, the flood poured into the streets of Vac – to freedom, families, friends and food.

One British woman who had been locked in a Rakosi prison for seven years nearly missed her chance of freedom – for the curious reason that she had officially ceased to exist. Dr Edith Bone was sixty-eight, and after visiting Budapest in 1949, to write articles for the *Daily Worker*, she made her way to Budapest airport to return to England. As she was about to board the aircraft, she was arrested on Rakosi's personal orders, and charged with espionage.

From that day she vanished, without any identity, not even a prison number. Repeated British protests were always met with the same bland explanation, 'She is not in this country. She went to the airport and boarded a plane, so we have no further responsibility.'

Dr Bone spent years in solitary confinement at Vac. Deprived of writing materials, she made letters of the alphabet out of the sticky, under-cooked prison bread. She made an abacus so she could count, and a calendar. A woman of indomitable courage, she later, when allowed books and writing materials, studied Greek and mathematics. Finally she was moved to Budapest Central prison and there, as the revolution escalated, she was 'lost' again. One by one the other prisoners were freed, and their names were ticked off the lists. Her name appeared on no list, and it was at first thought that her cell was unoccupied; but by chance an insurgent peered through the peep-hole and saw the emaciated creature within. He took her to a room filled with freedom fighters, the last woman in the prison. Yet the insurgents were worried, for they too did not know who she was. They asked her to wait until they could find her file – a document which did not exist.

At this, Dr Bone, who had a choice command of English, told them in no uncertain manner what she thought of them. As she remembered later, 'What happened next is mostly unprintable ... never before can those young men have seen such a hullabaloo ... the young man decided to get rid of me quickly,' and as he ushered her to freedom he apologised. 'Don't think too badly of us. We too were victims.'

He found a car and drove her to the British Legation, where she was taken to Joan Fish, and 'five minutes later I was sitting with that national emblem, a nice cup of tea, in my hand.'

7

The Fourth Estate

Friday, 26 October

For two days there had been no newspapers, but now, when *Szabad Nep* reappeared, people hardly bothered to buy it, because for the first time in Hungary's history the Party newspapers faced at least twenty rivals, all passionate, idealistic, articulate, and, above all, speaking not with the crushing voice of authority, but from the heart. None who edited them thought in terms of profit. No matter if a man in the street did not have a forint in his pocket, an eager youngster would still thrust a paper into his hands. The police, the Army, writers, factory-workers, and of course the students, all produced independent newspapers, some of four pages, others only single sheets, some professionally printed, others roughly stencilled.

Dora Scarlett felt that 'people hungered and thirsted for the printed word as though they had crossed a desert – as indeed they had.' She found that the newspapers had no tinge of fascism, anti-semitism, or political irresponsibility. They called for order, national unity and defence.

Many papers printed poems on their front pages. Sandor Petofi's famous poem starting 'The sea has risen, the sea of the people,' appeared on no less than five broadsheets (on the same morning). Other papers printed new poems of varying quality 'hammered out in the stress of the uprising'. The police newspaper *Magyar Randor* headed its first issue, 'With the people through fire and water'.

In the offices of *Szabad Nep* Peter Fryer discovered that several newspapers were now being printed there. The editor of one, an old friend of Fryer's, interviewed a stream of youngsters, then turned to Fryer and said, 'They bring us poems, news items, articles, short stories about the revolution by the score. Some of them are good, some not so good. But we try to help them. New talent. We never suspected it, never.'

The first issue of the Army's newspaper appeared on Thursday evening – but only after a bitter battle in which six Hungarian soldiers were killed, for shortly after the revolution started the Avo had taken over the army printing press in Bajscy Zsilinszky Avenue. On Thursday morning, the Army counter-attacked with three tanks and drove out the Avo. That evening exultant printers started the machines rolling, and as they spewed out the first wet copies Hungarian Army officers in uniform hurled them out of windows to the waiting, cheering crowds below who read them by the dim light of street lamps or under the headlamps of cars – lapping up the newspaper's demands (among others) for an end to martial law and the dissolution of the Avo. 'We swear by the corpses of our martyrs that we shall win freedom for our country,' ran the main editorial.

Anna Gabor, who had resigned from her secretarial job with the giant United Electric Company at Ujpest, joined one of the first freedom newspapers to appear. *Igazsag*, or *Truth*, which ran for nine issues, was the mouthpiece of 'Hungary's Revolutionary Youth' and within twenty-four hours was the most popular newspaper in the country. It was edited by Gyula Obersovszky, a dynamic writer with a reputation for crusading zeal. (Khrushchev is supposed to have had Obersovszky in mind when he declared that 'If ten or so Hungarian writers had been shot at the right moment, the revolution would never have occurred'.)

When Anna Gabor walked into the dingy print shop in a small street behind the Ady Cinema and asked if she could help, Obersovszky glared at her and asked what she could do.

'I'm a secretary,' she replied. 'I can do shorthand—'

'Ever wallpapered a room?' he asked.

Taken aback, Anna admitted that she had once papered the living-room of her flat, whereupon Obersovszky, as she remembered, 'gave me a sudden warm smile, and I felt his fierceness was just a mask.'

'Fine!' he cried. 'I've just the job for you. We haven't got enough papers to go round, so we're going to paste copies on every notice board, every inch of wall we can find. That'll be your job.'

Truth had in fact a national distribution, for the editor organised a courier service to almost every major town in Hungary. One copy was delivered to the Kilian Barracks, eliciting the revolution's first reader's letter, in which the hard-pressed defenders of the citadel wrote, 'This sooty, bloodstained, tattered piece of paper is being passed round from man to man. We read it aloud to the dying.'

Thanks to people like Anna, thousands of people read this and other newspapers on the walls of Budapest, which flowered with strange new 'blossoms' as the first posters outlining the student demands disappeared under the swift strokes of paste brushes preparing the way for free newspapers.

Walking down the Korut, a street of luxury shops in which all traffic had stopped, Dora Scarlett found it 'like a public reading room. Walls and shop windows were plastered with notices, poems, caricatures and jokes, from end to end.' This was the first time for a decade that any citizen could publish anything he liked, and the result was startling. Dora Scarlett found a caricature of Rakosi departing with his suitcases labelled 'Lies' and 'Promises', and the caption, 'We want no more bald heads.' There were some amateur artists' impressions of the fall of the Stalin statue, and a memorial card inviting people to its funeral.

Here and there in the Korut and other streets were strange symbols of the time: open suitcases on the ground, placed there for donations for the wounded or homeless. All contained notes. None was guarded. There was another strange innovation: street names were being changed, so that Dora Scarlett found 'a walk through the city became a voyage of discovery'. For example, the first part of Stalin Avenue had originally been Andrassy Street, but the name had been changed before the revolution; now people had unearthed the old enamel street plates, which had lain hidden for years. At the very start of the street, where 'Stalin Avenue' had been engraved on a huge block of granite, the stone had been prised out of the wall and lay on the ground with the name defaced. At the entrances to the many government offices in the area the Kossuth coat of arms reappeared. Long since forbidden by the Russians, hidden in attics or cellars, they now adorned door after door. Further east the bronze boots of the Stalin statue still stood on their plinth of pink marble, but now they were put to practical use – filled with bouquets of Hungarian flags.

For the old and sick who could not get to the Korut or other free 'libraries', the editor of *Truth* produced a radio version of his newspaper. Among his many friends in the radio world Obersovszky numbered George Kovacs, who had been sitting in the 'pagoda' when the students burst into the radio station. When the first freedom radio stations went into action, Kovacs was given the task of broadcasting the contents of *Truth* in their entirety.

The newspaper also opened the eyes of the people to the 'high life' of Hungary's Communist leaders. Workers struggling to earn their daily bread now learned that members of the Politbureau had not only paid no rent for their luxury villas, but were given free clothing, free coal, free nannies to take their children to the Party's Gorki School – in fact all the expenses of the family were paid out of Party funds. For the first time they read details of the Party 'food warehouse' in Fo Street which sold goods at forty per cent below cost, and stocked luxuries like oranges and bananas not available to the rest of the population.

The allocation of cars fascinated readers. Each high official had two 'comrade' drivers, who worked in shifts, for they not only looked after the breadwinner, but took the children to school, attended to the wives, did the shopping. The cars were issued strictly according to protocol. Members of the Politbureau rated air-conditioned, heavily armoured American Chevrolets or German Mercedes. Ministers drove in Russian Zis cars (until it was found they used too much petrol; they were then allotted the more economical Zim car). Deputy ministers were provided with Soviet-made Pobodas (also popular with the Avo) and deputy heads of departments drove in Czech Skodas.

All had one thing in common: special, easily identifiable small-numbered licence plates, enabling the police to obey their instructions never to stop them, even for traffic infringements.

Radio Budapest titillated its listeners with a description of Rakosi's villa in Buda, with its illuminated swimming-pool, two bathrooms filled with expensive slimming equipment (and drawers crammed with imported vitamin tablets). Rakosi had two pianos in his sitting-rooms, together with an American hi-fi. Insurgents found his cellars stocked with French wines and Havana cigars, and discovered that he had given lavish dinners in Party headquarters where he had installed a banqueting-room with American-style kitchens so that the expenditure could be conveniently debited to the account of the subsidised office canteen.

The stories were exciting – but the intellectuals sounded an occasional note of caution. Zoltan Tildy, Hungary's first President of the post-war Council (before Rakosi sent him into the political wilderness) said on the radio that he did not approve of the fighting, adding, 'I know there are many acute problems which must be tackled immediately [but] the nation must provide the necessary atmosphere of calm and civil order and peace in union among all Hungarians. This is our supreme, our essential duty today.' Gyula Hay, the idol of Hungarian youth, was even blunter. 'There must be a changeover to peaceful methods without the slightest delay,' he warned. 'The armed struggle must stop immediately. Even peaceful demonstrations are not suitable at this time because they can be misconstrued.'

At first the Western world had no real inkling of the revolution's escalation, for the rigid Gero censorship had turned Hungary into a silent land. Conflicting rumours reached the West, and these had somehow tended to give the impression that since Khrushchev had listened to the Poles the same thing might happen in Hungary.

Everything changed overnight. The British Legation had its own radio link with Whitehall, though the American diplomats did not have one to Washington, and had to rely on a teleprinter that was tapped. Even so the first radio hams were picking up the first faint messages from home-made transmitters, the first neutral businessmen reached Austria with the first harrowing details. And it was of course not difficult for officials experienced in monitoring radio broadcasts to detect nuances, to read between the lines, if only when Budapest Radio announced on Friday morning, 'There will be no school today.'

President Eisenhower, referring to Poland in an after-dinner speech, had already said that 'the fruits of Communist imperialism now daily become more evident in the satellite world'. Within twenty-four hours when, as Eisenhower remembered, 'the picture became clear', the President was saying, 'The heart of America goes out to the people of Hungary.' In London, Sir Anthony Eden issued a statement from No. 10 Downing Street that the Government 'have been following with sympathy and admiration the struggle of the Hungarian people for their rights and for freedom', while Hugh Gaitskell, Leader of the Opposition, deplored 'the ruthless intervention of Soviet tanks and troops against the Hungarian workers'. In Paris, Christian Pineau, the French Foreign Minister, declared that the Russians had committed 'a major error' in ordering Soviet forces to crush the rebellion.

Pineau, however, was not alone in displaying caution. He pointed out that just as history and geography obliged France to remain linked with the Western world, so countries like Poland and Hungary would remain linked with the East, and it would be dangerous to cut these links and so possibly give the Soviet Union an opportunity to reverse its de-Stalinisation process.

Pineau's words were soon echoed in the United States by Foster Dulles, the Secretary of State. 'The United States has no ulterior purpose in desiring the independence of the satellite countries,' he told an audience at Dallas, Texas. The American Government, he added, did not look upon them as 'potential military allies'.

The speech had been vetted previously by Eisenhower, who quickly ordered the Government to prepare a position paper on Hungary and Poland 'reaffirming our assurances to the Soviet Union that we had no intention of making these countries our allies' but at the same time warning Khrushchev that America would go along with any United Nations action 'including the use of force'. Already the United States was seeking Europe's backing to submit the Hungarian problem to the UN.

Yet the truth is that none of the major powers had any real idea yet of the implications of the revolution, and certainly not of the reactions within the Soviet Empire. When Allen Dulles, the sixty-two-year-old head of the CIA, attended a meeting of the National Security Council on Friday morning, he blithely told Eisenhower, 'The Chinese Communists might not be unhappy over what's happening in Hungary. If so we might at this moment be seeing the beginning of the first rift between China and the

USSR.' In fact the pipe-smoking Dulles, with his rimless spectacles and clipped moustache, could not have had the remotest idea of China's reaction, or of Russia's thoughts, though this did not prevent Dulles from naïvely telling Eisenhower at the meeting, ' "Chip" Bohlen [Charles E. Bohlen, American Ambassador to Moscow] recently saw Bulganin and Khrushchev together at a reception in Moscow, and Khrushchev, he said, had never looked so grim. His days may well be numbered.'

Eisenhower's reaction was to wonder whether 'with the deterioration of the Soviet Union's hold over its satellites, might not the Soviet Union be tempted ... even to start a world war?' He obviously took the possibility seriously for that night the Defence Department and other security agencies were put on special alert.

Fortunately for the freedom fighters in Hungary, details of these discussions – duplicated in almost every Western capital – never reached Budapest; instead the world's radio stations concentrated on beaming to Hungary their admiration for the courage of the insurgents, their declarations of hope, their bitter denunciations of the Soviet Union. This was just what the Hungarians wanted to hear. It gave them the feeling they were not fighting alone and unsung. Nothing breeds courage more than the knowledge that it is being recognised; and the possibility that the UN might take up the Hungarian cause also stimulated the insurgents to more courageous action. Delegations surrounded foreign embassies in Budapest, asking for support at the next meeting of the UN (which was not even in session). Two thousand people congregated before the British Legation and refused to disperse until the Minister, Mr Fry, promised to send their petition to Whitehall.

True, nobody in the West had promised any kind of military action or even help to Hungary, but, as Tibor Meray felt, 'Most Hungarians were, in any case, suffering from a nostalgia for the West ... the twisted propaganda about the West, to which they had been subjected by the Russians for years, had an effect precisely the opposite of that which had been intended: it had made them think of all the richness, the pleasure, and the gentleness of life to be found in that forbidden world.'

Soon, too, the first detailed stories by foreign correspondents appeared in Western newspapers. Before the massacre at Magyaro-var the chief correspondent of the London *Daily Mail* – one of the first to reach Budapest – had filed details of his first night with the freedom fighters. Part of the report read as follows:

Tonight Budapest is a city of mourning. Black flags hang from every window. For during the past four days thousands of its citizens fighting to throw off the yoke of Russia have been killed or wounded. Budapest is a city that is slowly dying. Its streets and once beautiful squares are a shambles of broken glass, burnt-out cars and tanks and rubble. Food is scarce, petrol is running out.

But still the battle rages on. For five hours this morning until a misty dawn broke over Budapest, I was in the thick of one of the battles. It was between Soviet troops and insurgents trying to force a passage across the Danube. There is no doubt that the revolution has been far more bloody than the official radio reports suggested. I made for the Chain Bridge[1] that spans the Danube. In front of the bridge stood a barricade of burnt-out tramcars, a bus, old cars, uprooted tramlines. It was at least the 50th barricade of its kind I had seen since I entered the city after driving from the frontier. As I drove towards it, lights full on, with the Chain Bridge on my left, heavy firing started from the centre of the bridge. Machine-gun bullets whistled past my ear. Then, when some heavier stuff began falling, I switched off the lights, jumped out and crawled round to the side ... to the road block. I found nine boys there, their average age about eighteen. Three wore Hungarian uniforms, but with the hated red star torn off. Others wore red, green and white armbands, the national colours of Hungary. All had sub-machine-guns. Their pockets bulged with ammunition.

[1] The Chain Bridge, completed in 1848, was designed by a British consulting engineer W. Tierney Clark, who sent his brother Adam to Budapest to supervise the construction. Adam fell in love with Hungary, married a Hungarian girl, and is buried in Budapest. The Hungarians, touched by his devotion to their country, named the square at the Buda end of the bridge 'Adam Clark Square'. The name has never been changed. An exact, though smaller, replica of the bridge still spans the Thames at Marlow in Buckinghamshire.

Half-way across the bridge I could see the dim outlines of two Soviet tanks. For an hour they fired at us until a shell smashed straight into the overturned bus. One of the boys was killed instantly. I tried to help a second boy who was hurt, but he died five minutes later in my arms.

This was an area of fighting dominated by one of the most colourful leaders of the insurgents, 'Uncle Szabo', in charge of nearly two hundred young fighters in Buda's Szena Square, which they barricaded with upturned railway coaches from the nearby South Station. Students and factory workers awaited Russian attacks from behind the coaches or from the rooftops of nearby buildings.

'Our first engagement was with two Russians in a motor-cycle combination,' said one seventeen-year-old.[1] 'After them came some infantry with tanks. Those in front were wiped out and the tanks were attacked with Molotov cocktails and machine-gun fire. Two were completely burned out, and among the casualties were two high-ranking Russian officers. Then the battle really started. "Uncle Szabo" was a man who knew all the answers. We were not short of inspiration but we were lacking experience. He was an older man, not a military person; he was constantly on the move, sending kids off to pick up food or bring up ammunition or even sending some of the young ones home when he thought that the parents would start worrying. I don't know very much about him myself, and I don't think many do, because he was rushing to and fro all the time, and it was difficult to talk to him.'

'Uncle Szabo' became a living legend second only to Pal Maleter, who had now been joined by an old friend from his military academy days. Mark Molnar not only knew the Colonel, but also his father who was the Molnar family dentist. With the Russians ousted from the wrecked Astoria Hotel, and street fighting becoming more and more concentrated on a few strong-points, Molnar felt his battle-toughened troops would be better employed at the Kilian Barracks.

Maleter welcomed him with open arms, and within a couple of hours the two men were fighting side by side, fending off a

[1] Quoted by George Mikes.

heavy attack by six Soviet tanks. As they approached, Maleter called for complete silence. Not a man stirred, even when the first shells thudded into the thick walls. One fighter, Peter Szanto, remembered how Maleter 'came and looked down. He picked up a bottle of nitroglycerine and threw it at the first tank.'

The mass of metal erupted in flames with a roar 'that almost shook the building'. Then everyone pelted the other tanks, disabling three in a few minutes. 'After that,' said Szanto, 'the morale in the barracks was sky-high. When citizens called on us to report the presence of Russian tanks or the whereabouts of the AVH, the freedom fighters forayed out to do battle.'

Inside the citadel, Maleter had an excellent hospital, and he needed it − not only for the wounded, but because his boys were often on the point of exhaustion. When Eugen-Geza Pogany, correspondent of the Vienna newspaper *Ungarns Freiheitskampf* toured the barracks he saw a small, pitiful figure with blond hair, his face deathly white, in a hospital bed. He enquired if he were wounded.

'Not at all,' replied the army doctor. 'The boy's totally exhausted. With a machine-gun he defended an important street intersection virtually alone for three days and nights.'

The boy's name was Jancsi. He was thirteen.

Maleter himself was as adamant as ever that he would never surrender.

'For us there is only one alternative,' he told Pogany. 'Either we win or we fall. We have confidence in Imre Nagy, but we will lay down our weapons only to regular Hungarian troops, and we will put ourselves at the disposal of the new government immediately if it really is a Hungarian government.'

8

The Fragile Freedom

Saturday to Monday, 27–9 October

In Moscow, as October drew to a close, the Soviet leaders were confronted with two alternatives: either to crush the rebellion in Hungary, or to accept it.

It they chose the former course, the Soviet Union would have to send in massive troop support, and Khrushchev was well aware how repercussions would damage East–West relations, particularly now the United Nations was involved. For two days the Soviet Presidium debated the 'Hungarian problem'. Khrushchev was anxious to avoid a total military engagement, hoping that if the revolution did not escalate further the Soviet Union could still maintain the fiction of having been invited to help restore order in an internal disturbance.

If, however, the Soviets decided to accept the revolution, Khrushchev knew he had to act quickly before the situation got out of hand, causing the Soviet Union to suffer a humiliating moral defeat in the eyes of the other satellite countries. Khrushchev knew that Budapest's tired insurgents were sustained by a will to die if necessary for a cause now emblazoned across the world. If the insurgents had lost thousands, the Russians had lost hundreds. If the insurgents could not win with small arms, neither could the Russians win with heavy tanks. In order to achieve total victory, the Hungarian 'infantry' would need thousands of armoured vehicles, yet no Russian victory was possible without large reinforcements of infantry. The opposing sides were, in fact, waging two different kinds of war. The result was a military stalemate.

Within the Kremlin, Khrushchev faced opposition from the

military clique, which never really believed that a soft line would achieve any positive results – and that included keeping Hungary in the Soviet Empire. But for the moment Khrushchev had his way. Despite military opposition, he decided to accept the revolution, as he had done in Poland. He instructed Mikoyan and Suslov to fly back to Budapest with a new policy document to be published on Tuesday, 30 October.[1] Details of the document must have been drafted a considerable time before the Tuesday. Why then, in the face of the mounting danger signals in Hungary, was it not published earlier, since in it, Khrushchev made specific references to the withdrawal of Russian troops from the country? For instance, he promised:

> Being of the opinion that the continued presence of Soviet units in Hungary could be used as a pretext for further aggravating the situation, the Soviet Government has now given instructions to its military commanders to withdraw their troops from the city of Budapest as soon as the Hungarian Government feels they can be dispensed with.
>
> At the same time, the Soviet Government is prepared to engage in negotiations with the Hungarian People's Government and the other signatories of the Warsaw Pact regarding the question of the presence of Soviet troops elsewhere in the territory of Hungary.

This was tremendous news, yet it was kept secret. The delay in publication – even Nagy had no idea that this promise was on the way – certainly showed, as Professor Paul Zinner put it, that 'for once the well-oiled machinery of a totalitarian state could not keep up with the rapidly changing events. The deliberations of the Soviet Presidium ... were too ponderous to cope with the problems on the spot.'

The extent of this monumental blunder lay in the fact that this was just the kind of news Nagy needed as he faced additional pressures. But the pace of the revolution was such that Khrushchev could not keep abreast of events. He did not realise that the provinces were now taking matters into their own hands, inciting the people of Budapest to more fighting, and poor Nagy, un-

[1] For full text, see Appendix III.

aware of the good news on the way, could not offer the provincial leaders any concessions.

Many provincial areas now controlled their own free radio stations and were beaming anti-government bulletins, whipping up tension, imploring the insurgents in Budapest 'to throw off the Russian yoke', boasting that *they* had already done just that. It was true that large areas of the provinces had been cleared of Soviet troops, though not always by fighting. In many areas the Russians were thin on the ground, or in isolated training barracks where they wisely decided to make local peace rather than risk the possibility of quick defeat or being overwhelmed.

In Veszprem the Revolutionary Council sent a delegation to the local Soviet commander who gave an assurance that Russian troops would take no action; he also refused asylum to Avo officers who sought refuge in his barracks. In Jaszbereny the Soviet commander gave an undertaking that he would not interfere in Hungarian internal affairs and confined all his men to barracks, while in Debrecen the Soviet troops withdrew from the city after negotiating with the Revolutionary Council. When towns like Gyor, Vac, Hatvan and Szolnok broadcast that they had 'beaten' Russian troops, it could only inflame the insurgents – at a time when Nagy was trying to prevent further fighting.

Radio Gyor was now transmitting over the entire Transdanubia area, between Budapest and the Austrian frontier. It not only had its own powerful transmitter, but two relay stations which had joined the Provisional National Council of Gyor-Sopron County, headed by Attila Szigetti, a huge man with bristling red moustaches, whom Paul Zinner considered to be 'the most imposing political figure of the revolution outside the capital'. Szigetti had no hesitation in warning Nagy that the Hungarians had no confidence in many members of Nagy's government. 'Though Nagy has the nation's support,' he broadcast on 27 October, 'that is not enough. Soviet guns are still active in Budapest. The people have spoken their judgment with arms in hand, and the Soviet troops should be sent home.' These were strong words – but they came from a man who had been a deputy in the first post-war Hungarian government and who commanded respect.

The threat from the provinces was real. Then Nagy suddenly faced a new danger in Budapest.

Before dawn on Sunday the twenty-eighth, Nagy was awakened by the telephone. Losonczy was on the other end of the line, with frightening news. Karoly Janza, the new Minister of Defence whom Nagy had been forced to accept, had been holding secret talks with the Soviet High Command in Budapest. Between them they had concocted a murderous plan. Janza had persuaded a handful of Hungarian troops to join the Russians in a plan to wipe out the Kilian Barracks. The presence of the Hungarians would, of course, enable the proposed attack to be described as 'Hungarian, supported by the Russians'.

'When?' Nagy asked.

'It's timed to start at dawn today,' Losonczy replied. 'The objective is the total destruction of the area.' The assault would be launched not only on the barracks but on the surrounding buildings, including the Corvin Cinema.

One wonders whether Nagy, sitting in his pyjamas on the edge of the bed, had even a fleeting moment of doubt. For he must have known that if the Kilian Barracks fell the fighting would end – and that was his declared aim. And if the fighting had ended on this Sunday Nagy might well have been in a position to achieve the Gomulka-type compromise for which he had been striving. Ironically, had Nagy never been warned of the attack, the future of Hungary could have been very different.

As it was, he never hesitated. Half an hour before the assault was due to begin, he telephoned Yuri Andropov, the Soviet ambassador, and Janza, telling them: 'If you launch the offensive, I resign.'

Andropov also did not hesitate, no doubt visualising the reaction in the Kremlin if the leader of their choice left the Hungarian Communist Party. The attack was cancelled, and hundreds of Hungarian lives were saved.

At last Nagy realised the futility of relying on the Central Committee with its Stalinist remnants. That morning he by-passed them by forming a provisional committee of six men to direct the practical work of the Government.[1] He then picked

[1] Antal Apro, Karoly Kiss, Ferenc Munnich, Zoltan Szanto, Janos Kadar and Nagy.

up the secret 'K' telephone and spoke to Khrushchev, warning him that Moscow must urgently promise to evacuate Russian troops or he (Nagy) could not be responsible for the carnage that would certainly follow.

To his astonishment Khrushchev seemed in an expansive and almost jovial mood. He agreed instantly, telling Nagy that Mikoyan was on his way with a policy statement in writing. Nagy said he did not think he could wait for Mikoyan's arrival. Khrushchev told him to go ahead and make the announcement. Andropov would inform the Russian High Command in Budapest to implement the order.

And so at last Nagy was able to go on the radio at 5.25 on Sunday evening and promise the one item of news for which all Hungary had been waiting.

'The Hungarian Government', he announced, 'has come to an agreement with the Soviet Government whereby Soviet forces shall immediately withdraw from Budapest. The Hungarian Government has started negotiations to settle relations between the Hungarian People's Republic and the Soviet Union with regard to the withdrawal of Soviet forces stationed in Hungary. All this is in the spirit of the mutual equality and national independence of Socialist countries.'

There was more good news to come. 'After the re-establishment of order we shall organise a new and single police force and we shall dissolve the organs of state security. No one who took part in the armed fighting need fear reprisals.'

There was one proviso, and it did not seem unreasonable. There must be an immediate ceasefire so that Nagy could open negotiations with Russia on the withdrawal of her troops and the formation of a new Hungarian militia force.

A man of stature, preferably a man above politics, was needed as an extra rallying force in Budapest itself. The new, free capital of the country required a mayor and who better than Jozsef Kovago who had filled the post so illustriously after the war? After discussing the matter with Nagy, Zoltan Tildy sent for Kovago to come and see him in Parliament. There he asked him bluntly, 'Would you be interested in becoming Mayor of Budapest again?'

Kovago, who had firmly decided never to meddle in politics,

was overwhelmed. 'I could hardly think of a greater honour than to lead this great city,' he replied.

That night Nagy slept on a camp-bed in Party headquarters, and the following morning made his way to Parliament Building. It was a sunny, sharp autumn morning, so he decided to walk, picking his way through the broken glass and rubble. Soon he was surrounded by people bombarding him with questions. Meray, who was with him, saw an attractive, distinguished-looking woman with tears in her eyes say, 'It's good to see you, Comrade Nagy. Everyone was saying you were a prisoner.'

With a broad smile Nagy doffed his hat politely and replied, 'You see how much I'm a prisoner!'

By dusk on Sunday evening Budapest was engulfed in a wave of euphoria. In the Duna Hotel, on the east bank of the Danube, a group of insurgents bustled into the lobby carrying a huge tricolour with the inevitable hole in the middle. One man stood on another's shoulders to nail it on the wall behind the reception desk. There was a roar of laughter when he fell down. And then one voice, lonely at first, started the national anthem. The piping voice became a chorus as all joined in, filling the imposing entrance hall with its majestic melody. When the sound died away, a stranger 'with Franz Josef moustaches curling almost to his ears', went up to the author and said in stilted, precise English, 'I am glad you are here, sir. This is the proudest moment in our history.'

By Monday morning, there seemed to be clear evidence that the Russians were sticking to their end of the bargain. The United Press correspondent saw for himself: 'Soviet tanks and troops crunched out of this war-battered capital today, carrying their dead with them.' On the Danube embankment Dora Scarlett watched the guns and ammunition-carriers rumble past, and when she walked to Stalin Avenue, she stood looking at a procession of trucks, 'each drawing a field kitchen, each with a little bright fire glowing below, and steam puffing gaily from the top. They were pulling out. I had to tell myself that it was really true.' Lazlo Beke remembered, 'The noise of the departing tanks and the rhythmical staccato of marching feet were like a heaven-directed symphony.'

Soon the first peasants reached the capital, their carts or farm cars loaded with food. Dora Scarlett found they were 'giving it away in the streets'. One old farmer in a convoy of farm carts stopped Lazlo Beke and asked him if he would like a drink of milk. Lazlo accepted gratefully and 'felt the strength pouring back into my veins'. The farmer wanted to give away his milk where it would be most needed, so Beke jumped in his car and guided the old man to a hospital where they shared it out among the wounded. Many other insurgents helped to distribute free food. Bela Szasz was in hospital, recovering from an infection, and soon it was crowded with freedom fighters. He was astonished when one youngster entered the ward with ham, eggs, and cigarettes.

Lieutenant Peter Gosztony, a twenty-four-year-old career officer in the Hungarian Army, was equally surprised when horse-drawn carts loaded up with chickens, meat and bread started rolling up to the Kilian Barracks. Gosztony, who fought the entire revolution from the barracks, remembers, 'They refused any payment. They only wanted two things – to give us food and shake hands with Maleter. I heard Maleter tell one old peasant, "Make sure you do your job well. You are as important as we are." '

When Dora Scarlett went shopping in the big market at Dimitrov Square, she found 'mountains of chickens and ducks' all trussed, wrapped in greaseproof paper bearing the government export stamp *Terimpex*. There was plenty of red meat too, and for the first time since she arrived in Hungary Dora bought a sirloin of beef. The plentiful supply was due to Zoltan Vas, a veteran of the Communist movement in Hungary. During the 'liberation' of Hungary in 1945, Vas had organised the starving city's food supplies, and now, as Minister of Supply, he was repeating the performance. His first edict was to ban all exports of food – hence the neat packages of trussed poultry.

As the old farm carts, laden with bread, milk, meat and vegetables passed the wrecked buildings, many people felt with Tibor Meray that 'the atmosphere of 1945 had been revived. There was an aura of new beginnings after so much sorrow and so much blood, and it was exciting.'

Hundreds of shops had been wrecked by shellfire, so many supplies were channelled into state shops or the markets. But though this meant queueing for three hours or more to buy bread or potatoes Dora Scarlett found that 'suddenly, everyone was remarkably patient and good natured'. The elderly behaved with great stoicism. The old bent grandmothers, their heads shrouded in black kerchiefs, and carrying the inevitable string bags, often had to take shelter during occasional bursts of gunfire, particularly in the Hunyadi Square market where Dora did much of her shopping. One had to cross an open space to reach the market, and Dora noticed that 'quite young people would lose their nerve crossing this square, look over their shoulders once or twice, and then start to run. But the little old women just ambled along patiently, and came back with their two or three kilos of potatoes and bottle of milk.'

On one occasion Dora Scarlett saw an old woman standing hesitant on the edge of the pavement. 'She was short, frail as a sparrow, with the sharp nose and chin and sucked-in cheeks of age and emaciation.' Dora presumed that she wanted to cross the street but, as she was on the point of helping, some freedom fighters passed in a truck and the old lady, raising a hand, cried in a thin voice, *'Eljen!'* ('Long live!') 'Her eyes,' Dora remembers, 'of the milky pale blue of age, were alight with joy.'

Though only food shops were open, nobody looted the valuable goods displayed in hundreds of smashed windows. Time and again Dora Scarlett felt, 'I could easily have put out my hand to take a blouse or a pair of shoes,' but when she passed the same spot later the merchandise was still there. She heard one woman who had stopped before a broken shop window displaying cakes remark that they should be given to the children before they went stale. Someone retorted, 'Better let a few cakes spoil than set an example which might look like looting.'

Leslie Bain watched a crowd busily collecting boxes of chocolates which had been blown into the street by shellfire. Every box was replaced behind the shattered glass. Next door a florist's shop had been partially destroyed, but this time the goods were not replaced. All the flowers strewn in the streets were carefully picked up, then placed reverently on the bodies of insurgents killed in battle.

Lazlo Beke saw a sign behind the broken window of a watch-maker's shop, 'We found your window broken and we took your merchandise home. You can call for it at Kovacs, 78 Rakosi Street, any time.' Not far from Andrassy Street, he saw something of a different nature – a large wooden box bearing a sign, 'For the families of those who gave their lives for freedom.' The box was full of currency notes. There was no guard. To the Mayor of Budapest, Jozsef Kovago, the capital was 'a metropolis pervaded with such sacred feelings that even the thieves abandoned their trade'.

Peace, however fragile, meant different things to different people. To Lazlo Beke it meant a present for his wife – a pint of milk given to him by the old farmer. He took it back to the hostel with a loaf of bread. When he saw Eva he realised from the circles under her eyes that she 'was getting weaker and weaker with the baby and her work among the injured. She welcomed the milk as a godsend.' But after he had made sure that she had drained the last drop he had to leave her again, this time not to fight but to help with the ceasefire arrangements at the Technological University.

Thomas Szabo knew nothing of the ceasefire at first, for he had been sent on a mission outside Budapest and was amazed on his return to find himself driving back through the silent capital. He asked Captain Kovacs, 'Tell me, sir, is it true that the revolution has been won?'

'At the moment fighting has ended in the capital,' Kovacs cautiously replied. 'Russian troops have received an order to stop firing, so it seems we have won.'

Thomas was given four hours' leave and walked towards his parents' flat through streets packed with people. What struck him most was 'the women holding their children by the hand or pushing them in prams'. His father, mother and three younger brothers were listening to Radio Free Europe as he entered the flat. His mother 'let out a cry and threw herself into my arms'. Like any mother the world over, her first words when she had dried away her tears were 'How dirty you are, darling!' When the time came to return to Corvin Passage, his mother broke down, but his father looked at him gravely, and all he said was, 'Take care of yourself, my boy.'

Anna Gabor had a celebration of a different kind. Feri Lorenc, a writer for *Truth* (where Anna had graduated from billposter to secretary), had acquired a bottle of *barack*, Hungary's famous apricot brandy, some sausages and bread. They crossed the Danube to Buda for a picnic on Gellert Hill overlooking the city. Their lunch was interrupted by an extraordinary sight – scores of men 'swarming like ants' round the Liberty Monument. Originally this had been a graceful statue of a woman with up-raised arms, but in 1946 the Russians had insisted on adding a dominating bronze statue of a Red Army soldier. Dozens of ropes now encircled it and 'hauling like Egyptian slaves moving giant blocks' the people of Budapest rocked the statue backwards and forwards until finally the Russian soldier fell flat on his face.

Hundreds of Budapest boys too young to fight emerged into the streets, swarming over the rubble, intent on one objective only – to see who could collect the most spent bullets.

Drunken joy swept the city. Real laughter was heard for the first time in a week. But not everybody celebrated. Thousands of mothers mourned their sons; wives mourned their husbands. As for the 'missing', the agony for those who waited and hoped was almost worse than the certain news of death. All over the city men and women walked from corpse to corpse, drawing back the flags with which they were so often covered, seeking to identify a body riddled with bullets.

Vast areas of the city were littered with the remains of war – huge piles of debris, gaping houses, smashed Russian tanks. The Russian dead who were not removed by the retreating forces lay where they had been killed, but in death, as one man observed, their faces, sprinkled with lime, took on the serene quality of snow-white statues.

To the practised eye of John MacCormac of the *New York Times*, the devastation was worse than any he had seen as a correspondent in the Second World War. In a side street near the Corvin Cinema, he found a makeshift surgical clinic in which forty men and boys had died and 500 wounded lay mostly on the floors after a battle in which Soviet troops shot up the operating-theatre. Driving along Ulloi Avenue towards the Kilian Barracks, he saw more evidence of the savage Russian attacks in burned-out tanks and armoured cars 'as well as in the bodies of

20 Soviet soldiers that still lay unburied in the shattered street'.

As he drove carefully past broken glass, hanging telegraph wires, unexploded shells and corpses, young insurgents who had stopped fighting surrounded his car. 'Their faces were grey with exhaustion, their young chins were covered with a week's beard, but their spirit was still indomitable.' MacCormac asked one of them, 'When did you surrender?'

'We never surrendered!' the boy cried. 'The Russians went away and we came out.'

Though the ceasefire was by now 'official', Colonel Maleter was warily insuring against any sudden changes, and the fighters talking to MacCormac still carried arms, including 'a boy who could not be more than ten years old holding at the ready a rifle as tall as himself. Beside him was a fifteen-year-old girl with a sub-machine-gun and a forage cap on her head, who looked on the brink of exhaustion.'

Maleter was still in the barracks – and still maintaining a reserve of defiance. 'We have not surrendered,' he declared, 'and if our demands are not granted we shall carry on our fight until they are.' He had agreed to receive a deputation from the Hungarian Army, and to help transform the insurgents into newly formed National Guard, and he certainly supported Nagy. At the same time, he refused to allow his fighters to lay down their arms until the last Russian soldier had gone, and until Nagy would confirm 'the honour and patriotism of the freedom fighters'. When that happened, as he hoped it would, his forces would take on police powers 'until a new police force has been organised'.

9

The Last Hope

Tuesday, 30 October

Mikoyan and Suslov, who had flown in to Budapest with the '30 October Declaration', seemed determined to do everything possible to stabilise the position. When the non-Communist Zoltan Tildy met them, Mikoyan assured him categorically that all Soviet troops not in Hungary by virtue of the Warsaw Treaty would be withdrawn. Kadar also had 'amicable negotiations' with the Russians. The two men, together with Nagy, spent hours frankly outlining their problems: the possibility of multi-party elections, even the fact that Nagy was being pressed by extremists to leave the Warsaw Pact. But, as Tildy told the Russians, 'though some future decisions may have to be taken to calm the people, you must have faith in us on one point. Hungary wants to tighten its friendship with Russia – but it must be based on mutual confidence, not force. Hungary has absolutely no intention of following an anti-Soviet policy.'

Tildy was delighted. 'We can negotiate with the Russians,' he declared. 'We can get along with them as long as they are convinced we are sincere.'

Janos Kadar, a quiet unassuming man, was not so certain. It would be fatal, he said, to push the Russians too far, and he was not sure that Mikoyan could be trusted. A strange man, Kadar was, as Nagy once said, 'a born sitter on the fence'; he did not entirely trust Kadar. Besides the Russians did seem sincere. A journalist from *Truth* captured the atmosphere of hope and goodwill when he wrote:

Within the last few hours, I was able to penetrate the inner sanctum of the Party office on Academy Street. The reception hall, bordered with tall marble columns, was plunged in deep silence. Sitting about were vigorous-looking men, all wearing the same dark blue overcoats and the familiar Russian caps. They were members of Mikoyan's and Suslov's entourage. Otherwise, the building was more or less under the protection of the members of the Revolutionary Army.

Janos Kadar sent me word to be patient. He was in conference, I was informed. 'With whom?' I asked. 'With Mikoyan and Suslov,' I was told. 'They are discussing the withdrawal of Russian troops.' After a few minutes, Imre Nagy came out of the conference room. The negotiations must not have been fruitless. Suddenly the door of the conference room opened and Mikoyan and Suslov emerged. Suslov's face wore a smile. I found myself in their path, and the Russians – was it by habit, or did they take me for a party official? – shook my hand.

Some Westerners viewed the '30 October Declaration' with scepticism, but one man was delighted. Allen Dulles of the American CIA told President Eisenhower, 'This utterance is one of the most significant to come out of the Soviet Union since the end of World War Two.' Eisenhower's feet were more firmly planted on the ground. 'It is true' was his only comment.

Still, everything did seem to point to peace. Even *Pravda* admitted, 'The Nagy government has won the support of the people,' while Moscow Radio announced, 'Reports pouring in from all over Hungary show that the workers support the new government and approve its programme.' In Moscow, Marshal Zhukov, the Soviet Minister of Defence, said, 'In Hungary the situation has improved. A government has been formed in which we have confidence.' On the same evening, Shepilov, the Soviet Foreign Minister, said, 'One must satisfy the workers, peasants and intellectuals,' and promised that if the insurgents honoured the ceasefire, the Russian troops would leave Budapest.

Cables of congratulation reached Nagy from Tito in Yugoslavia and Gomulka in Poland. Even Communist China, which had accused Russia of 'not taking the principle of equal rights into account in dealing with other Communist states', now voiced wholehearted approval for the new Moscow policy declaration. Nagy's hopes were buttressed by world opinion. At the specially convened a meeting of the UN Security Council on Sunday, Henry Cabot Lodge, the American Ambassador to the UN had made it clear that the struggle in the isolated capital of Hungary had now leapt on to the stage of international politics.

> The situation in Hungary [he declared] has developed in such a way as to cause deep anxiety and concern throughout the world. Available information indicates that the people of Hungary ... are being subjected to violent repressive measures by foreign military forces and they are reported to be suffering very heavy casualties. The members of the United Nations cannot remain indifferent. They must assert their serious concern and consider how best they might discharge the obligations which they have assumed under the Charter.

Only words, it is true, and the Russians had been poised to use the downstroke of the veto in New York, but the fact that the meeting was held at all gave the isolated Hungarians great comfort, especially when they learned of the tremendous public interest in New York, where huge crowds paraded in front of the UN building carrying the banners denouncing the 'Kremlin butchers!'

All this was heartening to Nagy, particularly as more and more confirmation reached him that the Russians were actually leaving. Radio Budapest announced, 'The withdrawal of Soviet troops is in full swing. Units of the Hungarian Army, the police and youth detachments are taking over the job of maintaining order.' John MacCormac, walking through the scarred streets of the city, saw for himself that 'The Hungarian people seem to have won their revolution. Soviet troops are now leaving Budapest.' More confirmation came from the provinces. Free Miskolc Radio announced that special trains were being prepared for Soviet troops at the frontier town of Zahony. The free radio at Szabolcs-Szatmar announced that 'at least a division' of Russian troops had crossed the River Tisza, ready to be evacuated via

Zahony. 'Other divisions to the south are also on the move,' the spokesman added.

So, Nagy had achieved a peaceful solution – and by the seemingly impossible feat of pleasing everyone. Many of the original aims of the revolution had been achieved. Soviet troops were leaving; the new government included Bela Kovacs and Zoltan Tildy, neither of them Communists, which meant that non-Communist groups now felt they had a voice in the corridors of power.[1] Yet Nagy had managed this without sacrificing the Party. True, it was not in the best shape but on its foundations he could build tomorrow's Communist Hungary – and, equally important, convince today's Kremlin leaders that it was possible.

As Miklos Molnar of the *Literary Gazette*, who saw Nagy regularly, put it,

> The first balance sheet of this strange government, which started with fighting the rebels and ended with a reconciliation which adopted most of their major aims, is not far short of the optimum solution if we think of politics as an art of the possible ... for surely Nagy had succeeded in obtaining the support of every force involved, from the USSR to the rebels, by way of the Party.

But now Nagy had the close support of a group of friends he could trust. Geza Losonczy – his outburst of temper long forgotten – was always at his side. Tildy, of the Smallholders' Party, was not only wise but was blessed with unbounded energy. Nagy put another old friend, Ferenc Donath, in charge of radio and information, and a neighbour of his in Buda, Gyorgy Heltai, handled foreign affairs. His son-in-law, Ferenc Janosi, was told 'to keep an eye on military matters'.

Now, at last, Nagy was able to wipe away the slur that he had called in Russian troops. When a workers' delegation from Angyalfold mentioned the rumours, he told them he had had nothing to do with it, pointing out that he was not appointed premier until after the Soviet troops were on their way to the capital.

---

[1] For the principal names in the four governments of the revolution, see Appendix IV.

With him at the meeting was Jozsef Szilagyi, the tall, brown-skinned son of a peasant whom Nagy had befriended when teaching at the agricultural university, and had now made his personal secretary. Szilagyi remembered later[1] that 'Imre Nagy replied by saying that it was not he who had called in the Russians, though an attempt had been made to make him sign the resolution later'. Szilagyi made certain that Nagy's denial was given full publicity on Radio Budapest and in all the newspapers.

(Proof of Gero's lie that Nagy had actually signed the document was seen by Eugene-Geza Pogany. After meeting Maleter in the Kilian Barracks, Pogany was later taken to the Parliament archives to see 'a document of historical significance'. It was the resolution which Gero had commanded Nagy to sign, but there was no signature – only the name of Imre Nagy typed in.)

Among Nagy's first tasks was to set up a National Guard. He sought advice from the friend who had rescued him from the Avo – Colonel Sandor Kopacsi, chief of the Budapest police. As Kopacsi remembered later, Nagy 'instructed me to organise the new special police, enlisting the insurgents into its ranks also, and to establish the top body of the National Guard'. Nagy told Kopacsi, 'Look for an experienced, well-trained man, possibly among people rehabilitated recently.'

Kopacsi already had his man in mind – forty-four-year-old General Bela Kiraly, who had had a distinguished army career until he was jailed by Rakosi in 1951; he had been released only about three months previously. General Kiraly was a spare, handsome man who had learned excellent English while in prison; he felt his job was 'to organise the military and security for the defence of a capital in case there was a second military intervention'. As he told Bela Szasz, 'The Government wanted to avoid war with the Russians. We wanted only to be able to hold the capital for days or even hours to secure the possibility for the Government to seek a political solution.'

One danger was apparent: the insurgents, backed by provincial hotheads might go too far; that after this victory achieved against odds they might increase their demands beyond the original

[1] *Hungarian White Book*, vol. 5, page 84.

sixteen points, beyond the original *reason* for the revolution. Nagy was only too aware of the danger; his anxiety was shared by his friend Tibor Meray, who analysed the problem with great perspicacity:

> It sometimes happens in history that a whole country becomes the victim of an optical illusion. That was what happened in Hungary. Nagy's announcement of the cease-fire order, which he linked this time to a promise that the Soviet troops would leave the capital, spread drunken joy throughout the country. The little people of Hungary, who had fought with such indomitable courage, now thought that they had triumphed over the Soviet Union, not only morally but also militarily.

This was the danger. Tito's cable of congratulation to Nagy had contained an anguished warning: thus far but no farther. Gomulka in his telegram told Nagy in effect, 'Whatever happens, do not abandon the path to Socialism or all will be lost.'

In vain Nagy tried to pass on these warnings. To a delegation from the South Budapest Revolutionary Council which visited him, he said categorically, 'Do not demand too much or we will lose everything we have gained. If the Russians for one moment believe we want to leave the Communist axis, their troops will come straight back.'

Yet people would not listen, particularly in the provinces. The Revolutionary Committee at Vas stopped referring to the 'Hungarian Government' on its free radio, instead calling it 'the government in Budapest'. At the same time, Attila Szigetti warned Nagy from Gyor that he must call for free elections within three months or 'tens of thousands of demonstrators from Gyor will march on the capital and encourage the uprising to continue'. This was against everything Nagy believed in. Indeed, when his friend Miklos Gimes brought the matter up, Nagy retorted sharply, 'No question of that as long as I'm in power here.'

As if this were not enough, Radio Free Europe, which had already served Nagy ill, incited the insurgents to further bloodshed. At the very moment when Nagy was striving to cool tempers, it allowed its 'military expert' to give some gratuitous

Above Imre Nagy broadcasts to the nation   *Below* Erno Gero *(left) ;* Janos Kadar *(right)*

A squadron of Soviet tanks in the centre of Budapest. The author
took this photograph from a shattered shop window

Above A defiant Hungarian guards a captured Soviet tank
Below The debris of war

Freedom fighters raise the Hungarian flag

Above Pal Maleter *(left)*, hero of the Hungarian uprising and defender of the Kilian Barracks, in conference *Below* An exhausted Noel Barber *(right)* talks to freedom fighters

Freedom fighters drape the makeshift graves for their fallen comrades
with the Hungarian flag

The only case of looting — when enraged Hungarians on the first
night sacked the Soviet propaganda bookshop in Budapest

Hungarian refugees flee to Austria

advice to the people of Budapest. Talking of the ceasefire order, he said:

> Imre Nagy and his supporters want to revise and modernise the Trojan horse episode. They need a ceasefire so that the present government in power in Budapest can maintain its position as long as possible. Those who are fighting for liberty must not lose sight even for a minute of the plans of the government opposing them. Otherwise there will be a repetition of the Trojan horse tragedy.

This was in turn followed by more unsolicited 'advice' when Radio Free Europe proclaimed on 31 October, 'The Ministry of Defence and the Ministry of the Interior are still in Communist hands. Do not let this continue, freedom fighters. Do not hang your weapons on the wall. Not a lump of coal, not a drop of gasolene for the Budapest government, until Interior and Defence are in your control.'

This broadcast was followed by another, in which a Radio Free Europe announcer said, 'This little government [the new smaller cabinet] offers no guarantee. The actual situation is such that it must not be accepted even on a provisional basis. It is urgent, as the free radios have demanded, that a new National Provisional Government, capable of facing the situation, be formed immediately.'

It is not difficult to imagine the effect of such provocative statements in places like Gyor, let alone in Budapest.

Radio Free Europe, which was so damaging to the cause of Imre Nagy, was partly financed with funds from the American Central Intelligence Agency. RFE operated on a huge scale, beaming nearly twenty hours a day to satellite countries on twenty-nine transmitters, mostly from Munich. At Munich alone the staff totalled around 1300; nearly ninety people in the Hungarian section were actively employed in actual broadcasting. Many were Hungarian émigrés who had lost everything when Communism arrived after the Second World War. The United States had financed many Hungarian émigré groups, some of whose members filtered into the CIA.

They shared one thing in common with many Americans – a firm belief that all Communists are bad Communists; the Hungarians speaking on RFE might well have argued that their bitter attacks on Nagy were only a reflection of the American way of thinking. Even after the ceasefire RFE attacked Nagy saying, 'It should be realised at least that the Hungarian people has risen against the Communist system as a whole.'

This was, of course, not true; the uprising was inspired by Communists and largely fought by Communists anxious, perhaps naïvely, for a better form of Communism.

On another occasion, when Nagy was trying his utmost to calm the population, RFE gave a point-by-point lesson on how to make Molotov cocktails. It seemed as though the broadcasters *wanted* the fighting to continue, and even the American Government came to the woeful conclusion that it was 'clear that, after the rebellion was underway, RFE improvised its own policies, and found itself caught up in the emotions of the times. With the advantage of hindsight, it can be said that the results, at best, were unfortunate for all concerned.'[1]

Leslie Bain, who monitored RFE regularly in Budapest during the revolution, felt that 'Radio Free Europe and to some extent the Voice of America greatly embarrassed the Nagy revolutionary government with their broadcasts by insisting on goals which by no stretch of the imagination that government could ever have reached.'

Questions of directives from the head office in New York were made more difficult because in the middle of the revolution RFE was moving into new offices.[2]

[1] *Radio Free Europe – A Survey and Analysis*, Library of Congress, 22 March 1972.

[2] John Dunning, who worked in the New York office at the time and is now assistant to the President, told the author, 'There were some childish commentaries, such as the one on how to make Molotov cocktails, which went on the air without anyone seeing it.' The broadcaster was dismissed with several others after Adenaueur had studied RFE tapes and found some broadcasts open to misinterpretation. And as John O'Kearney wrote in the *Nation* in February 1957, 'During the days of the fighting it played a large part in keeping the blood flowing. People listened to it because they had no other source for news of what was going on anywhere but where they were themselves. RFE egged the battle on with almost hysterical enthusiasm.'

As before, events forced Nagy to forsake the rule-book of Communism. This time there were two decisive dramas, each occurring on the morning of Tuesday, 30 October. One was a mission of peace, the other a mission of hate.

The first one centred round the figure of Cardinal Jozsef Mindszenty, Primate of all Hungary.[1] Eight years previously he had been arrested on Rakosi's orders, sensationally tried, treated with contempt for one of such high ecclesiastical office and sentenced to death; the sentence was later commuted to life imprisonment. He had spent most of the years in solitary confinement, though for the past twelve months he had been confined in Felsopeteny Castle, fifty miles or so north of Budapest.

Early on Tuesday – a mild, October morning – the Cardinal's Avo guards told him to pack a bag. He was to be removed because his life was threatened. When the Cardinal asked by whom, the Avo officer replied, 'The mob.'

The Cardinal refused to move from the castle. The guards pulled him from his chair. The Cardinal resisted, and was still struggling when another Avo rushed into the room and shouted that a Russian-style armoured car was driving up to the castle.

Within a few minutes, John Horvath, the Communist head of the Office of Church Affairs, ran into the room shouting, 'Your life is not safe here. I have orders to move you.'

'I will not go,' the Cardinal replied. 'You have taken everything from me there is to take. You can take nothing else.'

Horvath hesitated, presumably not relishing the prospect of using physical violence against the old man. He left the room to telephone Budapest for advice.

Unknown to the Avo (or Horvath) all messages from the castle were being tapped by insurgents, and an army unit led by Major Antal Palinkas at Retsag was barely a dozen miles away. Palinkas immediately set off for Felsopeteny with two tanks and an armoured car, after detailing other units to intercept Horvath who had been ordered by telephone to return to Budapest.

By this time several hundred villagers were gathering in the castle grounds, armed with pitchforks, spades, hoes and other farm implements. The Cardinal heard them shout, 'Freedom for

[1] It has to be remembered that eighty-five per cent of the population were Roman Catholic.

Mindszenty and bread for the Hungarian people!'

At the prospect of violence the Avos panicked. As the Cardinal remembered later, he heard them 'running from one room to the other, shouting to each other about the demonstration outside'. Then an incredible thing happened. The senior Avo officer approached the Cardinal 'with humility and respect' and to the old man's astonishment announced they had formed a Revolutionary Committee, that the Cardinal had been wrongfully imprisoned and that he was now free to go. As he was speaking the tanks arrived and Major Palinkas led the assault into the great hall of the castle. It was bloodless. Freedom fighters disarmed the Avos, searched the cellars, discovering a cache of machineguns and other arms under a pile of coal.

Outside the convoy waited while the Cardinal packed a bag. As he climbed into the armoured car, he noticed that the red stars had been painted out and replaced by the Hungarian colours. The villagers cheered, waved their pitchforks, and within a few minutes Hungary's most illustrious prisoner was driving away to freedom. His first words after blessing the crowd at Retsag were, 'My sons, I shall carry on where I left off eight years ago.'

Much had happened in eight years, and though the Cardinal was greeted with enthusiasm by the vast majority of Hungarians, who now had a focal point for any Catholic political ambitions, there were some who harboured misgivings about his possible conduct, who felt that the Cardinal might find it difficult to bridge the gap between 'carrying on where he had left off' and the forces of a new emancipated church. Nagy and his colleagues could only wait and see.

Meanwhile people queued patiently for meat outside the state-run Kozert shop near Republic Square. At one corner of the square, opposite the Erkel Theatre, stood the headquarters of the Greater Budapest Party Committee.[1] Inside the building was a detachment of 47 Avo. Nobody quite knew why they were there, for most were young recruits, perhaps pressed into service against their will, and they had been there since 23 October, presumably too afraid to venture out. Even more incredibly, the building was

---

[1] The 'local' branch of the party, not to be confused with the national Party headquarters in Academy Street.

used occasionally by leaders meeting delegations who seemed
to have ignored their presence. In a work of fiction, such an
anomaly would be looked upon as a clumsy device to further the
plot; nobody will ever know how the Avos were able to remain
there unmolested.

Shortly after 9 a.m. a truck drove up to the front doors of the
building. It was laden with meat – beef, sides of bacon, mounds
of sausages, all of which were hurriedly unloaded. At this point
a patrol of insurgents arrived. The hungry women shouted to
them as the meat disappeared inside the heavy doors. The freedom fighters sent in a group of youngsters to discover what was
happening. They were greeted on the first floor by two men in
civilian clothes.

'What's going on, boys?' one asked. The leader noticed that the
men's clothes were new. He asked them to produce their identity
cards. They were unable to do so. At that moment someone
from above hurled four grenades down the narrow staircase well.
Fortunately they did not explode until they hit the ground floor.

The boys ran out of the building; as they escaped, insurgents
in the square tried to force their way in. The Avos pushed them
all back – except one who was grabbed and pulled inside the
building before the heavy doors were slammed and locked.

Inside the building a delegation of workers and two Hungarian
Army officers were meeting to discuss the best ways of guarding
factories against possible Soviet attack. The meeting was chaired
by Imre Mezo, secretary of the Budapest Party organisation, a
pro-Nagy man of great integrity who had fought not only in the
Spanish Civil War, but with the French resistance in the Second
World War. No one knows whether Mezo realised the Avo were
inside the building, but when two Avos in civilian clothes brought
the youngster before him Mezo ordered him to be kept under
guard.

Outside the insurgents demanded the return of their 'hostage'.
The mood was ugly. The insurgents surrounded the building,
then brought it under attack. The Avos returned their fire. It was
the start of a bloody three-hour siege; in the course of it the Avos
suddenly appeared on neighbouring rooftops and sprayed the
crowd with machine-gun fire.

Inside the building Mezo telephoned frantically for help until finally the Defence Ministry sent three tanks to clear the square. When the crews saw the carnage, they sided with the insurgents, with only one thought in mind – revenge.

Among the crowd was photographer John Sadovy who reported the climax of the battle as follows: [1]

Now they were closing in fast. We met another group led by a man carrying a huge flag. 'Come on, come on, it's ours,' he shouted. Other groups of revolutionaries were coming in from the side, screaming and going into the building. There was only occasional machine-gun fire from the top floor, but people were still being careful. At the front of the building there were thirty to forty dead. They were lying in a line. As one had been hit the man behind had taken his place – and died. It was like a potato field, only they were people instead of potatoes. Now the Avo men began to come out. The first to emerge from the building was an officer, alone. It was the fastest killing I ever saw. He came out laughing and the next thing I knew he was flat on the ground. It didn't dawn on me that this man was shot. He just fell down, I thought. Then the revolutionaries brought out a good-looking officer. His face was white. He got five yards, retreated, argued. Then he fell forward. It was over for him. Six young policemen came out. Their shoulder tabs were torn off. Quick argument. 'We're not so bad as you think we are; give us a chance,' they said. I was three feet from that group. Suddenly one began to slouch forward. They must have been close to his ribs when they fired. They all went down like corn that had been cut. Another came out, running. He saw his friends dead, turned, headed into the crowd. The revolutionaries dragged him out. Then my nerves went. Tears started to come down my cheeks. I had spent three years in the war, but nothing I saw then compared with the horror of this. I could see the impact of bullets on clothes. There was not much noise. They were shooting so close that the man's body acted as a silencer. They brought out a woman and man from the building. Her face was white. She looked left and right at the bodies that were spread all over. Suddenly a man came up and hit her

[1] *Life Magazine*, Special Issue, December 1956.

with the butt of a rifle. Another pulled her hair and kicked
her. She half fell down. They kicked her again. I thought that
was the end of her, but in a few moments she was up, plead-
ing. Some of the revolutionaries decided to put her in a bus
which was standing nearby, though there were shouts of 'No
prisoners, no prisoners!' There was still shooting inside the
building. Occasionally a small group would come out. One
man got as far as the park, which was a long way, but there
he was finished. Two more came, one a high-ranking officer.
His bleeding body was hung by his feet from a tree and
women came to spit on him. Then came a last scuffle at the
entrance of the building. They brought out a little boy.
They were carrying him on their shoulders. He was about
five years old, with a sweet expression on his face as he
looked left and right. There were shouts: 'Don't kill him,
save him!' He was the son of one of the Avo officers from
inside the building. To see this little face after what you'd
seen a minute ago brought you back to reality. They spared
him and the crowd passed him from shoulder to shoulder
until he was out of harm's way. Going back through the park,
I saw women looking for their men among the bodies on
the ground. I sat down on a tree-trunk.

Almost every one of the Avos was beaten to death. The two
officers also died. One of them, a Colonel Papps, was beaten,
spat on, strung up head downwards on a tree, doused with petrol
and set on fire. And the honest Imre Mezo died later of wounds.

Despite the hatred for the Avo that burned inside every
Hungarian, even the revolutionary newspaper *Hungarian Independence* felt constrained to rebuke its readers, 'We must raise
our voices against those who stoked the fires of anarchy, who
incited the throng.'

In fact, many acts of violence were due to a change in the types
of 'freedom fighters', not all of whom were genuine, though they
often operated under the guise of a National Guard armband.
Mark Molnar noticed a subtle change in the composition of the
armed bands roaming the streets. The writers and students had
retired, the workers were preparing to return to their factories; but

when the prison doors had been opened some hoodlums also escaped. Before long several truckloads of food from Vienna disappeared. Marauding gangs of ex-convicts, liberated by pretending to be political prisoners, at times gunned down suspected Avos without proof of their identity.

George Kovacs, the one-time broadcaster, was with his group on patrol near Moricz Zsigmond Square when they saw a gang of youths 'pushing, hitting and threatening to lynch a man in uniform. I was uneasy – none of us felt that just because a man wore a uniform he should be hanged or shot without trial.'

The leader of Kovacs' group pushed through the crowd to reach the prisoner. One of the opposing gang threatened to open fire, and a stand-up fight was barely averted, before Kovacs' group took the man away for questioning. His papers proved him to be a captain in the artillery who had fought with the insurgents in the first phase of the revolution.

Many gangs called themselves 'Maleter's men' and Molnar mentioned the matter to him; but Maleter was a fledgling politician, and waved the problem aside, though on one occasion he did slap a teenaged 'insurgent' who was found with some earrings in his pockct, and warned him, 'You are lucky not to be shot.'

Among those who felt that Maleter was not taking a tough enough line was Leslie Bain, the American, who went to see Losonczy and told him bluntly, 'It seems to me that Maleter could stop the atrocities if he wanted to by issuing an order to his own men, unless he prefers to let them go on and use the disorders as a reason for grabbing all power himself.' As Bain remembers, 'Losonczy seemed aghast and later I found Imre Nagy equally bewildered.'

Whether Maleter could have prevented the disorders or not, there was one almost insuperable problem, summed up by Colonel Kopacsi. 'There is no way we can check on everyone,' he said, 'though there were instances when we did recognise known criminals, and were able to deal with them.'

A short, skinny man arrived with a group at Budapest police headquarters. His tommy-gun was slung over his shoulder, and while the leader of the group talked to the police officer in charge the man looked around, as though searching for a face, and was unwise enough to mutter, 'I've got a bone to pick with someone – and if I find him I'll exterminate him.'

A policeman recognised him as Sandor Itoso, known all over Hungary as 'The Elizabetta Street murderer'. His trial had excited enormous excitement, and he had inadvertently escaped with other criminals from jail where he was serving fifteen years.

10

The Victory Dance

Tuesday, 30 October (continued)

Once again events were moving too swiftly for Nagy. The revolution was overtaking him. Hour by hour the price of peace was rising, and though he knew that more concessions would be fraught with danger he had no option now but to ignore Tito's danger signal of 'So far but no farther'. By lunchtime on Tuesday, 30 October, he had formed a new coalition cabinet[1] with three Communists, two members of the Smallholders' Party and one Social Democrat or Peasant Party. Now he was faced with a momentous decision.

Shortly before 2.30 p.m., he went to the microphone, and told all Hungary, 'The tremendous force of the democratic movement has brought our country to a crossroad. The National Government has decided to take a step vital for the future of the whole nation. The cabinet abolishes the one-party system and places the country's government on a basis of democratic co-operation between coalition parties.'

He begged his listeners to prevent further bloodshed, telling them, 'We have to establish order first of all.' His sentiments were echoed by Zoltan Tildy, who had been the first president of the Hungarian Republic after the war. Following Nagy to the radio, he said in a voice choked with emotion, 'I embrace Hungary's dear youth, my heart overflowing with warmth.'

But if Nagy hoped his latest concession would appease the hotheaded he was sadly mistaken. Within an hour, he was besieged by more and more demands. Some wanted an immediate declaration of neutrality. Others insisted that the fight should continue

[1] See Appendix IV.

until there were no more Russians on Hungarian soil. Almost everyone, it seemed, wanted him to abrogate the Warsaw Pact.

Inside the Prime Minister's office in Parliament Building the scene bordered on bedlam. Delegates argued violently. At least two fist fights broke out. Nagy was deeply shocked. After wrestling with his conscience he had just made a broadcast of historic importance, yet instead of being rewarded with praise he could hear in the tumult nothing but more demands, all of which he knew would exhaust Russian patience.

The climax came when Szigetti, leading a five-man delegation from Gyor, warned Nagy that a 'parliament' of Revolutionary Councils was at this very moment debating in Gyor, representing all western Hungary. 'If you don't agree with their demands,' he shouted, 'Gyor might revise its stand and break with the Nagy government.'

Hecklers challenged Nagy to abrogate the Warsaw Pact. He lost his temper and threatened to resign. From the back of his office a voice shouted, 'That would be wonderful!'

Almost in tears Nagy was hustled from his own office by Losonczy. Nagy was, as Zinner felt, 'clearly aligned ... with other tragic figures in history, caught in the swirl of revolution and horribly mistreated by it.... The die was now cast. The Premier stood in the middle between irreconcilable forces rapidly converging on one another and on him.'

Among the exultant people in the streets of Budapest, the temper was very different, for they were still blissfully under the illusion that Russia had been vanquished by force of arms. Unconcerned by the grim tussle taking place behind the closed doors of Parliament Building, time was too precious for thought, though not for rejoicing. Glasses of *barack* or bottles of thin-necked 'Whistler' wine were brought out of hiding. People offered total strangers their precious Munkas or Terv cigarettes. In the few undamaged cafés still open waiters surreptitiously produced bottles of Szilvorium, Hungary's plum brandy, or the more fiery Torkoly, the rough working-man's spirit, now gratefully drunk by anyone anxious to toast this new and stupendous victory. 'At first we couldn't believe it,' Anna Gabor remembers. 'Free elections! It was like a dream that comes true!'

None of the revellers in the streets had any idea that the **dream** was already being transformed into a nightmare. Tito's warning had come true. Shortly before midnight several government leaders were discussing plans in Nagy's office in Parliament Building. Sandwiches, the inevitable small bottles of soda, and some 'Giraffe' beer (so called because of the emblem on the label) stood on a table opposite Nagy's desk. It was almost Wednesday, the last day of October, when Losonczy walked into the office and whispered in his ear.

Nagy nodded. In walked Pal Maleter, who had met Nagy for the first time earlier in the day when he was appointed deputy commander under Kiraly of the newly formed Revolutionary Committee of the Armed Forces. Jozsef Kovago, now Mayor of Budapest, remembered later the moment when Maleter, with soldierly directness, said gravely, 'Comrade Prime Minister, I have to report that Soviet armoured units are invading Hungary in large numbers across the Russian border in the north-east.'

There was silence, but no sense of panic, none of the unseemly bedlam that had disgraced the Premier's office earlier that day – only anguish, perhaps at the speed with which retribution had come.

For Nagy and Gyorgy Heltai, his new Deputy Minister of Foreign Affairs, it must have been a terrible moment. Heltai had been involved in all the discussions with Mikoyan and Suslov. He felt so confident of the outcome, so sure they were sincere, that earlier in the day he had offered Bela Szasz (with whom, incidentally, he had shared a cell for five years) the post of ambassador to France.

As Heltai told Szasz, 'The situation became more optimistic with their visit. They agreed to the withdrawal of Russian troops, and declared they were ready to recognise a coalition government of the democratic parties. During the talks, Mikoyan and Suslov even showed their willingness to have talks about the revision of the Warsaw Pact. They said frankly that perhaps Hungary had the right to question its membership of the Pact.'

Now, suddenly, all had changed. Why? Nagy no doubt felt the demands of the provinces had driven the Russians too far. He knew, of course, that though the revolution had been started by Communists demanding only a better form of Communism the picture had changed, and in any free elections the Communists would be beaten. Such a possibility would be totally unacceptable to Moscow.

Yet, as Heltai felt, Mikoyan and Suslov had seemed disposed to accept the possibility of free elections. Had they been duping the Hungarians all the time? Heltai was right in feeling that they had in fact been sincere, for there was a more sinister reason behind the sudden change, which at this time was not so much a change as a Soviet insurance.

We know now that a bitter policy division was raging within the Kremlin at this time. Khrushchev was anxious to pursue a soft line. The military clique bitterly opposed this, though Khrushchev won the right to send his disciples, Mikoyan and Suslov, to Budapest. There was no question of the Russian generals forcing Khrushchev to change his mind, but (like Nagy) they knew that in the long run Moscow would never tolerate free elections and lose a Communist satellite. So they insured against it. Since it is always easier to withdraw troops than mount a hurried offensive (Budapest had already proved that) they quietly alerted several infantry divisions, and moved them into position. Khrushchev, it seems, was not informed. The generals felt that if Khrushchev's policies proved to be right they could easily withdraw. If the soft line failed, Russian troops would be poised for the kill. And of course Mikoyan and Suslov were completely ignorant of this when they smiled and beamed in Budapest.

Nagy decided he would not publish the news. As the meeting in his office finally broke up in the early hours, the eerie silence that had shrouded Budapest since the guns stopped firing was broken by the sound of music.

Down in the far corner of Parliament Square, the scene of so much blood, a hastily assembled tzigane orchestra was playing, and those in the building who peered out of the windows could just make out shadowy, swirling figures.

The people of Budapest were dancing away the night to celebrate victory.

PART II

The Road to Despair

I I

The Day of the Lies

Wednesday and Thursday, 31 October, 1 November

At 10 o'clock on Wednesday morning, 31 October, the Hungarian cabinet met to discuss the latest developments. A messenger interrupted the proceedings with a cable which he handed to the tired Prime Minister. He studied it in silence, then he stood up and read aloud: 'British and French forces are bombing Egypt.'

As Gyorgy Heltai, the new Deputy Foreign Minister, remembered, 'The silence was deafening.' It was shattered by Losonczy, who exploded, 'God damn them!'

Someone asked, 'Aren't we going to put out feelers to the west, even now?'

'Certainly not *now*,' Nagy retorted.

As the first bombs thudded into the sand wastes of the Sinai Desert, a new crisis point in the Cold War erupted. It had been simmering since the British evacuated their Suez bases, a move which was followed by the massive Russian arms sales to Egypt in 1955. Until this happened, the United States had been sympathetic to Nasser, but now that Egypt was flooded with Soviet technicians the White House had second thoughts. Having offered to finance the Aswan Dam in the Nile, America abruptly cancelled its offer in July 1956 – three months before the Hungarian uprising.

A furious Nasser immediately nationalised the Suez Canal. In Whitehall Eden, already a sick man but understandably concerned with protecting British oil supplies, consulted the French and prepared for joint military action. For three months nothing happened. Then on 29 October, the Israelis swept across the Sinai Desert, and within hours reached the banks of the canal. At the very moment when Nagy was broadcasting to his country his hopes of a Russian withdrawal, the British and French were sending an ultimatum to Egypt and Israel: 'Pull back ten miles from the canal or we send in our planes.' The Egyptians refused, the bombing started, and with one stroke any possible compromise solution between Russia and Hungary was for the moment all but forgotten as the international situation entered a new phase; it gave Russia a perfect opportunity to stall demands for freedom by 10 million people locked behind the Iron Curtain.

The British and French action had the effect of drawing world attention away from Hungary, while it concentrated on what it considered to be a potentially more explosive area. It was a political gift to Khrushchev, for though Suez was by no means the only factor that influenced Russia's decision to send troops back into Hungary the Western preoccupation with this new crisis helped. The British were so occupied with Suez that they hardly extended a thought to Hungary, and even the Americans seemed to go out of their way to assure the Russians that they would not interfere while the Suez crisis continued.

It was one of the most unfortunate coincidences of modern history, for it gave the Kremlin a golden opportunity to consolidate the Soviet empire. Many of the Soviet leaders regarded it as treason to surrender an inch of Soviet territory; there were many who feared that if Hungary left the Warsaw Pact it might become a showcase for the West, a second West Berlin, a country filled with tempting Western goods that would stir envy in every other satellite country and perhaps encourage them to follow suit. Indeed some of the satellite leaders were themselves afraid, for they stood to lose their positions if that happened. That was clearly why Anton Zapotocky, the Czech premier, made the ridiculous assertion that the uprising 'has unleashed a Fascist white terror'.[1]

When the Soviet Presidium met in Moscow on the morning of 1 November, its findings were by no means unanimous. The Kremlin, faced with the double crisis of Suez and Hungary, was

[1] Zapotocky conveniently forgot that in the real white terror, which lasted ten days in 1871, the Versailles army which suppressed the Paris commune slaughtered over 20,000, transported another 20,000, causing Thiers to gloat, 'The ground is paved with their corpses.'

in confusion. Colonel Oleg Penkovskiy remembers.[1] 'We in Moscow felt as if we were sitting on a powderkeg. Everyone in the general staff was against the "Khrushchev adventure". It was better to lose Hungary, they said, than to lose everything.'

Nevertheless Marshal Zhukov had already held a high-level military conference at Uzhgorod on 26 October, at which plans were prepared to alert 75,000 men, including two divisions of 'uncontaminated Orientals', who were rushed to the Hungarian frontier directly from the Carpathian Command.

All morning grim snippets of news reached Parliament Building – news so incredible in view of the recent promises by Mikoyan and Suslov that even the most cynical found it hard to believe them. Radio Miskolc posed the question, 'The Soviet Army has moved several formations into our country. Yet according to latest announcements Soviet troops will be withdrawn from Budapest. Why then are the new Soviet troops necessary? Marshal Zhukov – do you know of this?'

From Zahony on the Russo-Hungarian frontier came news that 'thousands of tanks' had entered Hungary. Yet at the same time Russians *had* been seen making an apparently orderly withdrawal from the capital, with the exception of a few key places, such as the Soviet embassy, which they insisted on guarding. Yet now Nagy received news that the three Budapest airports – Ferihegy, Budaors and Tokol – had been stealthily surrounded by Soviet tanks, and that Soviet personnel had taken over key duties in the airport buildings. Hungary's puny Air Force sent a message to General Kiraly that unless the airports were freed Hungarian pilots would 'make an armed stand in support of the demands of the entire Hungarian working people'.

Kiraly flatly forbade the motley assortment of obsolete Hungarian aircraft to take any action. The Prime Minister, he told the Air Command, insisted that as discussions were still taking place with the Russians any belligerent action by the Hungarians might destroy hopes of reaching a compromise. Even so, when Nagy telephoned Andropov, the Soviet ambassador smoothly assured him the Soviet tanks were only there to ensure the safe evacuation of Russian civilians.

[1] *The Penkovskiy Papers*, Doubleday, New York, 1965.

Hungarian planes did fly several reconnaissance sorties, finding evidence of Russian tanks grouping outside dozens of Hungarian cities. Near Budapest – at the north–south road junctions of Vac and Cegled – they spotted nearly two hundred tanks.

The Russians were effecting three different troop movements. They were withdrawing from the capital and from public view in the provinces. At the same time they were sending new forces from the east to strategic centres inside Hungary, ostensibly, as Andropov put it, 'to assist in the organised withdrawal of Soviet forces'. In fact the Russian forces, strategically located along the main arterial roads, formed a crescent about a hundred miles east of Budapest. Thirdly, the Russians were massing heavy armoured units on the frontiers or just inside Hungary. At Zahony nearly 300 tanks – 80 of them the latest model heavy tanks – were located just inside the border. In some cases, as at the village of Csaroda, one convoy which apparently moved back to Russia never left Hungarian soil but turned a circle. There was no fighting. To those unaware of what was happening in lonely country areas, there was an illusion of peace. But by the Wednesday the roads leading into Hungary from the east were choked with Soviet military traffic, not only at Zahony, but at the frontier village of Nyirbator near Satu Mare in Romania, and at Battonya, near Arad in Romania.

The forces the Soviet Union were assembling to bludgeon a tiny, heroic nation were larger than the combined forces of Montgomery and Rommel at the battle of El Alamein. The Russians were leaving nothing to chance.

To the people of Budapest the scent of victory was still in the air, for Nagy imposed a strict censorship on 'all news of an alarming nature'. For three days newspapers were forbidden to report the return of Soviet troops, for Nagy still felt there was a hope of peace. The Russians on manœuvres in the past had often retraced their steps, changed their routes because of transport problems. Nor were the Russians particularly concerned with frontiers. Desperately he still clung to the hope that it was all a mistake – that perhaps the orders had been put into effect by the Kremlin before Mikoyan returned to Moscow, and that turning a cumbersome army around was a protracted business. It was a slim hope – indeed a foolish one – but it was enough to make Nagy believe that it would be wrong to upset his fellow countrymen at a moment when he was trying so hard to calm them.

And then, too, he was still caught between believing in Hungary and believing in Communism. Miklos Molnar, a senior editor of the *Literary Gazette*, went to talk to Nagy and left Parliament feeling that 'He was split. On one side was his confidence in the Party, on the other his faithfulness to the people and his own principles. He was depending on the Party and wanted to be faithful to the Party. So he became the last man to defend the Communist Party, yet at the same time he was slowly dissolving it. Nagy had to see that his aims couldn't be fulfilled if he remained faithful and loyal to the Party.'

By Thursday morning, 1 November, even Nagy could not ignore the warnings that came pouring in from transport officials unable to operate their rail and bus lines. Nor could he ignore one other factor: the ominous silence in Moscow. When he cabled Khrushchev, his message remained unacknowledged. When he phoned the Soviet leader on the 'K' line, he was told he was 'unavailable'. When he phoned to Mikoyan the result was the same. It did not take much imagination to realise that the Russians were deliberately refusing to speak to him.

There was only one thing to do. Nagy summoned the Russian ambassador, Yuri Andropov, to his office in Parliament Building – in itself a gesture without precedent, for normally Nagy would have gone to the Soviet embassy; it was a striking sign of Nagy's mounting anger. This was the first of five tense meetings between the two men on this fateful Thursday. Bitterly Nagy remonstrated at the evidence of Soviet troop movements. Angrily he demanded an immediate explanation. Why was the Soviet Government not keeping the promises it made in the '30 October Declaration'?

Andropov, a grey-haired, humourless, narrow-minded Stalinist, with an inscrutable expression, at first said Nagy's allegations were completely untrue. Nagy then offered documentary proof, at which Andropov gave the classic Russian diplomatic reply: he did not have any information on the subject, but would request an explanation from his government.

The Soviet ambassador must have been impressed with Nagy's

annoyance, for within two hours – around 11 a.m. – he was back.
Nagy, who had been hoping against hope for some reasonable
explanation, received him in his office. With a polite smile
Andropov insisted that the troop movements were 'completely
normal'. They involved police units of the MVD sent to bolster
sagging morale among the Russian troops being evacuated – an
unlikely story since the incoming troops were estimated at 75,000
with 2500 tanks. In a feeble attempt at explanation, Andropov
added, 'They are necessary to safeguard the departure of the
Russian troops in Hungary, and the tanks surrounding the airports are supervising the evacuation of the sick and wounded.'
With a smile that never changed, Andropov added, 'They signify
nothing more.'

To Nagy, who had lived in Moscow for years, who was adept
at assessing Soviet actions, one thing was abundantly clear: when
Soviet leaders could not even trouble to *appear* convincing, it
meant that matters had reached a stage where it was no longer
important to keep up appearances.

He must have asked himself a number of questions. Were the
Russians once again planning to dismiss him as callously as they
had done before? Were they also going to dump the '30 October
Declaration'? Whatever his thoughts, they were interrupted by
Andropov who telephoned him just before noon. Moscow had
sent an answer, and he would dictate it if the Premier wished.
Nagy sent for Gyorgy Heltai, then told Andropov to speak slowly
so that he could translate the Russian reply sentence by sentence,
which he did, dictating the Hungarian version.

The '30 October Declaration' was still valid, said Andropov.
Khrushchev wanted the Hungarians to form two special committees to meet with Soviet experts. The first would begin discussions on political problems, with special emphasis on the
Warsaw Pact. The second would start negotiations with Soviet
military experts on the withdrawal of Russian troops.

The most important question of all remained unanswered –
'What', Nagy asked Andropov, 'has become of the promise that
no further Soviet units would enter Hungary?'

Andropov could give no answer.

This was the chilling moment of truth. As Heltai remembered
later, 'Nagy and I both came to the conclusion that the Soviets

wanted either to provoke Hungary into attacking them, and so give them the excuse to annihilate us, or else hoped to occupy the entire country without resistance. There was only one way to save the country. We had to leave the Warsaw Pact and declare our neutrality.'

Nagy asked Heltai to draft the texts of both declarations, while he convened a special meeting of the executive committee of the Party, which included Janos Kadar, still apparently sitting on the fence, and Ferenc Munnich, whom Nagy likewise distrusted. The committee – the leading body of the Communist Party – agreed that Soviet Russia had violated the Warsaw Pact and that the only course was to renounce the Pact and declare neutrality.

That afternoon Nagy called a meeting of the cabinet, and summoned Andropov to attend. The meeting in the panelled council chamber on the second floor took place in 'a tense, agonising atmosphere'. Every time the question of Soviet troops came up, Andropov insisted the picture was distorted. 'It's an exaggeration', he cried, 'to speak of a massive military threat. The entire question is of no real importance.'

The Russian excuses were obviously not to be trusted. The motion was passed, and in a curious way, having made the decision, Nagy experienced a sense of relief, almost exaltation. Certainly he passionately believed he had made the right decision, and even extolled to Andropov the benefits to Russia of a free and friendly Hungary. Andropov was unimpressed; he knew what the reaction of the Kremlin would be to the prospect of a free country, susceptible to Western influence, on its frontier. Tersely he promised to convey the decision to Moscow immediately.

As Nagy sat down, other members of the cabinet rose in turn to give him their support. The last man to speak was the enigmatic Kadar who – no doubt to Nagy's astonishment – launched into a passionate, patriotic speech. Looking Andropov straight in the eyes, Kadar cried, 'What happens to me is of little importance, but I am ready as a Hungarian to fight if necessary. If your tanks enter Budapest, I will go into the streets and fight against you with my bare hands.'

It sounded like bragging, but Heltai was right in thinking that 'Since the 28th Nagy had the complete backing in Hungary.

There was no danger of a reactionary backlash. We had one big problem – the reaction of Soviet Russia. The most important factor in our foreign policy was to secure true independence and as long as Soviet troops were in Hungary we were unable to solve that problem.'

Yet small countries rarely denounce treaties drawn up by their more powerful neighbours. Indeed, on the face of it, the Russians were left with no diplomatic space in which to manœuvre for an 'honourable settlement'. True, the Kremlin probably never intended to 'manœuvre', but by taking this unilateral step Nagy forfeited the last faint hope of negotiation. Russia now had the choice between making humiliating concessions which would reverberate throughout her satellite empire, or of crushing the Hungarians.

If Nagy still entertained some hope, others did not. The atmosphere of unreality was captured by Bruce Renton of the *New Statesman*, who had walked across the deserted Parliament Square and into the building in the hope of meeting Nagy or Kadar.

> Two soldiers, carrying tommy-guns and grinning hopefully, led me through a maze of rich Byzantine corridors. Walking down these golden passages gave an impression of Russia 1917. After the atmosphere of the streets, the warm waiting-room was soothing for the nerves, apart from the fact that armed patrols kept passing incongruously across the rich carpets. One of Nagy's assistants spoke fluent English.... In the next room Nagy was arguing with Soviet Ambassador Andropov. The assistant told me 'Russian troops are pouring in from the Ukraine. They are digging in around Budapest. I am very pessimistic. I hope I am safe in telling you this. But you could not communicate it anyway.' There was a swift passing of messages for relatives in the West, a handshake and he advised me to leave Budapest at once.

Jozsef Kovago, the Mayor, suffered a similar brutal moment of disillusion. He was told the news privately before it was made public by Zoltan Tildy, and his immediate reaction was a sense of exuberance. He remembers thinking, 'I firmly believed we had found the best solution. We provided an excuse to the West to interfere, and we gave the Soviets an opportunity to save face while giving up Hungary. I was sure the free world's diplomacy would act quickly.'

His exhilaration was short-lived. When he returned home, an old friend he had not seen for ten years had been waiting for hours to see him. He had come, he said, to ask a great favour; to strengthen his hand he prefaced his request by telling Kovago that he was the anonymous donor who had sent regular payments to Lonci while Kovago was in jail.

With some embarrassment Kovago thanked him, and the old friend 'equally embarrassed' said, 'I hate bringing all this up but I have to because I want you to listen to me.'

'Well, go ahead. What do you want?'

'I want all of us to get into a car tomorrow morning, with both our families and leave immediately for Austria. We can't stay here for another minute. The Russians are coming.'

To Kovago, the request was 'preposterous', and when he indignantly refused the old friend begged him, 'It's unfair to your family. Let me take your wife and daughter at least.'

Kovago suggested he ask Lonci, but she refused to leave without her husband, though she felt that their friend was right. Kovago, like so many others in the revolution, was now convinced that Hungary would be saved by the United Nations.

'You are just like a child,' the down-to-earth Lonci told him. 'The whole country is full of Russians. The city is surrounded.'

By now the cabinet meeting had broken up. Nagy immediately informed the diplomatic missions in Budapest of the decision, and before broadcasting to the nation sent a cable to Dag Hammarskjöld, Secretary-General of the United Nations, requesting the Hungarian question to be put on the agenda of the General Assembly, about to begin its eleventh session.

It was Hungary's first appeal for help. Until now, it had never occurred to Hungarians to seek assistance, but now when they did ask it was too late. Heltai summed it up as follows: 'By now the West was occupied with the Suez crisis and we got no real answer from the UN.' Hammarskjöld did not go to Budapest. Instead he went to Cairo.

Indeed, the reaction in New York when the desperate plea arrived was more cynical than even Heltai could have imagined, and perhaps it was as well for the Hungarian people, still hoping for peace at this critical juncture, that they were unaware of the appalling blunders that took place there.

Shortly before 10.30 a.m. in New York – 4.30 p.m. in Budapest – the teleprinter on the twentieth floor of the United Nations building recorded a question from a caller identifying himself by the code words, DIPLOMAG BUDAPEST:

UNITED NATIONS NEW YORK ARE YOU THERE?

Never before had a message come directly to the UN, but always to a country's delegate. UN operators and secretaries clustered round the machine to see what would follow.

At 10.42 a.m. New York time, it came:

FOR SECRETARIAT U.N.: IF YOU ARE BUSY I CAN CALL A FEW MINUTES LATER, OUR MESSAGE WILL BE READY. OKAY? PLEASE ANSWER.

The United Nations replied,

WE ARE NOT BUSY, CAN WAIT IF YOU WANT.

After forty-eight minutes without transmitting Budapest broke the connection at 11.14. At this moment Nagy was holding his fateful cabinet meeting with Andropov in attendance.

The curious nature of the messages reaching the UN cried out for some official inspection, particularly as the newspapers were filled with details of Hungary's fight. Yet nobody warned Hammarskjöld's Secretariat that the Hungarian Government was apparently about to transmit what would certainly be a highly important message.

At 12.21 p.m. in New York, the UN teleprinter stuttered into action again, and the operators read:

BUDAPEST CALLING. ARE YOU READY PLEASE?

After the UN replied, Nagy's historic plea,[1] addressed personally to Hammarskjöld, arrived in flawless English (except for

---

[1] Text of Nagy's Note, Appendix v.

the tagline following Nagy's signature, DO YOU RECEIVED PLEASE?)
At 12.27 p.m., the United Nations acknowledged:

RECEIVED WELL. THANKS VERY MUCH.

By any standards this was not only a message of importance, but
of great urgency. Certainly the operators realised its significance
and sent it by special messenger to the Secretary-General's office,
where it arrived within eight minutes. Yet, it 'created little or no
excitement. Mr Hammarskjöld's office too had all its energies
aimed at Suez. Further, it was the lunch hour. Not only did
the Secretary-General's office make no announcement of the
message, it was soon to deny that it had ever come at all.'[1]
New York newspaper reporters, who had by now monitored
Nagy's actual broadcast, started bombarding the UN to confirm
Nagy's statement that he had appealed to Hammarskjöld.
'Through confusion or oversight, the Secretary-General's office
said it had not.'
Finally, around 2 p.m., the message was found. By 2.30 p.m.
it was mimeographed and distributed to UN delegates. Yet, even
now, it bore no markings to indicate urgency or importance, but
was merely stuffed into the delegates' boxes which were already
half-filled with unimportant circulars. Some delegates did not see
Nagy's appeal until late in the evening.
A handful of pro-Hungarian delegates tried in vain to bring
the Hungarian question before the General Assembly, scheduled
to meet that day. The Afro-Asians, who swayed the voting, and
were afraid the Suez issue might be sidetracked, refused to permit it. They took refuge mainly in an apparent technicality,
pointing out that Nagy's message had asked for the matter to be
raised at the 'forthcoming General Assembly' – and that meant
a wait of eleven days, unthinkable in the circumstances. They
insisted that, as Nagy's wording was vague, it might not refer to
the present meeting.
Hammarskjöld could have settled the matter instantly if it
had not been for a tragic blunder by his Secretariat. Nagy *had*
made his intention clear in a second teleprinter message, again
addressed personally to Hammarskjöld, which arrived at the

[1] Gordon Gaskill, *The Virginia Quarterly Review*, vol. 84.

UN at 12.45 p.m. – a bare eighteen minutes after Nagy's formal appeal. It read:

> I HAVE THE HONOUR TO INFORM YOU THAT MR JANOS SZABO, FIRST SECRETARY OF THE PERMANENT MISSION, WILL REPRE-SENT THE HUNGARIAN PEOPLE'S REPUBLIC AT THE SPECIAL SESSION OF THE GENERAL ASSEMBLY OF THE UNITED NATIONS TO BE CONVENED NOVEMBER 1, 1956, AT NEW YORK.

Nagy had named the date. It was a message that brooked no argument. Alas, the UN Secretariat overlooked its significance. It was not circulated to delegates, and 'more than 24 hours later the Under Secretary-General still did not know of it and assured the Security Council that no such messages had been received'.

In fact, though the lines to Budapest remained open for several more hours, Hammarskjöld did not even have the courtesy to acknowledge Nagy's appeal for another 12 hours, by which time the lines had been cut.

Among the first diplomats to be told the decision of the Hungarian Government was Mr Fry, the British Minister. He was not surprised. Because of his direct radio link with Whitehall, he was better informed than his colleagues in Budapest, and he took immediate action. He made his way to the top floor of the Legation where a small restaurant had been improvised to feed the families of British officials who had moved into the building. To them he announced that a convoy taking all Legation wives, including Mrs Fry, would leave early the next morning, while the road was still open.

Not everyone wanted to go, and though 'Bunny' Fry's word was law in the Legation he could not force British citizens to leave; among those who refused the offer were a small but bizarre coterie of elderly impoverished gentlewomen. They had originally come to Budapest as nannies at a time when there were well-to-do Hungarian families who considered it wholesome for their offspring to be brought up in the British nursery tradition. The families had gone, the children had grown up, died or emigrated, but most had bequeathed small pensions to their ex-nannies, to whom Hungary had replaced Britain as home. Their modest lives were made more cheerful by regular visits from Joan Fish, the consul, who normally arrived with a weekly parcel of small luxuries. But now the work in the Legation was piling up; there were day-to-day problems making it impossible for Joan to keep to her schedule of visits.

The old ladies seemed blissfully unaware of the dangers around them. When one ex-nanny, Miss Westbrook, phoned Joan Fish at the Legation, the consul imagined she was asking for help to leave the country.

'Oh no!' Miss Westbrook was horrified at the prospect. 'I'm not going to let the Russians ruin my life.... But I *am* in very serious trouble, Miss Fish. I've run out of tea.'

For a week Nagy had tossed and turned on a camp bed in Parliament Building; but this night, with the die cast, he decided at midnight to go home to his villa in Orso Street and get a good night's sleep. He called for his car and set off through the blacked-out city. The wide avenues were deserted, but the streets that should have been darkened glowed eerily with a million tiny, flickering lights. It was a few minutes before Friday, 2 November, All Souls Day, the Day of the Dead. From every window of the streets a candle glowed as Budapest prepared to honour its fallen martyrs.

That night Nagy slept the deep sleep of a totally exhausted man. He awoke refreshed, ready to wrestle with any problem – except the shattering, unbelievable news that greeted him.

Janos Kadar had secretly vanished during the night.

12

The Turncoat

Friday, 2 November

Janos Kadar was forty-four, an undistinguished-looking man of medium height, with light brown hair, and a habit of speaking very slowly. A one-time steelworker, he had changed his name from Janos Csermanek when he became a Communist in 1929.

For years he had been a faithful friend of Rakosi's – until Rakosi realised that Kadar could implicate him in a false arrest. Without a moment's hesitation Rakosi ordered Kadar to be jailed. When he was safely in prison, Kadar was told to sign a confession. He refused. Rakosi phoned Milhaly Farkhas of the Avo and bellowed, 'Beat him! Beat him until he talks.'

Farkhas was only too willing to oblige. Kadar was beaten mercilessly on the body, feet and testicles. When he was unconscious his body was smeared with mercury to stop the pores from breathing. As he was about to regain consciousness, still lying on the floor, his teeth were forced apart and Farkhas stood over him and urinated into his mouth. Kadar confessed – to nothing. It was Nagy who finally secured his release in 1954.

The writer George Paloczi-Horvath, who used to see Kadar in the corridors of Parliament Building, felt his jail sentence had turned him into 'the ultimate type of split personality ... a conscious mixture of delusion and cynicism, of obsession and opportunism. Many leading Communists suffer from this.'

Why had he disappeared so mysteriously? Nagy's first thought was that Kadar's flight had been motivated by fear. It seemed inconceivable that Kadar should betray the man who had engineered his release from jail, the more so as on the evening of his disappearance he had made a passionate radio broadcast, painting such a glowing picture of tomorrow's free Hungary that Tibor Meray felt he was 'a man who had decided to take part with his whole being in the great task which faced his country'. Yet he had vanished so secretly that his wife came down to Parliament Building in the morning to find out why he had not come home the previous night.

Then came another shock. Ferenc Munnich, the Minister of the Interior, had also vanished. His disappearance was equally perplexing, for while Kadar was broadcasting Munnich had been telling a Western journalist of the Government's plans for the future, and reiterating that the Russians would never dare to attack Budapest because they feared the loss of world prestige. The interview had, however, closed abruptly on a curious note. The telephone rang. When Munnich answered the journalist heard him switch quickly from Hungarian to Russian; he told the man on the other end of the line that he and Kadar would be at the rendezvous in half an hour.

Geza Losonczy was the first to piece together the extraordinary sequence of events. One of the drivers from the Parliament car pool told him that during the night Munnich had asked for a car and driver. When it drew up outside Parliament Building, Munnich and Kadar got in and Munnich instructed the driver to make for a secluded wooded park south-east of the Kerepes cemetery, the Bois de Boulogne of Budapest. Munnich, a taciturn man at the best of times, with a face that rarely betrayed any emotion, sat hunched up in the back of the Mercedes, with the windows carefully curtained. Kadar was silent.

When the car reached the park another car awaited them. It was a Russian Zis. Kadar and Munnich got out. For a few moments they walked up and down, talking earnestly, then the pool driver saw the shadowy figures gesticulate, heard their voices raised in argument. Finally Munnich took Kadar's arm and led him towards the Russian car. The Soviet driver did not get out of the car. Once near the Zis, Munnich opened the door and started to try to push Kadar in. There was no actual struggle. Kadar did not resist, but to the Hungarian driver it appeared that Kadar was in some way unwilling to enter the car. 'He looked as though he couldn't make up his mind,' said the driver.

Finally Munnich all but pushed Kadar into the back seat, scrambled in after them and slammed the door. The Zis roared off into the darkness.

Losonczy was not to know at this stage that Kadar and Munnich were taken immediately to the Soviet embassy. They stayed there talking to Andropov for over an hour. Then they were spirited to the town of Uzhgorod in the Carpatho-Ukraine – the first Soviet town beyond the Hungarian border.

Still not knowing why Kadar should flee so secretly, Losonczy, after telling Nagy, decided to seek advice from Bela Szasz, who said the news should be published. Losonczy said Nagy was against this, so Szasz telephoned Nagy personally.

'I'm sure he's gone over to the Russians,' Szasz told the Premier. 'If Soviet troops attack Budapest, Kadar would be an ideal man to make any new government seem legal. You *must* broadcast the news of his disappearance now – immediately. If you do, it's going to make it almost impossible for the Russians to use him later.'

Nagy was horrified. 'Of course not,' he said. 'We don't really know what did happen. We can't publish news based on a driver's unconfirmed story.'

As Losonczy remembered, 'It was decided not to publicise Kadar's disappearance.'

Nagy asked Jozsef Szilagyi, his personal assistant, to conduct an enquiry, and Nagy's secretary, Mrs Jozsef Balogh, who took down all the evidence, remembered later that after Szilagyi had questioned the driver he ended the minutes of the investigation with the words, 'They presumably went over to the Soviets.'

Nagy was by now aware of a sense of urgency, yet there was no trace of panic. The revolution was petering out; more and more men and women were returning to work. People outside Parliament hardly realised the grim diplomatic tussle being fought inside; they were more concerned with the fact that order was quietly being restored in the capital.

Nobody really knew what to expect. There were conflicting rumours everywhere – that the Russians had gone, that they were returning, that they were not returning. When François Bondy, the French editor of *Preuves*, met members of the Revolutionary

Committee, a spokesman forecast, 'There will be a fight to the death.'

Yet when Zoltan Tildy was asked by the *New York Post* correspondent if the Soviet agreement to negotiate on technical questions meant they would eventually withdraw Tildy replied, 'I believe that if a person is inclined to argue about a problem it means that he thinks the problem may eventually be solved, and I am convinced hostilities will not break out again.'

Rumours about the imminent arrival of the United Nations were even more startling. Jacques Leblond of the French newspaper *Le Dauphin Libéré* was in the office of *Truth* when he heard that a sixteen-man delegation was expected at Budapest airport. He drove out immediately, only to find the airport deserted except for its ring of Russian tanks.

Anna Gabor, who was in the *Truth* office at the time, and heard the rumour, managed to telephone friends in Vienna[1] who told her categorically, 'United Nations are already stationed on the frontier. They're British and Americans and one officer told me that they're ready to enter Hungary if Nagy formally invites them.'

Near Parliament Building, Ejaz Husain, of the Karachi newspaper *Dawn*, stopped his car which carried a UN sticker on the windshield. Hungarians from two nearby tanks jumped down and rushed towards him, shouting, 'Are the United Nations already here?' When Husain said he was only a member of the UN press corps, one soldier 'with marked disappointment' muttered, 'Not enough!'

Even Geza Losonczy told a French journalist, 'I have been informed of the arrival in Budapest of a UN delegation but I have not yet met it.'

The people in Budapest had no inkling, of course, of the farce being ponderously played out before the UN delegates in New York when they finally did indulge in a pathetic attempt to discuss Nagy's appeal to guarantee Hungary's neutrality.

Any hoped-for firm stand by the Americans failed to materialise. Quite apart from the fact that Eisenhower now had

[1] The telephone service was miraculous. During the same week-end the author managed to telephone his wife in Rolle, a small Swiss town on Lake Geneva.

only three days left before seeking re-election, Foster Dulles woke up at seven in the morning with excruciating abdominal pains. He was rushed to the Walter Reed Army hospital, where he was operated on for cancer – so the State Department lost its leader.

The Security Council did meet at 3 p.m., New York time, but hardly had its members sat down before Brilej, the Yugoslav delegate, moved for an adjournment, saying that as Nagy and the Russians were negotiating the Security Council should wait and see how events turned out. Henry Cabot Lodge, of the United States seemed inclined to agree. 'We believe that adjournment for a day or two would give a real opportunity to the Hungarian Government to carry out its announced desire to arrange for an orderly and immediate evacuation of all Soviet troops,' he said.

Other Western delegates were shocked. Sir Pierson Dixon of Britain felt, 'It would be quite wrong, misleading and unfair to the Hungarian people to take the comfortable view ... that we can now leave the Hungarian question to settle itself.' Mr John Walker of Australia said even more firmly, 'Unfortunately the world has had some experience of the course that "negotiations" sometimes take in a country where the Soviet Union has been able to establish military supremacy.' Monsieur de Guiringaud of France hit the mark: 'We have not only the right but the duty to find out whether [Soviet troop movements] are not rather a regrouping of Soviet forces so they will be able to intervene with such suddenness as to make possible the establishment of a regime to the liking of the Soviet Union.'

Throughout this, the dour Arkady Sobolev, the Russian delegate, remained silent. Not until 6 p.m. did he speak, and then it was to describe reports of Soviet tanks returning to Hungary as 'utterly unfounded' and counter-attack with a charge that hundreds of Hungarian Fascists were being flown into the country from what he called a 'Hungarian–American' base in Austria.

It was now a week since the United Nations had first discussed Hungary and, apart from pious announcements, not a thing had been done. As the *New York Times* reported sadly, 'None pressed for specific action.'

There was, however, ample time for the Security Council to

approve the very specific United States demand for a ceasefire in the Suez conflict.

One country, though it could offer no military assistance to Hungary, was taking 'specific action' of a different kind. The good neighbour Austria had opened its doors to its one-time brothers of the Austro-Hungarian Empire. By now tens of thousands of Hungarians had fled across the border to freedom, every one of them to be offered food and shelter with no questions asked. Other countries, of course, were willing to receive refugees, but at this stage, when no one was clear as to the outcome, Austria was running one of the largest staging posts in modern refugee history. In all, 200,000 people would cross into their country.

Among them was one man who had fought for more than a week without a thought of death, and who had, after an agonising decision, decided to make for the border. During the previous night Eva Beke had started sobbing bitterly, and when Lazlo woke up and tried to comfort her she cried, 'Everyone says the Russians are going to attack. I'll never see my mother and father again.'

In the morning the student fighters held an emergency conference in the radio bunker they had built at the Technological University. With a sick feeling Lazlo counted only forty-seven of their original band of eighty. The rest had died, and as he looked at the survivors he realised that 'their tired faces, overcast with gloom, showed that they had the same type of conflict in their minds: How can I serve my country better – by staying at home and fighting, or by seeking aid beyond the borders of Hungary?'

They sat in the ill-lit bunker, perched on broken chairs, stools, upturned boxes, sandbags. Finally they took a vote; thirty elected to remain. Eleven hands were raised by youngsters who decided to leave, while Beke was among the six who could not bring themselves to decide. 'If it hadn't been for Eva and the baby, I wouldn't have hesitated to stay,' he said later.

That night, sleeping close to Eva, with the old lady 'squatter' in the other corner of the room, Lazlo tossed and turned as he fought his own battle 'between a heart that desperately wanted to fight and a sober mind that reasoned more logically'. Above all he was haunted by the spectre of Eva, carrying the baby, being sent to a labour camp or jailed – and it was this that finally persuaded him in the middle of the night to shake Eva and cry, 'Wake up, my sweet one. Get dressed. We're leaving Budapest.' He remembers they embraced each other 'and began to cry like babies'.

At 6 a.m. they gathered up a few belongings. They gave the small radio that had served them so well to the old lady who shared their room. They went through the building saying their goodbyes.

When Lazlo shook hands with Lali Bertalon, one of his oldest friends, who had decided to stay, Lali said, 'Perhaps you're doing the right thing. But continue our fight in the West.' And then, with a sudden grin, he added, 'And think of us when you smoke those American cigarettes.'

Beke decided to make first for a village in the interior, from which he eventually reached Austria; perhaps as well, for by now the Russians were guarding most exits from the country, as Leopold Joseph, a British businessman found. During the late afternoon, Mr Joseph drove in a convoy of American men, women, and children towards the frontier at dusk. When they were ten miles away their convoy found itself among a column of forty-five Soviet tanks, guns and supply vehicles. Highway 10, the road to Vienna, was blocked by two Soviet Tiger tanks surrounded by Russian soldiers.

'They wore cloaks,' Mr Joseph remembered. 'In the snow and by our headlights it reminded me of a picture of the retreat from Moscow.'

The Russian tank commander ordered the convoy to return to Budapest, telling a passenger who spoke Russian, 'This is no time for argument – turn back.'

The convoy turned back, making for the Hotel Duna on the Danube, where Joseph from his window could see Russian families leaving by boat. Joseph remembers watching them and thinking, 'As those women and children left with their furniture I knew there was going to be a war – with myself in the heart of it.'

*   *   *

Nagy had a different, and unexpected, kind of problem. While he was trying to form a broad coalition government, he received an urgent and angry message from Andropov insisting that the Soviet embassy was besieged by rioters. Nagy phoned General Kiraly – who noticed that his voice was agitated – and said, 'Kiraly, if anyone ever had an important job, you have one now. The Russian ambassador says Hungarians are raging round his embassy. If we can't maintain order we will offer an opportunity for a second Russian aggression. Drop whatever you are doing and go there yourself.'

Kiraly immediately ordered a company of tanks to proceed to the Square of Heroes, near the Soviet embassy. He also sent a mechanised infantry battalion. But when within a matter of minutes Kiraly reached the embassy the streets were deserted. He asked to see Andropov and, once in his office, told him, 'I have a command from my premier to check the rioting here, but I can see no rioting.'

The Soviet ambassador, Kiraly remembered later, 'appeared embarrassed'. Then he made a curious remark. He rose from his chair, walked round his desk and, ignoring the delicate question of the riot, told Kiraly, 'We Russians don't want to mix in your business. We understand your troubles and we are on your side.'

There had never, in fact, been any disturbances in the area, or for that matter anywhere else. Though the Russians would time and again accuse Nagy of being unable to maintain order, he was in fact doing better than any of his colleagues dared to hope. As Vlado Teslic, of the Belgrade newspaper *Borba*, remarked, 'Hungary has made a great stride in the direction of relaxation.' Radio Budapest described 'a picture of the streets in Budapest.... Traffic is lively. Restaurants and espressos are all open. The newspaper vendors shout about twenty different headlines. There are more people in the streets than usual.'

It was true – though many were women bent on precautionary shopping sprees, for everyone had scraped up every last forint to buy food against the uncertain days ahead; some struggled home with a goose under each arm.

The longest queue of all stretched outside the municipal pawnshop. For decades Hungarian housewives had pawned their winter clothes in summer and their summer clothes in winter. Now, thousands were redeeming their winter clothes earlier than usual, and staggering home with heavy suitcases or unwieldy parcels. 'In 1944 the Russians looted all the pawnshops,' said one woman in the queue, 'so we're taking our things out now before it's too late.'

Despite occasional qualms (or prudent forethought), the streets reflected a mood of raffish optimism. In the window of a women's dress shop, someone had hung cards labelled 'Rakosi' and 'Gero' round the necks of two plastic models. Outside 'Horizon', the Soviet propaganda headquarters, a huge sign read, 'Store for Rent'. Stalin Square, with its bronze boots, had been jokingly re-named 'Boot Square'. Outside the Bastya Cinema, which had been showing a French film *The Escaped*, someone had added a subtitle, 'Gero and Hegedus', while outside the Nap Cinema, advertising a film, *Irene, Please Go Home*, a joker had crossed out 'Irene' and substituted 'Russki'.

Many of the newspapers were equally lighthearted. Friday's issue of *Truth* made its readers chortle with the true story of Gyorgy Faludy, a well-known poet who had recently been released from an Avo jail. When arrested, as he explained, he had been accused of being an Imperialist agent working for the Americans, and was told to write a confession. Knowing the methods employed by the Avo towards those who refused, Faludy complied with alacrity. He admitted that during a visit to New York he had been contacted by a highly placed officer in the American FBI called Edgar Allen Poe, who sent him to an espionage school for training under two CIA officers. William Shakespeare and William Blake. He agreed that ever since he had been sending spy reports to them. All this was received by the Avo with stony solemnity. They based their indictment on his confession, and sentenced Faludy to 15 years in jail for passing classified material to Edgar Allen Poe.

All in all there was a mood of guarded optimism. Only one section of the population was racked with disappointment, as the Italian writer Indro Montanelli, discovered. Tens of thousands of football-mad Hungarians went to bed on Friday night convinced the Government was wrong to ban the international match between Sweden and Hungary, due to be played the following day.

13

The Trap

Saturday, 3 November

Saturday was bitterly cold, with a fierce wind blowing down the Danube. Across the river from Pest the first sprinkling of winter snow powdered the hills of Buda. Dora Scarlett found that 'Budapest began to look more normal, and the general mood was happier. On Saturday the buses started running. The city was at peace; not a single Soviet soldier could be seen.'

In fact the only Russians left were the delegation due to meet on this Saturday, and civilian families near the Chain Bridge, waiting to board the pleasure-steamers that would carry them along the Danube to Romania.

But when Dora Scarlett reached the radio station she found an air of deep solemnity. The radio's Revolutionary Council, which had ousted Valeria Benke, was in session and a spokesman announced, 'We are in grave trouble. Budapest is surrounded.' People, she found, 'swung between hope and despair. They believed they had won a victory. They could not think it would be snatched from them.'

This was the key to Saturday's fluctuating hopes and fears; it seemed impossible for victory to be taken away so quickly and so, everyone tended to minimise the bad news and magnify the good. It was by now common knowledge that Budapest was virtually surrounded; but people deluded themselves that this must be due to errors in command, for otherwise, why should the Russians and the Hungarians be sitting across the table, thrashing out the problems involved in a Soviet withdrawal. Indeed, thousands of Hungarians had seen the impressive, colourful prelude to the first meeting when General Malinin, in a green uniform bedecked with medals, was given full military honours as he and his officers strode along the thick red carpet at Parliament Building.

So many things seemed to buoy up hopes of peace. When George Kovacs, who had given up his radio reporting job to join the National Guard, reported to his group headquarters in Moricz Szigmond Square in Buda, he found 'long queues of freedom fighters moving slowly into the main hall of the building, where officers sat at a long table piled high with arms. As I reached the table I was told to hand in my gun with the words, "You won't need this any more. We're making an agreement with the Russians. The fighting is over." ' Kovacs, like many others, refused to give up his gun.

Yet, while freedom fighters were being told this, an English journalist in Parliament Building was told by a government official he knew, 'You've got a car haven't you? Then get out – now. Another day and it'll be too late.'

In direct contrast, optimism was reflected at every street corner. Nagy's pleas for workers to return had been heeded by tens of thousands. In areas where the fighting had been less severe, the famous yellow trams of Budapest were rattling along, with workers clinging to the windows. Where there was no public transport, factories sent trucks to collect employees. In big stations the first commuter trains shunted into the city. Postmen started their rounds again. Glaziers were confronted by enough broken windows to keep them occupied for months. In the theatres rehearsals started. A film crew was making a documentary in the streets. Schoolmasters wiped their blackboards clean, ready for the pupils' return on Monday. In Vorosmarty Square, Gerbaud's were again offering their famous pastries with morning coffee, and Hungary's traditional chestnut sellers were taking advantage of the sudden bitter weather by doing a brisk trade in hot-to-handle nuts in their paper cones.

As the United Nations said in its special report,

Order was rapidly being restored in the damaged streets of the capital. People were already at work removing the rubble and glass. Despite innumerable broken shop windows, no looting took place. Good progress was being made in the direction of political consolidation, and the resumption of work could confidently be expected on Monday, 5 November. Negotiations had been completed for the formation of a National Guard under General Kiraly with a view to ensuring internal security. A sense of confidence had developed among the citizens of Budapest.

The telephones never stopped. 'In these days,' as Tibor Meray remembered, 'the radio was the pulse of public life and the telephone the pulse of private life. Relatives who were separated, friends whose flats were far from each other, and lovers on both sides of the Danube, kept contact by telephone. "How are you?" "Is there still any fighting in your quarter?" "Have you enough to eat?" "Do you still love me?" During the days of the heaviest fighting, most of the lines became silent; but on Saturday they came alive again, burning and gay.'

Even the Avo were surrendering. Early on Saturday Nagy summoned them to give themselves up 'in their own interest', promising that those not facing charges could return immediately to their homes. Within two hours, thirty Avo surrendered in the Budapest 13th district and, according to Radio Budapest, 'the situation is similar in other districts'.

There was a sense of bustle, of determination. Anna Gabor summed it up to a friend, 'We've won the revolution – now it's time to clean up the mess.' Though everyone knew the Russians had lied time after time, nobody wanted to believe they were still lying. Dazed by euphoria, they ignored reality.

The Szechenyi Library – the largest in the country – provided a perfect example of people's attitude. Launching an appeal for documents relating to the uprising, it blandly promised donors, 'We will regard as confidential all material received before the victory of the revolution is definitive.'

Victory, it was thought, had been achieved, and peace was at hand.

In the heat of the battle, Hungarians had drawn great strength from the fact that they fought alone. Now their fervent hopes for peace – as distinct from victory – were sustained because they believed they were *not* alone. On all sides there was visible evidence of the world's concern. Eisenhower had promised $20 million. Over 50 plane-loads of essential food and drugs had already been flown in. Truckloads of materials rolled across the frontier.

'How could we think we were alone', George Kovacs asked a friend, 'when Mr Lodge in New York says, "The United Nations cannot remain a passive spectator to the events in Hungary."' Kovacs was not alone in being unable to differentiate between a hope and a pledge. Nobody seemed to have read the *New York Times* comment, 'The big Western powers appear to have decided to keep the Hungarian question to one side for the moment, until such time as it becomes clear that the anti-Soviet rebellion has either attained its objectives or has been checked.'

It would, of course, have been difficult for the West to send arms or troops across neutral countries into Hungary, unless they were prepared for a new war, though that did not stop Eisenhower from wondering, 'What would have been my recommendations to the Congress and the American people had Hungary been accessible by sea or through the territory of allies?'

To the Hungarians it was unthinkable that the West would allow such a glorious victory to be thrown away. Yet the Austrian Minister called to tell Nagy that the frontier with Austria had been closed. Anna Kethly, the Social Democrat leader, whom Nagy had sent on a mission to Vienna, was unable to return; a Russian tank near the frontier barred her way.

Yet there was still hope, Nagy felt. He reshuffled his cabinet, keeping Janos Kadar, whose disappearance was still not generally known, in it. It was a curious decision, but when Jozsef Kovago, the Mayor, saw Nagy and Tildy, both mentioned the disappearance of Kadar and Munnich, but surprisingly suggested, 'They might have started direct negotiations with the Soviets, which in the long run might come out well for us.'

One more name in the cabinet excited special attention. Pal Maleter, the heroic defender of Kilian, was promoted to general and appointed Minister of Defence. The news reached Kilian early in the morning and Maleter immediately summoned Mark Molnar, who was now a major (though he did not have a uniform). Maleter broke the news to him, adding, 'Frankly, I believe in Kilian and Corvin more than Parliament – I do hope it's not a trap.'

To safeguard against such a possibility, Molnar arranged an escort of two tanks and two truckloads of troops to accompany the staff car which would take Maleter to Parliament. And as Molnar was about to leave the room Maleter said to him, with his engaging, spontaneous smile, 'Mark – you're coming with me. I'm appointing you my ADC.'

As they drove to Parliament, Maleter told Mark, 'First thing, get our rooms in order, furniture, message section, secretaries, and so on. And then take an hour off and learn the geography of the building. You never know – it might be handy to know where the exits are. There are still a lot of Stalinists in the place.'

Mark mentioned the matter of his uniform, but Maleter waved the problem aside. 'We'll find you one when we've time, but don't worry – uniforms, medals, stars – they don't really count in this war.'

Maleter went straight to see Nagy, who immediately asked him to lead the Hungarian military delegation, ready to start discussions with the Russians.

During the morning Cardinal Mindszenty gave his long-awaited talk, and among those who watched him broadcast from a make-shift studio in Parliament was Pal Ignotus, who found it 'a fantastic sight; the diehard Primate Cardinal arriving with an armed guard of honour amidst the Communist revolutionaries. . . . The Cardinal walked in with swaying steps and glaring eyes.' Ignotus listened to his speech, which the Soviets have blamed as inciting 'counter-revolutionaries', but found the charge nonsense. 'The Cardinal's speech was moderate and cautious. But it was not appropriate to the extraordinary moment when it was made. One could not help feeling that a ghost was speaking from the past.'

Many criticised certain sections of the speech – to say nothing of his scornful, arrogant tone of voice – but in fact Mindszenty's speech had little impact, certainly not on the Russians whose plans had been laid long before the Prelate went to the micro-phone.

The Hungarian–Russian military talks seemed to be going well.

When General Kiraly ran into Maleter in a corridor of Parliament Building and asked him, 'How are things?' Maleter replied, 'Everything is in fine order.' Late in the afternoon, Kiraly ran into General Istvan Kovacs, the army Chief of Staff, who was a member of Maleter's delegation. He asked him the same question he had asked Maleter earlier in the day.

'It's practically agreed,' Kovacs told him. 'First Russia will evacuate all her armed forces from Hungary. Second, to avoid disrupting transportation, they will want to leave by degrees. We will set up a committee of experts to arrange a time-table. Third, the Hungarian garrisons must stop denying the Russians food and fuel. Fourth, the Russians are not prepared for a winter movement, and Hungary must be patient.'

The Soviet delegation expressed anxiety on another point: they did not want the Russian Army to leave Hungary with its tail between its legs. The honour of the Army must be upheld, and when the last units marched out of Hungary it would be with an appropriate colourful military ceremony between two friendly armies. To Nagy, the dedicated Communist, this seemed the most natural request in the world. It had never entered his head that the Russians should leave as a defeated army and, as Meray knew, 'he was delighted that the Russians had proposed a solemn ceremony with martial hymns, speeches and waving flags'.

The afternoon session could certainly be regarded as successful, for everyone felt that, unless the Russians were sincere, why on earth should they bother with details like military parades? But now Kovacs told General Kiraly that the evening meeting, timed to begin at 10 o'clock, would not be held in Parliament, but at the Soviet military headquarters in the hamlet of Tokol on Csepel Island. There seemed to be nothing sinister in the change, for the Russians were only conforming to the diplomatic courtesies by offering to be hosts.

One man, however, felt a qualm of anxiety, possibly remembering the countless occasions when the Russians had in the past arrested delegations from countries which had not taken proper precautions. Captain Lajos Csiba, a senior officer in the Kilian Barracks before Maleter's spectacular arrival, felt that, while it would be impossible for the Russians to stage a coup inside Parliament, Tokol was isolated – and a Russian stronghold.

Csiba was also in Parliament Building, and when he heard that Maleter was going to Tokol he asked him pointblank, 'Couldn't this invitation be a trap? Don't you think there's a danger the Russians might arrest you?'

As Csiba remembers, Maleter thought for a moment, smiled and replied, 'I don't think the Russians would do such a thing. The talks have been frank and understanding.'

As a distinguished general visiting the Soviet Army command, Maleter merited a guard of honour, and an ADC. But an ADC without a uniform was unthinkable.

More than once Mark Molnar had pondered on Maleter's apparent reluctance to find him a uniform. It had not mattered in Kilian, and since their arrival in Parliament Molnar had been cooped up in his office, spending the night fitfully dozing on a Louis XVI chair in a corridor, and so had no opportunity to acquire one. But he knew that Maleter could have arranged the matter in an hour, and presumed that perhaps Maleter thought a uniform inappropriate to a man who had resigned his commission.

Around 7.30 p.m. an astonishing thing happened. Maleter stalked stiffly into Molnar's small office. The two men were such close friends they invariably called each other by their Christian names, but now Maleter, every inch the general on parade, stood in front of him and said coldly, 'Major Molnar, I will not be requiring your services this evening. Report for duty tomorrow morning as usual.'

A bewildered Molnar saluted angrily. Maleter, who was not a man with whom to argue, saluted back. Then he did something which Molnar knew to be quite out of character. Without changing expression, he held out his huge hand, gripped Molnar's like a vice, and said one word, 'Goodbye!'

With that he turned on his heel, leaving Molnar with 'an uneasy sense of foreboding in the pit of my stomach'.

Within half an hour Maleter set off in a Russian military car for Tokol, and once on the island everything seemed to confirm the opinion he had given to Csiba. Maleter and his guard of honour were received with full military honours, and when Maleter retired to the conference room his Hungarian soldiers were entertained by their Russian counterparts with vodka and beer in an ante-room. Time and again the Russians drank toasts to their imminent departure, time and again they assured the Hungarians, 'Don't be afraid. We're going home soon.'

If General Kiraly, back in Parliament, was still nagged by any lingering doubts, these evaporated at 11 p.m. when Maleter telephoned him directly from the conference room. 'Everything is in good order,' he said.

It had been a hard, tense day for everyone, but at last Kiraly could feel a sense of relief. He told his staff, 'Now I'm going to sleep. Tonight for the first time I will sleep myself out.' He gave orders not to be disturbed before 9 a.m.

Outside the conference room the Hungarian soldiers were equally at ease. One of them, Sandor Horvath, a member of Maleter's bodyguard, remembered later, 'Everything appeared to go off perfectly in the office where the talks were taking place. At least that was our impression in the ante-chamber from the noise of conversation we could hear.'

At midnight there was a dramatic interruption. About twenty Russian policemen in green caps burst through the ante-chamber, smashed open the door of the conference room and swarmed inside, covering the Hungarian delegation with their sub-machine-guns.

They were followed by a man in civilian clothes, who sauntered nonchalantly into the room. Ivan Serov, head of the Soviet secret police, had flown into Budapest during the afternoon.

General Malinin – as startled and horrified as the Hungarians – jumped to his feet with an oath and demanded to know what was happening. Through the broken door Sandor Horvath was watching Maleter. 'The others were pale. Only his face didn't change.'

Maleter stood up calmly. 'So that was it, was it?' was all he said to the Russians.

General Malinin broke into profuse apologies – until Serov walked across to him, bent down, whispered in his ear. A disgusted Malinin stood up, made a gesture of indignation, as though to tell Maleter that this unseemly conduct had nothing to do with the code of honour existing between army generals. Then, very quietly, he stalked out of the room after ordering the Russian delegation to follow him.

Once gone, Serov acted quickly. 'The Hungarian delegation is under arrest,' he announced.

Outside in the ante-room, Sandor Horvath, who had seen and heard everything, was determined that 'before dying I would still shoot a few rounds at the men in the green caps'. He seized his sub-machine-gun, but two Russian policemen grabbed him, tore the gun from his hands. In the struggle, Horvath managed to get hold of the gun barrel and was fighting like a fury until he heard Maleter's voice.

'Stop it!' the General ordered. 'It's useless to resist!'

Serov had duped not only the Hungarian Government, but the Russian army generals in order to trap the one man whose dynamic personality would provide a rallying point for resistance. Maleter was never seen again.

At almost the same time as Maleter was trapped, Nagy retired to bed in Parliament Building. Zoltan Tildy also stayed the night, together with several others. Just before 4 o'clock on Sunday morning, Nagy was wakened by the telephone at the side of his camp bed. It was the Yugoslav embassy telling him that Russian armour had launched its attack on Budapest.

Hardly had Nagy put down the telephone before the private telephone linking him with Kiraly's headquarters rang. Kiraly's dreams of a good night's rest had been rudely shattered and, as he remembers, 'everything happened at once. Russian tanks moved to the Kilian Barracks and the Corvin Theatre, two main freedom-fighter strongpoints, and started shelling. I grabbed my direct phone to the Premier. I told him the city was being invaded and begged for orders to open fire.'

According to Kiraly, Nagy cried, 'No, no! Calm down. There is some misunderstanding. You must not open fire.'

Kiraly hung up 'bewildered'.

There was bedlam in Parliament, with men running from makeshift bedrooms, the blankets and sheets all over the floor, to offices in different parts of the building. The phones never stopped. Zoltan Tildy sent a message to Bela Kovacs to come to Parliament immediately, but though Kovacs set off he never made

it. By the time he had walked within a mile of Parliament, the
Soviet tanks were lined up across the bridges and refused to allow
anyone to pass.

Outside Parliament, flames lit up the approaching dawn.
Explosions seemed to merge into one continuous roar. Anna
Gabor felt 'the ground shaking beneath my feet'. Thomas
Schreiber of *Le Monde* woke suddenly to the sound of Soviet
tank gunfire in Budapest. When his telephone rang, 'a high official
implored me to intervene with my government: "Send us arms!"'
In his hotel lobby, a woman with a face as white as chalk rushed
up to Indro Montanelli, of the *Corriere della Sera*, crying, 'I left
the concentration camp only last week. I was in for seven years.'
Dora Scarlett had gone to bed happy because her foreign broadcasts were being resumed the following day and 'my last thought
as I fell asleep was of what I intended to say'. The next thing
she heard was the gunfire.

By dawn, Soviet tanks all but controlled the city. Hundreds
advanced along the main boulevards radiating from the Danube.
Every bridge was barricaded. Other tanks trundled towards
Boraros Square in Pest with the object of cutting off Csepel
Island. There was no organised resistance.

In Parliament Building, Tildy asked Nagy what arrangements
he was making for a radio broadcast.

'I'll take charge,' said Nagy. Ferenc Donath had already
scribbled out a rough text. Nagy had no time to consult the others,
but pencilled in a few changes, threw a coat over his shoulders
and walked through the long cold corridors to the studio on the
first floor at the far end of the building. The technicians were
alerted, the microphone ready. At 5.20 a.m., to a sullen background of heavy gunfire, Nagy broadcast to the Hungarian nation
– and the world:

Attention! Attention!
Attention! Attention!

Imre Nagy, President of the Council of Ministers of the
Hungarian People's Republic is now going to address you!

This is Imre Nagy speaking, President of the Council of
Ministers of the Hungarian People's Republic. Today, at
daybreak, Soviet forces started an attack against our capital,

obviously with the intention to overthrow the legal Hungarian democratic government.

Our troops are fighting.

The Government is in its place.

I notify the people of our country and the entire world of this fact.

Somehow Gyula Hay, Nagy's old friend and the idol of Hungarian youth, managed to reach Parliament with his wife. Nagy asked him to make a broadcast, but at first they could not find any paper. Finally, Hay did find a torn scrap and scribbled out the text of a brief broadcast.

This is the Hungarian Writers' Association speaking to all writers, scientists, writers' associations, academies, and scientific organisations of the world. We appeal for help to all intellectuals in all countries. Our time is limited. You all know the facts. There is no need to review them. Help Hungary! Help the writers, scientists, workers, peasants and all Hungarian intellectuals. Help! Help! Help!

Mrs Hay was reading her German translation as Russian tanks reached Parliament Square.

In the offices of *Szabad Nep*, a reporter tapped out a dawn message on the teletype to the Associated Press in Vienna:

Since the early morning hours Russian troops have been attacking Budapest and our population. Please tell the world of the treacherous attack against our struggle for liberty. Our troops are already engaged in fighting. Radio Petofi is still in our hands. Help – help – help!

Nagy's message had been translated into several languages and at 5.44 a.m. listeners glued to their radios heard it had reached the UN. In fact, Henry Cabot Lodge interrupted a meeting of the General Assembly to say:

A few minutes ago we received word of the appeal of the Prime Minister of Hungary while his city was burning. Budapest, according to its own radio broadcast, is surrounded by a thousand Soviet tanks firing phosphorus shells to burn it out. We can hear the Hungarian National Anthem playing. It ends with the words, 'Here is where you live, and here is where you die.' If ever there was a time when action in the United Nations could literally be a matter of life or death to a whole nation, this is clearly that time. If ever there was a situation which threatened the peace of the world, this is that situation.

Shortly before 6 a.m. the blackest blow of all hit Nagy. From Szolnok on the River Tisza in central Hungary, came the voices of Janos Kadar and Ferenc Munnich, announcing the formation of the Hungarian Revolutionary Worker-Peasant government. Munnich said in a flat tone that he and Kadar had severed all relations with the Nagy government because Nagy 'had come under the sway of reaction and become impotent'. Kadar, confirming the fact that he would be prime minister in the new government, declared that it was he who had called in the Soviet troops now in the process of murdering thousands of Hungarians.

'Acting in the interests of our people, our working class, and our country,' Kadar said, '[we] requested the Soviet Army Command to help our nation in smashing the dark reactionary forces and restoring order and calm in the country.'

The broadcasts had in fact been tape-recorded and Kadar was not even in Hungary. He was in Moscow receiving his orders.

Hardly had Kadar's message ended before a figure in flowing clothes appeared. It was Cardinal Mindszenty. Nagy had earlier warned him of the threatened danger, whereupon the Cardinal had ordered his private secretary, the elderly, white-haired Monsignor Egon Turchanyi, to dress hurriedly. They slipped into their cassocks and drove to Parliament.

Russian tanks were already ringing the Square. While Mindszenty remained hidden in the small car, Turchanyi got out and explained to a Russian officer. 'The Hungarian Government has asked us to come.'

With a sneer the Russian replied, 'I'm afraid we're in control here, not the Hungarian Government.'

Turchanyi warned the Cardinal to stay in the car while he

walked into the Parliament Building. He had hardly passed the door before two Avos rushed towards him, pistols drawn. He darted back to the car, drove round to a side door. It was unguarded. The Cardinal and the Monsignor entered, and made their way to Nagy's office.

The meeting was brief.

'I don't feel very secure in my palace,' the Cardinal began, 'so I have come to seek your protection.'

Tildy answered that the Government would do anything it could, whereupon Mindszenty replied, 'I can see you have nothing good to tell me.'

'You must flee!' Nagy interrupted.

'Where to?' asked the Cardinal.

'To the nearest diplomatic mission – the American embassy,' Nagy replied.

Mindszenty wasted no time. After putting on his overcoat, he rolled up his cassock above the hem so it could not be seen. Three young Hungarians led the way to the side door, shielding him from the few Russians who had already penetrated the building.

Once in his car, he and Turchanyi dodged the oncoming tanks by keeping to back streets until they reached the sanctuary of United States 'territory'.

To one man there was an added poignancy to this dreadful morning. When Mark Molnar reached Parliament and heard that Maleter had vanished, he was convinced the General knew what was going to happen and had spared his life. *That* was why he had refused to allow him a uniform – so that he had a legitimate excuse not to take his old friend into a trap. Molnar and about a dozen officers wanted only one thing – to fight and if necessary to die. But though they had arms every demand to use them was refused.

At last Molnar realised the futility of remaining in Parliament. 'I'm not going to be shot down like a pigeon,' he cried. He arranged with the other officers to meet at a rendezvous in Buda, and they left the building in small groups. The time had come to fight again.

*   *   *

If Nagy refused to permit any firing, he was determined to do one thing more before the end. Summoning his private secretary, he dictated a long statement which he hoped would put the Russian aggression in its proper historical perspective:

This fight is the fight for freedom by the Hungarian people against the Russian intervention, and it is possible that I shall only be able to stay at my post for one or two hours. The whole world will see how the Russian armed forces, contrary to all treaties and conventions, are crushing the resistance of the Hungarian people. They will also see how they are kidnapping the Prime Minister of a country which is a Member of the United Nations, taking him from the capital, and therefore it cannot be doubted at all that this is the most brutal form of intervention. I should like in these last moments to ask the leaders of the revolution, if they can, to leave the country. I ask that all that I have said in my broadcast, and what we have agreed on with the revolutionary leaders during meetings in Parliament, should be put in a memorandum, and the leaders should turn to all the peoples of the world for help and explain that today it is Hungary and tomorrow, or the day after tomorrow, it will be the turn of other countries because the imperialism of Moscow does not know borders, and is only trying to play for time.

Just before 8 o'clock a phone message warned Nagy that if necessary the Russians would shell Parliament Building. Some government leaders decided to flee and take their chances, mingling with the people and hoping to reach Austria.

Nagy and many of his closest colleagues decided to accept an offer of asylum from the Yugoslav Embassy. A convoy of cars was already waiting, and into them piled a group of nearly forty people. It included Nagy, Losonczy, Ferenc Donath, Janosi (Nagy's son-in-law), Gabor Tanczos of the Petofi Circle, Sandor Haratzi, president of the Journalists' Association, together with fifteen women, mostly wives but including Julia Rajk, and seventeen children.[1]

[1] For a complete list, see Appendix VI.

Two men decided to stay – one for a few moments, the other for longer. They were Zoltan Tildy and Istvan Bibo, the latter appointed Minister of State only the previous day.

Tildy's main preoccupation was to save the building from damage, after which he and his wife (who was in the building with him) would make for home. Firstly, he called the senior officers of the Parliament guard.

'I can't give you orders,' he said, 'only the Minister of Defence or the President of the Council can do that. But I *can* give you advice. Send a senior officer with a white flag and a Russian interpreter to the Russian commanding officer in Parliament Square. Tell him they won't be fired at and ask them not to fire on the building.'

Though Parliament Building was saved, Tildy had reckoned without the last member of the Government, Istvan Bibo, who refused to move.

Despite Tildy's pleas, Bibo armed himself with a machine-gun, installed it at an upstairs window on the second floor and decided to fight it out. After the others had left, Bela Kovacs managed to reach Bibo on the telephone. What on earth was he doing? he asked. Didn't he know that Tildy had given an assurance that there would be no firing?

Bibo was adamant – and his reasoning was simple, and understandable. 'The Russians intend to set up Kadar as head of a new government,' he explained. 'If I, as a government official, refuse to yield, I shall be demonstrating to the world that the new government was installed in place of Nagy's legal government by force.'

Within minutes of Nagy's departure, Radio Budapest went dead, at 8.07 a.m. – and the brave, short-lived legal government of Imre Nagy had, in effect, ceased to exist.

14

The Day of Infamy

Sunday, 4 November

No one who lived through the day and night of Sunday, 4 November, will ever be able to forget its savagery. The Russian order was 'Conquer or exterminate'; and from the moment the first Soviet troops entered the capital they showed no trace of pity for the puny enemy ranged hopelessly against them.

The Soviet officers, in their long, grey-waisted coats, were professionals of the first order, who went about their task of subduing the country with efficiency that left no room for sentiment. Many of their troops were of Mongolian stock. They were merciless. If one lone sniper fired a single bullet, retribution was swift and inevitable. Half a dozen tanks rolled to the building from where the shot had been fired and obliterated it.

The UN Special Report later observed that 'The Soviet troops avoided a systematic hunting down of secondary targets ... in the belief that complete order would shortly be restored. When that proved not be the case, Soviet tanks began to move again along the main boulevards, firing indiscriminately into houses to strike fear into the people.'

The writer Lajos Lederer had a room overlooking Karoly Boulevard near an insurgent strongpoint and, as he watched, 'The Soviet tanks shelled every house with total savagery ... by evening there was scarcely a building in the main boulevards of Budapest which had not been torn open by Soviet shells.' Resistance was hopeless – but the Hungarians fought with the instinct of men betrayed and a desire for revenge.

As hundreds of Soviet tanks trundled through the city, no men's thoughts dwelt on victory, yet as they snapped home the magazines of their sub-machine-guns and fastened grenades to their belts it was not in a mood of despair. To George Kovacs, making his way to Buda to rejoin his group, it was 'the curious kind of elation that comes only when the tension of uncertainty vanishes'.

Many insurgents had been quietly preparing – just in case the hoped-for peace talks failed. With the help of the National Guard, freedom fighters in places like the Corvin Cinema, the Kilian Barracks, Csepel Island, had replenished their ammunition, while those with military training had hastily brushed up their scant knowledge of artillery as anti-tank guns arrived from Csepel and were sited in makeshift defence positions.

Attempts at co-ordinated resistance were doomed, though General Kiraly made his way secretly to a former Jesuit monastery, called Manresa, on Freedom Hill in Buda and called a conference of senior officers. As he remembers, 'The Revolutionary military leadership faced a grave decision. Should it call on the nation to resist the Soviet aggression in a guerilla war, or start negotiations or just lay down arms?'

Half at the meeting opted for an armistice. The rest, as the General noted, 'felt that, even if further fighting seemed in the final outcome hopeless, they would not lay down arms before the Soviet invaders. They were unwilling to put their arms or themselves at the mercy of Soviet troops.'

Kiraly now faced an agonising choice. As a soldier every instinct told him to continue the fight. As a politician, his clear duty was to save as many lives as possible in a struggle that could have only one ending. General Kiraly had no illusions, but there was one factor which speaker after speaker stressed. 'They were also in principle reluctant formally to renounce the goals of the revolution.'

The soldier in Kiraly won. He decided to fight on, and started to organise headquarters in the old monastery. There was not much he could do to co-ordinate the fight, but he was there, ready to help anyone who needed him.

Though the Russians were soon in control of all strategic points – bridges, the radio station, police headquarters, Parliament Building – it was still a day of heroic deeds by isolated groups of defenders. In Buda thirty-two students formed a barricade round the statue of St Imre, the patron saint of Hungarian youth, in Moricz Zsigmond Square, which guarded an important route into Pest. Armed only with sub-machine-guns, Molotov cocktails and a few tins of petrol, the boys managed to hold up two Soviet columns for eight hours, destroying five Russian tanks before the last boy died.

Sometimes small groups succeeded, thanks to freak conditions. Mark Molnar and his men scored a spectacular success when Russian troops elected to drive through the 390-yard-long tunnel under Castle Hill in Buda – a tunnel which had an exit just short of the Chain Bridge, thus affording an easy entry into Pest for mechanised vehicles which might have found the twisting narrow streets on Castle Hill difficult.

Once Molnar learned that the Russians were using the tunnel, twenty men armed with grenades made their way over the summit of the hill to the Danube end, and hid above the neo-classical entrance with its twin Doric columns and simply dropped grenade after grenade on to the Soviet vehicles blindly following each other out of the tunnel into the square. They accounted for eleven armoured vehicles before the Russians counter-attacked.

Thomas Szabo had been given leave to spend the night of the 3rd with his parents. His mother had managed to buy a few pounds of potatoes and in his honour opened a pot of his favourite jam 'which was only as a rule allowed at Christmas'. His father found an old bottle of Tokay and they spent the evening singing and dancing with the neighbours.

When the gunfire woke Szabo he at first thought it was thunder, and opened the window to let in the cold air. Firing seemed to come from every quarter. He ran to his father's bedroom where the radio was kept. Nagy was speaking, 'but I could pay no attention to what he was saying. I saw only my father, that strong, brave man, slumped on a table; he was crying.'

His mother tried to stop him from returning to his unit, but his father took him gently by the arm and told him, 'Go if you feel you must. But only the West can help now.'

Tommy-gun slung over his shoulder, Thomas kept to the back streets until he reached the school behind the Corvin

Cinema. Captain Kovacs gave Thomas and his group crisp instructions: to take four machine-guns to the attics of the building, force an opening in the roof for the guns – and then wait.

'Don't make a single move until the enemy attacks the school,' he warned them. 'You will then receive reinforcements and we'll defend ourselves to the last moment.'

Turning to the others, he explained his plans. He was mobilising every group for support roles. Each group would stay at the school, ready to proceed wherever they were required. 'No one', he ordered them, 'is to change position without explicit orders, even if there's firing close at hand.'

As he left for the Corvin Cinema, Captain Kovacs turned round and said, almost cheerfully, 'Hold tight boys! It's only a matter of hours before the UNO troops arrive.'

The first Soviet attack came around mid-morning. Two Russian tanks rounded the corner, stopped, then started shelling the area. For half an hour Szabo and his colleagues returned the Russian fire, until their gun barrels were so hot they had to stop firing. On the opposite side of the street, under an arcade, a man with one leg was firing the school's last anti-tank gun. At first he was hidden by smoke, but when it cleared Szabo saw the old man score a direct hit on the tank. The other swivelled its gun turret round and opened fire. As the smoke cleared again, 'we saw three bodies, terribly disfigured, lying near the ruins of the little anti-tank gun.'

The school could not hold out much longer. More Soviet tanks arrived and Thomas heard 'a piercing whistle followed by an enormous explosion which shook the building. Explosions came one after the other; a blast of air knocked me sideways ... the girls were screaming with terror.'

There was only one thing to do – make for the Corvin Cinema. The street was littered with bodies. Everything was blanketed by acrid, choking smoke and the reek of high explosives. Barely a hundred boys and girls out of the original 400 were still alive, and together they made a dash for it. Thomas Szabo remembers the scene as he ran into the street, 'Piles of ruins everywhere, disfigured corpses, mines which had failed to explode.' Blinded by smoke, they made for the cinema.

*   *   *

The hard core of defenders at the Kilian Barracks numbered 1200 experienced soldiers and freedom fighters led by Hungarian officers. Supporting them were another thousand boys ready to relieve any hard-pressed sector. In front of the barracks was ranged a line of Russian tanks.

Hans Germani, of the German newspaper *Der Spiegel*, had somehow managed to reach the barracks where he found 'an assault group, equipped with hand grenades, machine pistols and bottles of petrol, just reporting to their captain'. He asked to join it.

They made their way from one cellar to another, each one filled with frightened women and children, through tunnel after tunnel, across back yards, over broken walls, working their way slowly towards the Soviet tanks. 'Suddenly we were in the bar of a small hotel,' Germani remembered later. 'An iron shutter protected the room from the street. In front of the window were Soviet tanks firing. A Hungarian, with a moustache right out of a novel, was bouncing madly about, shouting orders I could not grasp, waving a bottle of gasolene. The assault unit prepared to break out.'

Germani never knew what happened next. He woke up the next morning on a mattress on the floor of a makeshift hospital.

By nightfall, the Russians had penetrated the entire country. During the afternoon Peter Howard of Reuters drove from the Austrian frontier to Sopron, the most westerly town in Hungary, passing streams of refugees in little groups, carrying everything they could take with them – the luckier ones on carts or in wheelbarrows, others in a pram or on their backs. Outside the town, soldiers from a nearby artillery barracks had placed field guns in the hills, but the professional crews had gone, and Howard could see untrained students trying to discover how to fire them.

At the very moment he reached the main square in Sopron he heard machine-gun fire in the distance. Within two minutes screams pierced the still afternoon. Men and women tore round the corner yelling, 'They're here! They're here! Four Russian tanks have entered the town.'

He stopped by his car and waited as 'a sudden panic gripped everyone. We were swept along in a scurrying crowd of men, women and children, some weeping, some screaming, some yelling senselessly. Everyone else disappeared from the streets. In a few seconds Sopron had become a ghost town.'

Howard saw the tanks enter the town, then made his way back to the frontier across hills and fields lightly dusted with the first snows of winter. The field guns he had noticed on the way in were now deserted. The stream of refugees had vanished. As he stopped to take one last look backwards, he could hear the chatter of a machine-gun.

Outside Hungary men and women – ashamed, frustrated, impotent – listened at their radios to the anguished pleas from Hungarian transmitters not yet in the hands of the Russians. Each breathless, interrupted message took on the urgency of an SOS from a sinking ship, doomed unless help arrived.

Many new freedom radios using portable transmitters suddenly burst into life. Among them was Radio Free Rakosi, whose shifting location was never pin-pointed by the Russians. It cried,

> Please tell the Geneva Red Cross that several hospitals are in flames. Radio Free Europe, please forward this news, forward our request. Forward our news. Help! Help!

Radio Roka ('Fox') was another unidentified station which sent out urgent appeals for help,

> We ask every Western station which receives our message to transmit it in English, German and French.
> We need help!
> The people of Budapest have no food. We need food and arms. Only military help can save us. The whole nation is asking for help.

Suddenly listeners heard an interruption in morse – to those who could read it, a signal between freedom fighters,

> Keep fighting. Keep fighting. Do not believe Communist broadcasts. This is the radio of the national freedom fighters.

Do not surrender your arms.

Perhaps the most anguished appeal came from Radio Free Rakosi:

> In the name of all honest Hungarians we appeal to all honest men in the world.
> Do you love liberty? So do we.
> Do you have wives and children? So have we.
> We have wounded who have given their blood for the sacred cause of liberty, but we have no bandages, no medicine. The last piece of bread has been eaten.
> In the name of all that is dear to you we ask you to help. The UN is able to stop further bloodshed ... or shall we lose faith in the world's conscience and decency ... when we are fighting for world freedom?

To the American President, Radio Free Rakosi broadcast a personal appeal.

> Attention, attention! We ask you to forward our call for help to President Eisenhower. We ask for immediate intervention, immediate intervention. Continue to listen to our broadcasts. As soon as we have time to come from the firing line, we will continue.

Until the lines were cut, newspapermen tried valiantly to tell the world what was happening, to keep their lines of communication open, none more so than the Hungarian News Agency which had a teletype link with the Associated Press bureau in Vienna. For five hours one man tapped out a running account of the fighting from the besieged offices of *Szabad Nep*, starting shortly before six o'clock: [1]

> Russian gangsters have betrayed us. The Russian troops suddenly attacked Budapest and the whole country. They opened fire on everybody in Hungary. It is a general attack....

[1] Released by the AP 4 November, *New York Times* and *Daily Telegraph* London, 5 November.

I speak in the name of Imre Nagy. He asks help ... Nagy
and the Government and the whole people ask help.

If you have anything from the Austrian Government, tell
me. Urgent, urgent, urgent....

Long live Hungary and Europe! We shall die for Hungary and Europe!

The journalist went on to ask for news about help, telling the
West that Russian MIG fighters were over Budapest, and that
Gyor was completely surrounded by the Russians, then wrote:

Please tell the world of the treacherous attack against our
struggle for liberty.... Our troops are already engaged in
fighting.... Help – Help – Help! – SOS! – SOS! – SOS! –

Around 8. 30 a.m. the journalist wrote that even though the insurgents had almost no weapons, only light machine-guns and some
carbines, people were jumping on Soviet tanks, throwing hand-
grenades inside and then slamming the drivers' windows.

What was the United Nations doing? he asked 'Give us a little
encouragement.' There were nearly 250 people in the newspaper
building with him, he said: about 50 were women, and the tanks
were approaching the building, and shells were exploding nearby.

At 9.15 the first Russian bombers were reported over Budapest
and occasionally the reporter would tap out a quick note such as,

I am running over to the window in the next room to shoot.
But I will be back if there is anything new, or you ring me.

Don't be mad at the way I am writing. I am excited. I
want to know how this is going to end. I want to shoot, but
there is no target so far. I will file to you as long as possible.

Now I have to run over to the next room to fire some shots
from the window. But I'll try to be back if there is anything
new.

When he returned he wrote that he had just heard a rumour
that American troops would be in Budapest within one or two
hours, and then, as bullets hit his own building, he asked the
Associated Press to transmit for him a personal message to a

relative in Britain which said: 'Sending kisses. We are well and fighting.'

At 10.55 a.m. the connection was cut. The reporter did not come back.

So the news reached the Western world, sickened yet powerless to help.

In Luxembourg, the Soviet ambassador and his wife had to lock themselves in the embassy cellar when students stormed into the building, ransacked it and set fire to part of it just before a cocktail party was due to begin. They hurled the caviar canapes out of the window, then made a bonfire of diplomatic documents and the pictures of Khrushchev that adorned the walls. The staff of seventy and a few of the early guests barricaded themselves in an attic with beds and cupboards.

In Brussels mounted police charged thousands of students in front of the Soviet embassy. In Bonn students stoned the Soviet embassy, and flags were flown at half mast on all government buildings. In the Hague, the anti-Soviet indignation took a more practical turn. The city's bakers refused to deliver bread to the Soviet embassy. A hotel refused to permit the Russians to hold a reception that had been arranged weeks previously. In Rotterdam dock workers refused to unload Soviet ships.

From the statesmen of the world came words of sympathy and promises of help, but little else. Eisenhower summed up America's attitude as follows: 'Hungary could not be reached by any of the United Nations or United States units without traversing neutral territory. Unless the major nations of Europe would, without delay, ally themselves spontaneously with us (an unimaginable prospect) we could do nothing. Sending troops into Hungary through hostile or neutral territory would have involved us in a general war.'

Some felt that the United Nations could have taken a firmer stand. The General Assembly met on that fateful Sunday afternoon, and Henry Cabot Lodge introduced a resolution calling on the USSR to stop all forms of intervention in Hungary's internal affairs. Despite strong opposition from Sobolev, the assembly, passed the resolution by 50 to 8, with 15 abstentions; but not even the most sanguine delegates believed the resolution could achieve anything. Christian Pineau, the French foreign minister, broadcasting from Paris on Sunday afternoon, said, 'There will be regrets that the United Nations and certain governments have preferred to devote precious hours to saving the face of an Egyptian dictator instead of supporting a brave people who were simply affirming their desire for neutrality and their wish to be free.'

To a bewildered West the Russian onslaught was still incomprehensible. How could they picture Bela Kovacs, who had started out that Sunday morning as a cabinet minister, spending the night hiding in a cellar, a fugitive from the Russians?

There Leslie Bain found him, 'a hunched, stocky man with a thin moustache and half closed eyes ... a shadow of the robust figure he had once been.' As they sat, facing each other, Bain asked Kovacs why he thought the Russians had returned.

'Two things,' answered Kovacs. 'First we went too far, and the Communists panicked. Second, the Russians felt deeply humiliated.'

Kovacs still had the generosity to praise Nagy. 'My fondest memory of Nagy', he told Bain, 'will always be his transformation from an easy-going, jolly, studious professor into a flaming revolutionary.'

15

The Last Stand

Wednesday and Thursday, 7 and 8 November

The Kremlin chose the anniversary of the October Revolution –
Wednesday, 7 November – as a suitable date for Janos Kadar to
make his triumphant entry into Budapest. The puppet leader of
Hungary, elected by Russians inside Russia, was driven to the
capital in a Soviet armoured car with a Russian driver and was
escorted by Russian tanks to the steps of Parliament Building.

Kadar might have appreciated a welcoming committee, or the
crowds which invariably gravitated to Parliament on significant
occasions, but the huge square was deserted except for Soviet
tanks. General K. Grebennyik, the Commandant of the city, took
no chances; the square had been cleared several hours before
Kadar arrived.

Why had the Russians chosen Kadar? Khrushchev never
seriously considered bringing back either Rakosi or Gero. He had
tried in vain, through Mikoyan and Suslov, to win over Nagy,
who had been his first choice. But when Nagy was forced by
events into a position unacceptable to the Kremlin Khrushchev
had to make a quick decision to fill the vacuum swiftly. Military
success had to be followed immediately by a re-shaped political
machine. And Kadar was, as Paul Zinner put it, 'a housebroken
species of national Communist who suited their purpose ideally'.

As we know now, Khrushchev personally vetted Kadar, flying
specially to Uzhgorod shortly after Kadar fled there. He also
insisted on choosing the members of Kadar's cabinet. Kadar,
a man easy to manipulate, must have breathed a sigh of relief
when Andropov told him on the night he left Budapest that the
Russians were poised to resume total power in Hungary. As

Miklos Molnar wrote later, 'The feelings which had gripped so many Communists as they were caught by the impetus of the masses, did not have the same significance for Kadar. He had never seen eye to eye with this agitated and intoxicated crowd; he had submitted to the revolution without ever having really accepted it.'

The men who now arrived with Kadar in Parliament Building[1] were all hand-picked by the Kremlin leaders, who went to extra-ordinary lengths to 'collect' them. When Khrushchev said he wanted to talk to Imre Horvath, a trusted Muscovite, it was discovered that he was on his way to the UN; Khrushchev accordingly had him re-routed, via Vienna and Prague, to Uzhgorod.

The Kadar government's first task was to pass several resolutions, dealing mainly with urgent demands for all government officials to return to work on pain of losing pay and privileges if they refused. Revolutionary committees were ordered to help 'liquidate the present disorderly situation'. Hungarian soldiers separated from their units were told to remain where they were pending further notice. Civilians were promised an amnesty if they handed in their weapons immediately.

But the most urgent problem was food. Budapest was not starving, but shortages were grim. Food shops were ordered to re-open within twenty-four hours, though no one gave any advice on where to obtain supplies until the radio appealed to transport firms to deliver flour from mills to bakeries, and begged provincial food enterprises to organise truck deliveries to Budapest. The radio specifically mentioned shortages of bread, meat, milk, flour and live animals, and advised all lorries carrying food to the capital to be clearly marked, promising that Soviet military units had been given orders to facilitate food deliveries everywhere.

Those able to do so stored food against the future. When Pal Ignotus visited the Writers' Association building in Bajaz Street he found that peasants who admired the stand taken by the writers had inundated them with farm produce, and to his astonishment even saw 'in one of the offices dozens of live chickens twittering among the writing desks'.

[1] See Appendix IV.

But this was exceptional. Dora Scarlett's experiences followed the more normal pattern. By Wednesday, 7 November, 'I had boiled the bones of a fowl three times over for soup.'

Shortly after 9 o'clock that morning, she set off with her shopping net. So many shops she had known were closed that at first she unwittingly set off in the wrong direction, but then she saw some young men with string bags running the opposite way. They shouted to her, 'Bread is being baked in Bajnok Street!'

She followed them across Stalin Avenue and into the side street. 'Never had the smell of fresh bread seemed so delicious.' But there was one snag – a queue of at least 2000 people ahead of her. Resigning herself to a long wait she stood there, and soon scores of people were lined up behind her.

Because of its length, the queue had to advance over a piece of dreary waste ground, 'covered with mounds of refuse, potato peelings, tin cans and cinders' – evidence of the fact that no rubbish had been cleared for two weeks. Children scrabbled in the refuse for spent cartridges. A further macabre sight was two graves which 'we just managed to avoid trampling on as the queue moved forward'. One was of an insurgent who had been killed there, the other of an old woman who had died from natural causes; she could not be buried in the cemetery because no one could be found to take her body through the streets. Carefully Dora Scarlett picked her way past the two mounds, marked with simple wooden crosses, and partly covered with white chrysanthemums.

After two and a half hours she finally saw the bakehouse door ahead and caught glimpses of the lucky ones running off hugging the hot, oval, flat loaves. Then a voice from the bakery shouted, 'Only enough flour left for 400 loaves!' Her heart sank as she tried to make a rough count of those in front of her. The queue was five deep and she estimated that there were, in fact, just about 400 people ahead of her. She decided to wait and hope for the best.

During all this time heavy gunfire rumbled in the distance, though nobody took any notice, but now, without warning, firing broke out in the next street. For a few moments the people hugged the street wall. The firing increased. The queue scattered. Everyone fled. Dora Scarlett slipped into a big arched doorway, then into a courtyard where thirty or forty people were waiting, the silence broken only by the sound of one woman sobbing.

After twenty minutes or so, the shooting died down and Dora set off for home. But she had to cross the wide Stalin Avenue, and as she started Russian tanks opened fire along its length. She crouched in a doorway, barely two minutes from her flat. It took her another half hour to reach it. She was still clutching her shopping net – empty.

Even in the British Legation, now bursting with refugees, food was running short. Leopold Joseph, who had sought refuge there, remembers, 'By this time there was no bread. Our meals in the legation consisted of canned meat and spaghetti for lunch and macaroni for dinner. We slept on floors, in chairs, on desks, underneath tables, anywhere we could find. It was bitterly cold and there was very little heating. Some of us were on the edge of a nervous breakdown, not because of the shelling and the murder going on across the street, but because we thought we would never get out.'

The Minister, Mr Fry, moved into the Legation, and each evening presided over a meeting of senior officials to discuss what Joan Fish called 'the latest rumours'. Normally such a meeting would have been formal, but now as the diminished staff assembled at 6 p.m. the usual blotting-pads and pencils on the conference table were replaced by shallow, slim-stemmed glasses. 'I'm damned if I'm going to let the Russians get their hands on my stocks of champagne,' the Minister growled one evening. And from that moment onwards a glass of champagne helped to wash down the evening conference in the embattled Legation.

Kadar no doubt hoped that his imprisonment and torture by Rakosi would be his diploma for winning the support of the people; but he had reckoned without the fact that Nagy was still the hero who had fought to drive out the Russians, while Kadar, on his own admission, had called them back. He was despised as a traitor. Using their own special brand of cynical humour, the people of Budapest mocked him openly. In one street a sign read:

LOST – THE CONFIDENCE OF THE PEOPLE. HONEST FINDER IS

ASKED TO RETURN IT AT ONCE TO JANOS KADAR, PREMIER OF
HUNGARY, AT 10,000 SOVIET TANKS STREET.

Another placard read:

WANTED: PREMIER FOR HUNGARY. QUALIFICATIONS: NO SINCERE
CONVICTION. NO BACKBONE. ABILITY TO READ OR WRITE NOT
REQUIRED, BUT MUST BE ABLE TO SIGN DOCUMENTS DRAWN UP
BY OTHERS. APPLICATIONS SHOULD BE MADE TO MESSRS
KHRUSHCHEV AND BULGANIN.

In Rakosi Avenue, Thomas Szabo saw a hastily scrawled sign,

I HAVE LOST MY HONOUR. WHOEVER FINDS IT IS REQUESTED
TO SEND IT TO THE FOLLOWING ADDRESS: JANOS KADAR, HEAD
OF THE GOVERNMENT OF COMMUNIST HUNGARY, STREET OF
10,000 TANKS. CORRECTION: WE APOLOGISE FOR OUR MISTAKE
IN GIVING THE ADDRESS. COMMUNIST HUNGARY DOES NOT EXIST.

As the Russians tore the heart out of the city, the joke current
was, 'Except for nearly ten million counter-revolutionary landlords, factory owners, bankers, counts and cardinals, the Hungarian workers remain loyal to the people's democratic regime,
and all six of them form the Kadar government.'

The people put up defiant posters. They defaced every government proclamation on the walls. Dora Scarlett noticed the silent
bitterness of the people whenever a Kadar poster appeared. 'Within an hour or so of the proclamation being pasted up all over
Budapest, there was not a whole or undefaced copy to be seen.
This was not done by gangs going round the city, but by passers-
by. As soon as a poster was put up they would gather, read it
silently, and then by common consent, tear it across.'

The beautiful capital was by now a mass of scars and ruins. When
Jozsef Kovago, the short-lived Mayor, went to fetch his wife Lonci
and their daughter who had taken refuge in a hospital, 'I reached
the wide boulevard which looked like a battlefield. Houses were
in ruins, the only persons one could see on the street were in front
of food stores. Suddenly two Soviet tanks appeared. People tried

to hide. I fled into a house. The Soviet tanks opened fire on the people standing in the food line.' As quickly as he could, Kovago, 'went through the battle-scarred streets. Destruction and the dead were all over.' Finally he reached the hospital, which was now in a state of siege. Though he had to admit the battle was lost, Kovago still could not bring himself to flee from his beloved Budapest, so the Kovago family hid by moving each day to the house of a different friend.

Dora Scarlett saw the same appalling damage. When she headed for Mayakovsky Street, she found hardly a house left standing. For over a mile in the Boulevard of the Martyrs, every building was smashed. Stalin Avenue was a stretch of gaping holes. At the radio building, the front had fallen in, and on Castle Hill in Buda the National Archives building was on fire. She made her way to the yellowing old Rosalie Chapel where for decades peasant women had sat under the shade of its walls selling their lace. The tower had been knocked off. The old Rokus hospital, adjoining the church, was in ruins. 'The smell of stone dust and fire hung in the air, and down the long vistas of Rakosi Street and the Korut, the dust looked like fog. Over all hung the flags, as though the city were keeping some terrible festival of death. There were more black flags than ever among them.'

When she reached Rakosi Street, which people had to cross to reach one of the big markets, it was filled with a changing crowd of people, many in tears, filing silently past a long row of graves, all of young people, the mounds of freshly turned earth covered with candles, flowers and photographs.

People walked the streets, searching for friends. Dora Scarlett saw 'relatives and friends who had had no word of one another since the fighting began, fall into each other's arms, sometimes with tears.' She discovered that if she walked up and down the Korut or stood in the bread queue 'you would sooner or later meet most of the people you knew'.

From time to time the Russians would train their guns on a building and 'calmly pump shell after shell into it'. In this way they destroyed the grandiose Press Palace at the beginning of Lenin Avenue, and the famous 'gilt and crystal chandelier' Hungaria Restaurant. 'At other times,' Dora Scarlett noted, 'the crackle of rifle or machine-gun fire would suddenly start up in an apparently peaceful street, and it would be quite impossible to know who was fighting who. Some of the combatants were Avo men.'

Already the Avo were operating again. Major Lazlo Szabo, who had sat out most of the revolution in the Ministry of the Interior before being rescued by the Russians and taken to their camp in the country, remembers, 'On the morning of 4 November, we were ordered to assemble. They [the Russians] read an order announcing that Soviet troops had attacked Budapest that morning, and we could go back when the city was quiet.'

The Major returned to Budapest and made straight for the Ministry of the Interior, where he found some rooms burned out, files scattered everywhere or missing. 'Then we reorganised and went out to take over sections of Budapest from the Soviet troops.'

Many thought the Avo had been virtually exterminated, but in fact only a few hundred had been lynched or fled out of an estimated force of 30,000, and their espionage apparatus was virtually intact. Thousands of part-time spies who would willingly have renounced their ties with the Avo were forced to work again by threats of blackmail. Ranging from ex-ministers to prostitutes, they had code names, were now paid in advance (whether or not they wished it) and forced to sign receipts with their proper names. The Avo gained control of their lives.

One of their first arrests showed the Avo to be as cunning as ever. They tipped off the Russians where to find Colonel Sandor Kopacsi, the Budapest police chief. The Avo had a special score to pay back to the man who had rescued Nagy from them, and were delighted when they learned he had made no attempt to flee or seek asylum.

As Kopacsi was walking along Andrassy Street, he met a Soviet officer who had been stationed in Budapest for some years and whom he happened to know. The officer had been planted there. Professing himself delighted to see Kopacsi, he took his arm, and said that everyone was looking for him, and that Andropov, the Soviet ambassador, in particular was anxious to discuss with him the best means of reaching a truce. Kopacsi could be of immense service to his country and save many Hungarian lives if he would mediate, said the Soviet officer earnestly. Kopacsi had no reason to suspect treachery by someone he had known for years, and together they walked to the Soviet embassy. Once at the gates, Kopacsi was pushed and kicked into the embassy garden and arrested. He was interrogated personally by Serov, then thrown into the Avo dungeon in Fo Street.

In that week of bloody fighting it is doubtful if even Kopacsi could have stemmed the fury of the hopeless resistance. Motivated by a sense of outrage that bit into their souls, men and women attacked Soviet vehicles with nothing but their bare hands. When a boy of six was killed by a stray Russian bullet in Karacsnyi Sandor Street, the mother grabbed the bleeding child and ran towards her house. The Russians opened fire on her. The door of the house opened and about twenty men and women, armed with stones and sticks, rushed the Soviet armoured car. It was, in the words of Leslie Bain, 'a horrifyingly uneven battle', but when it was over eight Soviet soldiers lay dead or badly wounded, their armoured car wrecked, and the survivors had fled. All but three of the Hungarians were wounded.

Despite the horrors, the people of Budapest took a delight in taunting the enemy. When Russian troops looted a big liquor shop opposite the Franciscan Church, a group fastened a large placard at the entrance, reading:

THIS OPERATION WAS BRAVELY CARRIED OUT BY OUR GLORIOUS RUSSIAN ALLIES. WE SHALL NOT FORGET THEIR HEROIC DEED.

On a wall in the Korut, another sign appeared:

FORMER ARISTOCRATS, CARDINALS, GENERALS AND OTHER SUP-PORTERS OF THE OLD REGIME, NOW DISGUISED AS FACTORY WORKERS AND PEASANTS, ARE MAKING PROPAGANDA AGAINST OUR RUSSIAN FRIENDS.

In a pathetic attempt to cheer people up, Kadar ordered Budapest Radio to play hours of dance music, but the songs were frequently ill chosen. When Dora Scarlett switched on one day she heard a girl singing (the words being translated roughly by Dora),

Budapest, what a proud and beautiful city you are! How life throbs in your streets!

'It seemed unbearable effrontery.'

In a war of odd contrasts men would kill each other on one street, talk to enemies in the next. When Hans Germani of *Der Spiegel* returned to the street near the Kilian Barracks to search for the car he had left there before being knocked unconscious, he found a 'strange war'. As he walked warily towards the barracks, people were calmly queueing up for bread, oblivious to the fact that in the next street Soviet tanks were methodically destroying a house.

Not far away, in Ulloi Avenue, a Soviet tank had blown in the second floor of a shabby tenement, and in the huge gaping hole that had once been a wall a gaunt woman sat with a rifle across her knees, waiting for Russians to come within her sights. She spurned attempts to move her from her exposed position, and later that night, when the fighting had died down, she told Leslie Bain why.

'The Russians took everything I ever had,' she said, 'everything I ever cared for. In 1916 they killed my husband, a prisoner of war in Russia. My son fell three blocks away from here under Russian fire in 1945. My grandson will be deported because he foolishly surrendered three days ago when they promised amnesty. And that' – pointing to the black hole above their heads – 'was my home since I was a child. There is nothing left for them to take from me.'

In the industrial town of Dunapentele, the enemy sides actually 'talked things over' before starting to fight each other. The town had always been regarded as a Communist stronghold since its transformation from a small village into an industrial complex of 28,000 people. On Tuesday, 6 November, a Russian armoured column surrounded the town and demanded its surrender. The Revolutionary Council invited the Soviet commander to visit them, and he was escorted into the town hall with an Avo interpreter, where leaders told him there were no 'Fascists' or 'counter-revolutionaries' but only 'good hard-working Communists'. Two card-carrying Communists were now paraded before the Soviet commander. One told him, 'We have been taught to believe that you in the Soviet Union are pledged to defend human rights and that you are the liberators of people. We are Communists, but we want to be free of Soviet intervention.'

Embarrassed, the Russian officer replied that he was sorry, but he had to carry out his orders. The two Communists then took out their Party cards and ceremoniously tore them up in front of him. The Russian must have been shocked, for he agreed to take no action until he received further orders; they must have arrived swiftly, for the next day the Soviet Army launched a three-pronged attack on the town with tanks and self-propelled guns, killing 240 freedom fighters who held out until their ammunition was exhausted.

In Pecs, near the Hungarian uranium mines, the Hungarian Army, which had originally promised to fight, was disarmed by their pro-Moscow commanding officer and the Soviets took over the city – but not before 5000 miners and students had fled with guns to the nearby Mecsek Mountains, where they were able to employ real guerilla warfare, including one major ambush of a Russian convoy in which they killed the Soviet commander. Only when their ammunition ran out did they disperse and escape across the Yugoslavian frontier.

Yet the uneven struggle could have only one end, and inexorably the Russians brought the country to its knees. Guerilla forces still operated in some mountain areas, and General Kiraly still helped from his headquarters in the old monastery in Buda until warned that Russians were about to attack him. Still he refused to give in. Stealthily he moved to the small town of Nagykovacsi, twenty miles west of Budapest where 'We tried to contact and co-ordinate those freedom fighters still resisting in the immediate vicinity and in the mining areas of Piliscsaba, Dorog and Tata.'

But in effect, by the middle of the second week in November, only two strongpoints were holding out: the Kilian Barracks in Pest, and the workers on Csepel Island.

All the area surrounding the Kilian Barracks was being pounded by Russian shellfire, including the famous old Istvan Korhaz hospital. The Russians showed no compunction about attacking it, even shooting at ambulances reaching the hospital gates. By Thursday, out of twenty-four stretcher bearers only one survivor was left. The wounded were bleeding to death because no one could reach them, and the medical director told Bain, 'Modern history has no equal to the barbarity committed here. Soviet troops have killed or wounded half of our personnel.' Another doctor estimated that during thirty-six hours 700 Hungarians had died for lack of medical attention.

The Corvin Cinema block, fifty yards from the barracks, and where young Thomas Szabo had fought so gallantly, was overwhelmed by Tuesday afternoon, though only after stubborn resistance when its defenders managed to capture an anti-tank gun from a disabled Soviet tank. They placed it against the steps of the cinema, with an improvised automatic mechanism so they could fire it from inside the building. When a Russian armoured vehicle or tank came from a side street and turned in front of the cinema, the insurgents fired at its tracks.

The boys and girls inside were by now highly efficient with their Molotov cocktails and operated them on a three-stage plan. When observers on the roof signalled the approach of a tank, they filled old bottles – in many cases tomato ketchup bottles – with petrol. They were loosely corked, with towelling round the cork. At a second signal, as the tank drew nearer to the cinema, the bottle was tipped downwards allowing the petrol to seep into the towelling. At the third signal – as the anti-tank gun was fired – the defenders lit the towelling and threw the bottle at the immobilised tank. As the loose cork fell out, the bottle exploded. Not until the cinema was finally shelled with heavy self-propelled artillery was it evacuated.

Inside Kilian Barracks the last defenders held out fanatically. The odds were hopeless, though at times defenders actually received reinforcements as it became impossible for isolated groups of fighters to carry on. George Kovacs was one of a group which decided to fight from the barracks, and was one of the few men who survived out of a fighting force that at its peak totalled more than 2000.

For the last three days conditions were pitiful. Almost all the surrounding buildings were in Russian hands. Worse, the Soviets discovered the labyrinth of tunnels and dynamited them, in one case trapping 100 insurgents setting out on a foray. The youngsters were half way through the tunnel when the Russians blew it up behind them. They could not return, and when the air became fetid and they advanced in order to breathe, the Russians were waiting for them with machine-guns. There were no prisoners.

Soon there were no bandages for the wounded, almost no food for the fighters, no one could get out. And the shelling never seemed to stop.

Even when the garrison was reduced to less than 100, they tried to hold on, running from one firing position to another to create the impression of bigger numbers. In one macabre attempt to deceive the Russians, Kovacs and several others carried corpses to the slits in the walls, propping them up to draw Russian fire. But by Wednesday, 7 November, only forty survivors were left. They had no option but to surrender, and after parleying with a Russian officer they were promised an amnesty.

The big gates, where – so long ago it seemed – Pal Maleter had halted his tank, were thrown open. Through them, head high, marched a column of ragamuffin soldiers, many in their teens, bandaged boys, the blood seeping through, two men on crutches made out of old wooden window frames, a girl helping a wounded man. Their clothes were in tatters, many had no jackets or other protection against the cold as they marched out into Ulloi Avenue.

The gates banged behind them. The Soviet machine-gunners clicked back their magazines. Every youngster who had been solemnly promised his freedom was mown down.

At the last moment George Kovacs and a handful of friends who suspected Russian treachery hid in the barracks as the rest surrendered. They escaped through one of the tunnels not yet blocked by the Russians, reached Pest and headed for the frontier.

Now only one place still offered dogged resistance – Csepel.

One man had heard of the heroic defence of Csepel and had decided to join the defenders. 'After all,' as Mark Molnar remembers, 'I might once have been an officer in the Hungarian Army, but I had become a coalman, so I was entitled to fight with the workers.'

Mounting an old bicycle he had found several days previously, he set off for the thirty-mile-long island, formed where the river split at the southern tip of the capital.

The southern half of Csepel, with the Soviet High Command at Tokol, was held by a heavily reinforced Russian contingent. But the north was in the hands of 30,000 workers living in flats surrounding the forest of chimneys of the Csepel Iron and Steel Works and other factories.

Molnar rode towards the island along Soroksari Avenue, the only major road linking Budapest with the island; it was of considerable strategic importance to the Russians because unless they could hold it their airfield at Tokol was isolated. They controlled the avenue by day, but had not managed to oust freedom fighters from a small bridge at the northern tip of the island. For five days the Soviet command tried to break the resistance of the Csepel workers but, in the words of the UN, 'the freedom fighters maintained an effective organised armed resistance in most of the area throughout these five days'.

Molnar was astounded by the discipline and professionalism. The Hungarian line across the island extended for seven or eight miles, split up into twelve sections, facing an estimated twelve Soviet battalions. Mark was given the title of Comrade Commander and put in charge of 450 men guarding a half-mile sector in the centre. He had a small headquarters dug-out, with field telephone to the adjacent sectors and one to headquarters in the rear, at the grandly named Incandescent Lamp factory. Headquarters, he was told, would arrange all his logistical support – food, care for the wounded, reinforcements, ammunition – but when it came to actual fighting he would be on his own, for it was not always possible to co-ordinate all sectors. Each would have to operate separately if necessary.

The men were busy digging trenches along the flat, bare, wintry countryside, dotted with a few houses and clumps of trees. Behind the front line, the defences went back for a quarter of a mile, with criss-crossed trenches. Every stronghold was heavily sandbagged. Houses at corners had been transformed into strongpoints. Like a backcloth, the workers' flats reared up. 'Easy to defend,' Molnar remembers thinking.

He checked on his guns – five heavy machine-guns, two anti-tank guns, four mortars, plenty of ammunition. He had no heavy artillery, but could hope for more mortars, for these were still being manufactured in the machine shops behind his line.

Molnar had arrived during the night, and at 7 a.m. a truck stopped near his dug-out. Half a dozen men tumbled out and to Mark's amazement produced hot food. The soldiers queued up in orderly fashion, and one who politely offered Molnar a cup of soup commented, 'There's one thing about Csepel – you get hot food in the front line three times a day.'

As the food was being served, a column of about 150 workers arrived from the factories and flats to relieve those who had spent the night in the trenches. The routine was simple. Each man spent eight hours fighting, eight hours working in the factories manufacturing shells and guns, eight hours sleeping at home.

Behind Molnar's line was an improvised field hospital and, as he remembers, 'From the very first moment I arrived, I was allotted volunteer medical students and I knew just where to put my casualties.' The organisation, he felt, 'was far better than it had been on the Hungarian general staff. I had nothing to do but fight.'

There was also a human touch – provided by elderly ladies anxious for their sons' welfare. Molnar was startled on the first day when a motherly woman, addressing him as Comrade Commander, pointed to a teenager in a nearby trench and said with some agitation, 'He forgot his overcoat again. Would you please see he gets it?'

She looked at Molnar, who had not changed his clothes for a week, but said nothing. A few hours later she reappeared with a neatly wrapped parcel. From that day Molnar had a heavy coat and never wanted for clean underclothes. He discovered later that the woman's husband and eldest son had both been killed during the first week; but she herself never mentioned the matter.

At first Mark felt that 'The Russians were content to keep us immobilised, and probably they thought they would starve us out.' Food could certainly become a grave problem. At the moment it was being supplied from workers' families and factory canteens, supplemented by meat from one of the big Budapest abattoirs. This was conveniently situated a mile or so east of Csepel, on the narrow branch of the Danube 'tributary', so that freedom fighters could bring supplies by night across the small bridge, which was guarded with mortars, anti-tank guns, and a squad of men under an old sergeant-major who confided to Molnar with relish, 'I'm really *enjoying* this revolution.'

On the second night the Russians launched a heavy artillery attack. Molnar, who had decided to spend each night in the trenches, was awake when the first shells came screaming over. He could see the Russian gun flashes, perhaps half a mile away, coming from a copse at the foot of a small hill. The only hope was a diversion, which he had already planned.

Molnar had no armoured cars to race forward and harass the gunposts, but he had found four old sand tippers – three-wheeled mechanised wheelbarrows, the sort which tipped forward to discharge sand from a large iron bucket. He had lined each bucket with sandbags which precariously held a machine-gun in place, together with a three-man crew to hold the gun in position and then operate it. The driver sat on a saddle behind them.

As the shelling intensified, the makeshift contraptions lurched off in the darkness towards the Russian gun emplacements, unseen until they were close enough to open fire, and confuse the enemy. They could not knock out the Russian guns, but they did effectively silence them by bouncing around the countryside, giving the Russians the impression they were scout cars. This was the first big Soviet artillery attack and Molnar's section suffered nearly fifty casualties, including nineteen men and four women killed in the trenches.

On Wednesday, 7 November, the Russians launched a concentrated artillery barrage against the whole Hungarian front, and the next day Molnar – who had lost another thirty-five fighters – saw a Soviet armoured car approaching his sector of the line. From its radio mast a large white flag fluttered. Warning his men to hold their fire, Molnar climbed out of his trench and stood waiting until the Russian vehicle stopped.

An officer wearing a long grey coat and a hat trimmed with astrakhan took off his gloves, saluted and – perhaps unthinkingly – offered a hand to Molnar, who kept his own hands in his pockets.

In passable Hungarian the Soviet officer said, 'My commanding officer has sent me as an emissary to ask you to surrender in order to spare Hungarian lives.' Molnar, of course, had no authority to make such a decision, so instructed an aide to take the Russian to the headquarters of the Revolutionary Committee – where the offer was indignantly rejected.

That night there was another heavy barrage, and early the following morning – Thursday, the 8th – another emissary warned the Hungarians that unless they surrendered 'no one will be spared'. Again the truce was rejected. He had hardly returned before the Russians launched a massive artillery attack. Guns located on Gellert Hill in Buda attacked the lines from the rear. In the first two hours Molnar lost 100 men and women, boys and girls, all killed.

Despite appalling losses – and great damage to factories, installations and workers' flats – the freedom fighters held their line, though they were increasingly isolated as the guns from Buda bombarded the defence in depth behind them.

Molnar had long since stopped counting the dead. 'It was a cold, wintry day,' he recalls, 'and the trenches were so filled with corpses that the only way I could get from one end of my sector to the other was to climb out and run, crouching, over the open ground.' He estimates that at least 300 men and women had been killed in his sector alone. Volunteer medical students – when they could distinguish the wounded from the dead – rushed the wounded behind the lines. Many of those rescued were killed later when an anti-personnel rocket scored a direct hit on the makeshift hospital.

The telephone lines with Molnar's neighbouring sectors had long since been cut, so Molnar could not discover how the rest of the line was faring, 'though it wasn't difficult for me to imagine what was happening'. But his phone link with headquarters was still functioning and at 5.30 p.m. headquarters warned him, 'The Russians have broken across the water and landed on the east bank of the island.' They had attacked from the 'mainland' in force, landing tanks.

'We're all determined to fight on,' Molnar told headquarters, 'but we're running out of ammunition. Can you get some up to me?'

Over the crackling field telephone, a voice replied, 'There is no more ammunition, Comrade Commander. The Russkies have already occupied the main factories.'

Half an hour later, Molnar's telephone rang again. The Revolutionary Committee had decided that further resistance was useless. 'Get your men away as quickly as you can, and then you must escape,' he was told. 'Leave your weapons in your dug-out. It would be stupid to get caught carrying a gun. Thanks for all you've done and good luck.'

And so, as night fell on Budapest on Friday, 9 November, the fighting ended in a capital little more than a heap of ruins and a desert of corpses. With Csepel in Russian hands, all major resistance ended and as the French newspaper *Figaro* commented bitterly, 'The Red Army now occupies Budapest. It is red with the blood of the workers.'

16

The Great Escape

Friday, 9 November to Friday, 16 November

Leopold Joseph remembers leaving the British Legation on the Friday feeling, 'Perhaps this is the day of the greatest tragedy. The rebels held on because they believed the UN would come to their aid. They stood on the rooftops looking into the skies, waiting for the sight of planes that never came. Today they finally realised there would be no help for them.' One man said to Joseph, 'The United Nations has let us down.' Another told him the West had permitted another Munich. Joseph remembers, 'I never felt so grieved as I did when I walked round the streets.'

Leslie Bain and an American colleague Seymour Freidin were also walking the streets and Bain 'cringed inwardly' as the Hungarians surrounded them. Freidin tried to explain the West's position but Bain realised that he 'failed because it sounded hollow, even to him'. As they walked back to the American Legation Bain 'stole a glance at Freidin's face and saw that he had tears in his eyes'.

Hungarians felt that if Hammarskjöld could go to Suez, he could also have gone to Hungary, and that had he done so the outcome might have been different. Jozsef Kovago, now hiding from Russian search parties, echoed the feelings of most Hungarians when he said they expected the UN to help them restore order as they had done at Suez, by sending an international police force. Instead, as Eden wrote, 'the pitiable failure of the United Nations to influence Hungarian events in the slightest degree lit up the tragedy in flaming colour'.

Most Hungarians had at first hoped for the impossible, perhaps because as Paul Zinner wrote:

The United States can be faulted for its enunciated policy of liberation. For whatever was meant by those who propounded it (and precisely what they did mean has never been satisfactorily determined), it could be understood only in one sense by those to whom it was addressed. They had to assume a stance on the part of the United States that did not and properly should not exist.

This misconception – certainly exacerbated by Western radio programmes – made many Westerners uneasy. When Seymour Freidin was driving towards the Austrian frontier and people waved at his American flag, he slid further down his seat in embarrassment and 'it was the only time in my life that I had ever been ashamed that I was an American'.

George Kovacs remembers, 'We didn't expect arms – we knew that was impossible. We wanted *moral* support. If the West had threatened to send volunteers to Hungary when Khrushchev threatened to send volunteers to Suez, we might have called their bluff.'

What the Hungarians (and many Westerners) never realised was that the United States and Britain were caught completely by surprise. As Eisenhower said,[1] 'The thing started in such a way that everybody was a little bit fooled,' while Robert Murphy, Under-Secretary of State, admitted, 'The United States government had no advance information about the uprising, no plan of action.' Even though America did not have a minister during the revolution (the replacement for the minister who left in July had not arrived) this was an extraordinary admission, for the few journalists in Budapest in the weeks before the revolution were convinced the situation would explode. Sefton Delmer of the *Daily Express* went there deliberately because he could sense impending trouble, while the correspondent of the *Daily Mail* met Nagy less than two weeks before the revolution started, on the day when Nagy was reinstated into the Party, and cabled his newspaper, 'Hungary is on the verge of revolution. Everything points to an imminent explosion.'

Yet if Western diplomats failed to understand, so did Soviet Russia, whose errors in tactics were monumental; and so did

[1] CBS-TV, 23 November 1961.

many of the Hungarian extremists who goaded Nagy into an untenable position. Miklos Molnar (no relation to Mark Molnar) summed it up as follows:

In October 1956, two trends, two waves, met; the wave of the Hungarian revolutionary, democratic liberalism, and the wave of Soviet liberalisation. One sprang from the West, the other was a harbinger of the East's future. If the storm had not swept him away, Nagy would have been the bridge between the two.

The tragic misunderstanding ... began on the day of the revolution. Everyone misunderstands ... authority provokes the peaceful demonstrators, fires at those with whom it could come to terms. The insurgents interpret the political success of the uprising as a military victory. Imre Nagy mistrusts the masses and puts himself in the hands of those who mistrust him. The Communist leaders misunderstand the entire situation, fail to understand that only Imre Nagy can save what is still to be saved. The masses fail to understand Nagy's situation. The Soviet leaders, betting on two horses, lose on both. The Soviet soldiers shoot blindly, understanding nothing. The West understands even less, is busy fighting at Suez; it has an entirely wrong picture of Imre Nagy and misunderstands the successes and failures, as well as the possibilities and limitations of the revolution. Imre Nagy was the only one who, after his initial hesitations, recognised the real nature of events and attempted to reconcile, co-ordinate the two programmes, the two trends.

No one in the West was aware of the different ideological forces clashing in the streets of Budapest. Had the West been better informed – and had the United Nations taken the revolution more seriously – Robert Murphy might not have felt constrained to write, 'Perhaps history will demonstrate that the free world could have intervened ... but none of us in the State Department had the skill or the imagination to devise a way.'

Now it was too late. Hungary was again an occupied country, Budapest the capital of a Soviet 'province'.

General Grebennyik, the Soviet commander of the capital, whose favourite words seemed to be 'I order' or 'I direct you', was signing tracts pasted on every city wall, insisting on the polite fiction that Budapest was returning to normal. 'But can one speak of normal,' asked Luigi Fossati of the Roman newspaper *Avanti*, 'in a city where dead lie in the streets, their faces covered by a handkerchief or a sheet of paper?'

Grimly the city braced itself to live with the spectre of defeat. Life had to continue somehow but nothing could disguise the sullen hatred of the people. The children cursed the Soviet crewmen guarding their motionless tanks. When Lajos Lederer walked through the streets he heard one girl cry, 'Do you really believe that you've come to liberate us from a handful of Fascists?' Another shouted, 'You unspeakable swine!' Both spoke in Russian which they had been compelled to learn at school and which now paid its first dividend. Lederer noticed that the tank crews at first tried to answer back, to argue, 'but in the end they gave up. Dumbly they put up with being spat at and cursed.'

The Hungarians had prided themselves on not looting during the uprising. Now the Russians looted shops all over the city, frequently resorting to a propaganda trick. At big shops, the Russians plucked passers-by off the street at random, and at pistol point forced them to carry goods from the shops and load them on to Soviet trucks. Hidden photographers snapped them, the pictures appearing within a few days in *Pravda* – showing, of course, photographs of Hungarians looting.

The Russians were at their most dangerous when looting liquor stores. Many wine shops disguised themselves by taking down their signs, borrowing new ones from neighbouring shops so that a store filled with hidden bottles of Barack, Torkoly or Giraffe beer outwardly appeared to belong to a shoemaker or an electrician.

Everywhere evidence of Soviet callousness was visible. Bodies were left to rot in the streets; Russians, guarding every major intersection, waved back each prospective cortège. Many fathers and mothers, if they found the body of their son, carried him themselves to his last place of rest in the Kerepes cemetery.

A highly respected Englishman who died, aged 82, of natural causes was likewise buried in the Kerepes cemetery. Professor

Arthur Yolland, originally of Hoylake, Cheshire, went to live in Budapest in 1896, and compiled the world's finest Hungarian–English Dictionary. At one time he was senior translator at the British Legation, but even after his retirement, and a long illness, he had been 'kept on the books' as an honorary attaché, largely for his own protection. When he died, Joan Fish was determined he should be given a Christian burial. With Receczy she took out the Land-Rover, drove through dozens of Soviet checkpoints until she found a coffin, then a Hungarian priest with a smattering of English, and drove the one-vehicle cortège to Kerepes cemetery, where the minister haltingly read out the burial service while Russian tank crews watched in silence.

The body could not be lowered into the rock-hard ground, for the gravediggers had long since vanished, but reverently the old man's body was placed in one of the many rows of freedom fighters' coffins.

The people's hatred was reserved not only for the Russians; Kadar's grandiloquently named Hungarian Revolutionary Workers' and Peasants' Party was equally despised. Tibor Meray summed it up, 'Conceived in treason, it had been borne amid a massacre and baptised by a lie.' It was not Hungarian, it was not revolutionary, and it was certainly not composed of workers, who fought it by striking.

The jails were soon overflowing again, and day after day cattle-trucks trundled eastwards with their human cargoes destined for the Soviet Union. On Tuesday, 13 November, three trains left Budapest bound for Siberia. Each one consisted of sixty goods wagons, each wagon carried between fifty and sixty people.[1]

Though the armed struggle had ended, the workers now carried on the fight with the only weapon at their disposal – a strike. The workers' councils, born during the uprising, ordered a general strike so that for weeks the Hungarians lived under a dual government – Kadar backed by Russian tanks, the workers' councils representing the people. The councils had, in fact, become the last citadel of the Hungarian insurgency, for even with

---

[1] On 20 November Henry Cabot Lodge told the UN that America had factual evidence that 16,000 Hungarians had been deported by 14 November.

Soviet support Kadar could not crush them. 'It was one thing', Paul Zinner wrote, 'for the Soviet forces to reoccupy a town hall and sweep away the local revolutionary council; it was quite another thing for them to dislodge by force a workers' council whose base of operation was in the middle of an industrial complex employing thousands of workers.' There were just not enough Russians in Hungary to undertake such a gigantic task.

Despite every appeal, the workers remained on strike. Each factory proclaimed its own resolutions, often on duplicating machines, and each time Grebennyik, the Soviet commander, pasted up new proclamations workmen arrived as if by magic and covered them with their own posters calling for the strike to continue. It meant bitter hardship for hundreds of thousands of Hungarians, for though by agreement food supplies were unaffected by the strike few of the workers' families had enough money to buy even the scant rations available. Fortunately the peasants came to their aid when they could. Sometimes the peasants' trucks were looted before they reached their destination.

The Hungarian people were not the only ones short of food. Life in the British Legation was daily getting more spartan. By mid-November, Joseph was noting in his diary, 'Now we have half a slice of bread and a cup of tea for breakfast. There is no lunch, and for dinner we had tinned goose liver.'

Seventy people were living in the British Legation, and Joan Fish had the job of bedding them down and feeding them. She had collected blankets from the private houses of the legation staff, and had also raided their larders. But cooking still presented a problem, for there were only two domestic stoves in the legation on which to cook for all these people.

There was one way to beat the food shortage – if it could be made to work: reduce the numbers by evacuation and load up with food in Vienna for the return journey. But with Soviet tanks patrolling the border only those with exit permits could pass – and these were hard to get.

Luckily Joan Fish had a trump card which she had rarely used until now. One of her Hungarian consular clerks, who dealt with applications for visas and permits, was a patent spy – though nothing could be proved; Joan Fish knew that his advice carried great weight with the Hungarians and Russians. She caught him dealing in the black market with stolen jars of legation coffee and confronted him. He broke down and admitted it. Nothing was said about spying, but he knew perfectly well that if a spy planted in a foreign mission were caught dealing in the black market he could be shot. Now, whenever an exit permit was needed, Joan Fish told her clerk bluntly, 'If the exit visa isn't granted, a report will be filed about you.'

It worked. Soon Joan Fish in her Morris Minor was heading a convoy of five cars driving along icy roads to the Austrian frontier. Once there she bought all the food she could – and drove back to Budapest.

One more woman had joined the band of refugees in the British Legation – the once-dedicated Communist Dora Scarlett. Torn by principles in which she believed, treachery she had seen at work, her love for Hungary, Dora realised she must leave. She no longer wanted to work for the radio, and though she would gladly have remained in some non-political post she knew she would never be granted the necessary resident's permit.

'No one knew yet whether the new government would be lenient or resort to terror,' she remembers thinking, for 'its statements and general conduct pointed to vacillation between the two.' After what she had heard from the lips of people in the markets and in the streets, 'I could not bring myself to pretend support for the Kadar government.'

The radio station was in such a shambles that when she wrote out her letter of resignation she could not find anyone to hand it to, so she simply left it on a desk. Then she went to the British Legation, where she remained until she left in a convoy on Thursday, 15 November, one of eighteen people sitting on chairs ranged round the sides of a truck, with their luggage piled in the centre. A Union Jack was draped over the canvas cover, and the only window through which Dora Scarlett could peep was a tiny square cut in the canvas.

Along the roads they passed people walking towards Austria, who waved and occasionally held out a letter, hoping they would stop. They did not dare to, for they had been warned that if they helped Hungarians it could lead to trouble, not so much for the convoy as for the civilians.

They passed through the mining town of Dorog; the pits were still on strike and all the townspeople seemed to be in the streets. In all they passed ten Soviet checkpoints before reaching Hegyeshalom, near the frontier.

Here the roads were empty except for an occasional cart rumbling over the cobbles and geese paddling in the mud. The refugees were waiting for nightfall, and as the convoy reached the frontier in drizzling rain the desolate empty scene made Dora Scarlett feel that 'it looked as if life had come to a standstill'.

Dora Scarlett's journey from Hungary was relatively orderly. Others were not so fortunate. Many of the 200,000 who fled barely succeeded in penetrating the Soviet screen guarding the Austrian frontier. Hundreds of children, identified only by labels round their necks, were separated from their parents.

Along the border the Russians stalked the fleeing refugees, particularly on the deathly still, frost-bitten zone by the Neusiedlersee, a reed-filled lake separating Hungary from Austria. Hungarians hid in the reeds, waist deep in icy water, while marauding patrols hunted them. When the sounds of the pursuers grew faint, the wraith-like figures straggled towards the frontier. For many, hope vanished with the sudden bursting light of a star shell that illuminated, with blinding brilliance, every crouching form.

Seymour Freidin met one man who reached Vienna with his wife and two children, but was upset because he had left two brothers, one paralysed, and his sister and their children behind. Unarmed and alone, he sneaked back across the border, reached Budapest and organised an escape that was little short of a miracle. Three days later he reached the frontier again, a modern Pied Piper leading not only his family but his neighbours – twenty-four people in all, the youngest only thirteen months, who, like his paralysed brother, was carried by the men in relays on a makeshift litter.

Among those who escaped across the swamp was George Paloczi-Horvath, one of the writers on the Russian 'wanted list' who felt that 'our ranks were already decimated by arrests and deportations'.

Paloczi-Horvath had a wife and a year-old son; he dared not

risk a challenge by the Russians or the Avo, so he chose the swampy lake. He made a fur sack for the baby. A doctor gave him a sleeping draught to give the baby at the critical time. At the last minute they were joined by another writer – and former cell-mate – Pal Ignotus, and his wife.

In the end, the party totalled thirty-three men, women and children, who set off into the swamp on a stormy night, wading knee deep in mud and water, with each step 'an enormous physical effort'. Paloczi-Horvath carried his son on his shoulder, and with his wife at his side struggled on for several hours until they were forced to rest. They found a piece of land where the mud was only ankle deep. After an hour they started walking again, struggling in the swamp for another two hours. 'Then at last an Austrian flag – and a haystack! We collapsed.'

Jozsef Kovago, his wife Lonci and their young daughter also escaped across the Austrian frontier. Before leaving, Kovago paid one last visit to Bela Kovacs and tried to persuade him to flee, but Kovacs insisted on remaining. As he was taking his leave, Kovago turned to him and said, 'Well, we both happen to love our country and that is enough.'

'Yes, that's enough.' Bela Kovacs gave him 'a happy smile' and added, 'It would be less dangerous to prefer fishing.'

The Kovagos started out from Budapest's East Station in a train so crowded that people were hanging on the steps. One small knapsack held all their possessions. Near the frontier they hid for a night in a friendly farmer's haystack while the Russians searched the nearby house, then the following night set off on a ten-mile walk 'through cornfields, half frozen mud, woods and irrigation ditches. The icy wind chilled us to the bone. Every step meant an effort to disengage our feet from the heavy clay.' When search-lights stabbed the ground ahead, everyone lay flattened in the thick mud. Finally their guide pointed to a light twinkling at the other side of a field. It was the first village in Austria, and they reached it almost at the end of their strength. Only Catherine, their seven-year-old daughter, enjoyed the adventure. 'Can we do it again some time?' she asked.

Anna Gabor escaped by car – or, to be precise, half a car by the time she reached Austria. Once *Truth* had stopped printing, she was offered a lift by two Western correspondents who from time to time used the *Truth* offices. One had been wounded when his car was shot up, and had decided to leave the hospital in his pyjamas and a couple of blankets. His car had no heat. The glass in front had been shattered. When they reached the frontier beyond Hegyeshalom, a Soviet tank lay astride the road, and they were told to go back. All arguments were futile. The driver of the car in front of them, after being ordered back, mistakenly put his car into forward gear. The car moved forward only a couple of feet. According to Anna, 'The Russian officer didn't even bother to take the cigarette out of his mouth as he barked out an order. The man was ordered out of his car, the tank moved forward, and while the driver watched aghast, nonchalantly crushed the front of his car to bits.'

Anna Gabor and her friends decided to make for an isolated part of the frontier, hoping it would be unguarded. They were right, but they had to cross a strip of ploughed earth marking the frontier and the injured man was too weak from loss of blood to walk. Still, they had to take the car. 'It looked so easy,' Anna Gabor remembers. 'Only a few yards away across the ploughed earth was a row of little red and white Austrian flags, planted as neatly as the markers on a running track.' One of the men backed the car into a field, revved up the motor, and roared towards the ploughed earth at top speed. It sank into the mud almost immediately. Fearful of Soviet armoured car search squads, they dared not abandon the car, but had to try to get it out of the ploughed earth and drive further along until they found an easier crossing.

'Time after time we almost got the car back on to level ground, but each time it slid off the last furrow,' says Anna Gabor. They took the blankets in which the injured man was swathed and packed them under the rear wheel; when this proved ineffectual, they took out the back seat and tried to reverse over it. The seat snapped like a matchstick. Finally they smashed up the inside of the car, ripping out all the metal sheeting and woodwork with spanners, packed it under the wheels 'and then by a miracle we got the car on to dry ground'.

Two tyres were punctured, but the car lurched westwards across mined fields for twelve miles until they found a crossing where the ploughed earth had been beaten hard by constant use, and this time, aided by two Hungarians who heaved and pushed, drove the car across, and abandoned it ten yards inside Austria.

Mark Molnar almost ended up in Siberia. After leaving Csepel he hid for several days in the tiny flat of the girlfriend with whom he had dined on the night of 23 October, and whom he had not seen since he went out to buy fresh hot bread for their breakfast. Now she had another girlfriend staying in the flat, and both wanted to try to reach Austria. Mark decided to go out and see what was happening. He jumped on his old bicycle, skidded, and all but ran into a policeman.

No one was hurt, Mark apologised, the Hungarian policeman assured him no harm was done, but then, in the routine manner of all policemen the world over, he asked to see Mark's bicycle licence (obligatory in Hungary). Mark did not have one – and spent the night in jail. By chance the Russians visited it, and promptly sentenced him to ten years' hard labour in Siberia. The next day, with thirty other prisoners, he was loaded on a truck which drove off to the cattle train that would take him to a labour camp.

The driver was Hungarian, the guards two heavily armed Mongol Soviets. The driver handled the truck like a madman, swerving, twisting, nearly overturning. The Mongols banged on the back of his cab with their rifle butts. The prisoners were thrown about with each new crazy swerve. What Mark did not know was that two tough Hungarians had arranged with the driver to try to escape, and this was their only hope.

Finally at one corner the truck slewed round, and as everyone fell the two Hungarians grabbed the Mongols and literally threw them out of the truck. It was as simple as that.

The truck careered on for a few more blocks, then all the prisoners scrambled out. Mark made for his girlfriend's flat and the three took the next train to Gyor, spent the night there and finally got a lift to Sopron in a police jeep, driven by an amorous Hungarian policeman who wanted to date the second girl.

She pretended to agree, and they made a rendezvous to meet in a café at eight in the evening. She had, of course, no intention of keeping the appointment, so the three fugitives had to hide until dark; they in fact spent their last night on Hungarian soil at the local cinema. After midnight they made for the village of Agfalva and crossed into Austria.

Like Molnar, young Thomas Szabo also escaped via Sopron – and also narrowly escaped deportation. After evacuating the school, he reported to a new headquarters in Landler Street, only to find it swarming with Russians. Before Szabo could escape, he was bundled into a Russian military truck with about thirty boys and girls and then locked up for the night in a freight car at the East Station. During the night there was an outburst of firing, someone tore open the doors of the wagon by firing off the locks, and shouted, 'Make yourselves scarce!'

Thomas ran all the way home and it was his father who insisted that he must leave the country immediately. He gave Thomas 500 forints, and after a tearful goodbye to his mother Thomas set off first for Gyor, then Sopron, finally crossing into Austria near the small village of Saarfold.

Tibor Meray, to whom Nagy had confided so many fascinating details of the revolution, decided to make for Yugoslavia, with his wife Joy, their two-year-old baby daughter, and Tibor's writer friend Tamas Aczel.

They laid their plans carefully. All of them had valid passports issued to them just before the revolution in order to attend a football match in Vienna which was cancelled when the fighting broke out. As an international journalist and writer of repute, Meray had many valuable contacts, and he now decided to put one of them to the test: a high official in the Yugoslav embassy.

He asked him to frank all their passports with Yugoslav visas, then, taking a deep breath, he added, 'I would be eternally grateful if you ante-date the visas to early October.'

As Meray remembered later, 'The Yugoslavs were very decent,' and he got the visas, though they could do nothing about the Soviet exit permit which was also needed by everyone leaving the country. That was a problem they would have to deal with at the border.

Aczel had a small white Skoda car he had bought with money presented to him with his Stalin Prize for literature; it was so small that no one could take any luggage. Meray took only one thing with him – a book signed by Nagy. Almost as an afterthought, Aczel took his Stalin Prize certificate.

They drove to Szeged without incident, then chose a lonely frontier crossing a few miles further south. It was guarded by only three Soviet soldiers, but they flatly refused to allow them through without an exit permit. For three hours they argued in vain, until Aczel had an idea. From the back of the car he fished out his Stalin Prize certificate. Here was something the Russians could read, a document in Russian proving Aczel to be a man honoured personally by Stalin. Fascinated, the soldiers stared at the great man's signature. Their scowls turned into smiles, their threatening gestures into respectful salutes. Minutes later the little white Skoda was bowling along a road in Yugoslavia.

Among the last to leave in November was General Kiraly.

A week after the General had moved his headquarters to Nagy-kovacsi, west of Budapest, the Soviet High Command discovered its location, launched a tank attack, supported by artillery and infantry. In what is still known in Hungary as 'the bloody battle of Nagykovacsi', Kiraly's headquarters withdrew in the night after heavy losses.

He bivouacked on ridges in the mountains behind. Soviet helicopters hovered overhead, tracking their line of retreat. 'Anxiously we listened to foreign radio broadcasts,' Kiraly remembers, 'waiting and hoping for an eventual change that somehow would force the Soviet Union to negotiate with Imre Nagy after all. We hoped that then we could offer him again the services of the only surviving central organ, the headquarters of the National Guard and the Revolutionary Council of National Defence, to help him to rebuild from the ruins.'

Hope faded as the days passed, until Kiraly was faced with the last bitter realisation: 'If there was no place for Imre Nagy and for his political solution, there could not be any place for us.'

He gave orders for his group of fighters to disperse and cross into Austria in small numbers. This they did, so that Kiraly at least did not give the Russians the satisfaction of a Hungarian surrender.

17

The Final Murder

Friday, 23 November – and after

One man had no thought of escape. During all the days of fighting and defeat, Imre Nagy and his colleagues remained in the sanctuary of the Yugoslav embassy at the end of Andrassy Street, facing the City Park. A white three-storey building with a glass porch over the front door, the embassy stood in its own garden, lined with a low privet hedge, and protected from the busy street by six-feet high iron railings. It was in this garden that the Hungarians took their exercise.

They were already making plans for the future, in the hope that a political settlement would be reached. Soldatitch, the Yugoslav ambassador, received personal orders from Tito to allow Nagy every consideration, and this enabled Nagy and his followers to declare themselves the administrative committee of the Party – a step they had a legal right to take because five of the seven members of the committee were in the embassy. Among those present at the meeting was Szilard Ujhelyi who had this to say about the meeting:

> This meeting took place after Geza Losonczy came back from seeing Soldatitch. He invited the members of the administrative committee who were present – namely, Zoltan Szanto. Gyorgy Lukacs, Ferenc Donath and Sandor Haraszti – to meet in Soldatitch's office. So far as Haraszti was concerned, Losonczy made the remark that though he was not a member of the committee, he could participate in his role as director of the party's central organ ... Imre Nagy was already in the ambassador's office. I know from Losonczy that no minutes

were kept of the meeting, but the debate was later summarised and recorded by Losonczy. It was also he who declared that the administrative committee had drafted a plan for a solution after the events of November 4.[1]

Yet it must have been a difficult and depressing time for all of them after the exhilaration of the revolution – foreigners cooped up on one floor of the building with little to do in the midst of the bustling life of an embassy. They had to be content with their own company, and not all of the wives were disposed to one another. Added to this, gnawing questions which could never be answered tormented them: had they acted wisely in accepting asylum? And should they remain in the embassy or take their chances of escaping?

Like many others Julia Rajk was so depressed that she sought advice on this question from Bela Szasz. She sent Szasz a letter carried by Mila Gerogavitch, a Yugoslav counsellor only too eager to help. She asked Szasz simply, should she leave the embassy? Szasz replied equally directly, 'Come out. There is no point in staying with the Yugoslavs. Nobody will dare to touch you of all people.' But as Szasz commented later, 'Womanlike she sought my advice and then refused to take it. She would have fared better had she come out.'

Possibly with forebodings about his own fate, Nagy was anxious that the long articles he had written when dismissed from the Party should reach the West, and once again a Yugoslav embassy official obliged. Nagy gave him the keys to his empty house in Orso Street, and explained in detail where the manuscript could be found. The diplomat collected it and it was published first in Yugoslavia and later in Western Europe.

Nagy also gave one extraordinary interview to a Yugoslav journalist while in the embassy. The journalist could not use it while Nagy was a guest of his country, but he handed it to a Hungarian diplomat, Gabor von Szarka. When von Szarka escaped to the West, he gave it to the German newspaper *Bildzeitung* with a guarantee of its authenticity. In the interview Nagy admitted, 'The revolution went far beyond its aims and that is why it failed. When it started, our people wanted nothing else

[1] At the trial of Nagy, recorded in Kadar's *White Book*, vol. 5.

than equality with other independent people. At first I thought I could speak openly with the Russians. It proved to be wrong.'

It is hard to know the true feelings of Janos Kadar during Nagy's asylum. He cannot have been comforted by the knowledge that the hero of the uprising was living only a few blocks from Party headquarters, and the country still worshipped him. In an attempt to win popularity and break the strike which was strangling the country's economy, Kadar received streams of workers' delegations, and all demanded news of Nagy. On 13 November, he admitted to a group that he did not believe 'that Nagy had knowingly aided the counter-revolution, but that he had been overwhelmed by events'. One worker asked bluntly, 'What has happened to Imre Nagy?'

'Imre Nagy is not being held,' Kadar assured him. 'He left Parliament building of his own free will. Neither the Government nor the Soviet troops had any desire to restrict his freedom of movement. It is up to Nagy alone as to whether he will participate in political life.'

The following day, when Kadar received a delegation from the Budapest Central Workers' Council, he made one significant remark. 'I can state definitely', he told them, 'that nobody will be punished for having taken part in the great popular movement of last week.'

One of the workers asked if he could meet Nagy.

'Imre Nagy is still in Budapest,' replied Kadar, 'but he's in a foreign embassy from which he asked for asylum. While he is there we can't negotiate with him. As soon as he leaves and returns to Hungarian soil, we will consult with him and arrive at an agreement.' To another delegate he said with apparent disarming frankness, 'I'll be glad to talk to Imre Nagy at any time, and he can always have a seat in my cabinet. It's up to him to decide.'

No guarantees of Nagy's future could have been more explicit, and perhaps Kadar genuinely believed in what he was saying. But Kadar was a tool of the Russians, particularly of Andropov, who was not only ambassador but also a member of the KGB. Andropov, today head of the entire KGB organisation, certainly showed great aptitude. Sending for Kadar, he warned him that there was no room in Hungary for both Kadar and Nagy. It would split the people. He suggested that Nagy would be better out of the way, preferably in Romania, and told Kadar to suggest this. If Kadar could not persuade Nagy to go to Romania, then they would have to make other plans.

When Kadar next met with the Yugoslavs, he suggested Romania as a country of asylum. They had no objection, but the decision could only be made by the refugees; and the Hungarians refused to discuss the question. 'We want to stay in Hungary if possible,' declared Geza Losonczy, 'but if that proves impossible, then we would prefer to live in Yugoslavia – a Communist country that isn't under Soviet domination.'

All agreed that guarantees of safety would be necessary if they remained in Hungary and on Friday, 16 November, Kadar appeared to agree. No one, he assured them, would be persecuted. Knowing that Tito was watching every move from Belgrade, the Yugoslav ambassador decided that he needed written guarantees, and drove to Kadar's office to watch him sign them. When he arrived, however, Kadar presented him with some new conditions, among them a demand that Nagy and Losonczy must make a public confession of error.

Nagy was outraged at the thought of being humiliated by the man who had betrayed him and had no compunction in saying so. At this point Tito intervened personally, for he was getting impatient at the prolonged stay of his Hungarian visitors, and did not wish to become too involved. Though he had supported Nagy at first, he had – while Nagy was in the Yugoslav embassy – made a speech saying that Nagy had not been strong enough. It would be better for all concerned, he said, if Nagy left the embassy, and to this end despatched his deputy Foreign Minister, Doubrivoje Vidic, to Budapest. Before leaving, Vidic was told by Tito to see Kadar personally, and to be sure to get cast-iron guarantees of safety for the Hungarians. There were only two ways, Tito said, in which the problem could be solved. The Nagy group could be given a guarantee of personal safety and return to their homes. The alternative was to allow them asylum in Yugoslavia, a step to which Tito had no objection.

Vidic's arrival with these proposals forced Kadar to forget his earlier demands. After talking to Vidic he agreed to guarantee the safety of Nagy and his colleagues. It is only presumption, but Kadar must surely have consulted with Andropov, who must have also agreed – for the moment. So, on 21 November, in a formal letter to the Government of Yugoslavia, Kadar wrote:

> In order to settle this affair the Hungarian Government, in conformity with the proposal contained in the Yugoslav Government's letter to me of 18 November 1956, repeats herewith the assurance already given several times by word of mouth that it has no desire to punish Imre Nagy and the members of his group in any way for their past activities. We therefore expect the asylum granted by the Yugoslav embassy to this group to be withdrawn and that its members will return to their homes.

No guarantee could have seemed more clear-cut, and it had the added advantage of being addressed to a foreign power which had assumed responsibility for the safety of Nagy and the others. The Hungarians telephoned their friends asking them to prepare for their arrival on Friday evening. 'We'll be home for supper,' Nagy told one of them.

Late on the afternoon of Friday, 23 November, the group signed a joint letter of thanks to the Yugoslav ambassador, while Ferenc Munnich, Kadar's deputy premier, sent a bus to the embassy to transport the group to their homes. It arrived around 6.30 p.m.

Nagy was strolling in the embassy gardens, and as he walked towards the gate a Hungarian police officer saluted and then, under the pretence of shaking hands, whispered, 'Take care, sir. You are not going home.'

An astonished Nagy returned into the building and told the ambassador, who immediately decided to send two Yugoslav diplomats in the bus. One was Gerogavitch, who had carried Julia Rajk's letter, the other was Milan Drobac, the military attaché.

Nagy walked back towards the gates, then outside into the street. Several Soviet tanks were parked nearby, but that was hardly remarkable for most diplomatic buildings were still being guarded – or watched. One thing, however, horrified Nagy.

Calmly sitting in the bus waiting for the Hungarians were several officers of the Soviet MVD police.

Nagy announced flatly that on no account would he board the bus unless the Russian police got out. The Yugoslav military attaché joined in the argument. So did Soldatitch who had arrived at the gates to bid Nagy a personal goodbye. Finally the MVD police climbed out of the bus and stood on the pavement.

The Hungarian women and children climbed into the bus first. Nagy took a seat near a window on the right-hand side. The two Yugoslav diplomats sat near the exit door. The driver revved up the motor. As the bus was actually beginning to move off, two Soviet policemen jumped back on board. As they did so, a Soviet police car suddenly appeared alongside the bus as it gathered speed. Another trailed it. The Yugoslav diplomats indignantly protested at the violation of the Hungarian–Yugoslav agreement. A Soviet officer replied that the agreement was no concern of his, and he had his orders to take the passengers in charge. When the Yugoslavs continued to argue, the Russians simply forced them to leave the bus. As Gerogavitch told Miklos Molnar later than same evening, 'We had hardly gone a couple of hundred yards when the bus stopped and the Russians physically pulled us both from the bus.'

The bus drove off in the direction of Gorki Street, but when it reached the house of one of the Hungarians, Sandor Haraszti, it drove straight past his front door. At this moment the two escorting police cars were replaced by two armoured vehicles. The men shouted. Some banged the glass behind the driver's seat. The youngsters, instinctively sensing the tension, began to whimper and tug their mothers' skirts. All the time the two Soviet policemen remained perfectly calm. Sharing a bench seat near the exit, they said and did nothing as the Hungarians cried out in despair.

Finally the bus drew up in front of a building requisitioned by the Soviet High Command. A lieutenant was waiting. He ordered the passengers to enter the building, waved aside all protests, and warned that anyone attempting to escape would be shot.

Nagy refused to get out of the bus. Two burly Russian soldiers climbed aboard, seized him, pulled him out and hustled him through the big oak entrance doors.

Hungary was stunned by the news; Kadar would no doubt have preferred to keep the sordid affray secret, but the Yugoslavs, outraged at the physical violence used against members of its embassy, and at the manner in which they had been hoodwinked when acting as honest brokers between the two Hungarian factions, would not allow it. Soldatitch warned Kadar that his country was issuing a Note of protest in the strongest possible terms – at which Kadar decided to issue a communiqué first. It announced:

> It is well known that Imre Nagy, former premier, and several of his followers asked the Yugoslav embassy on November 4 to extend to them the right of asylum. This was granted them. The right of asylum expired on November 22. For more than two weeks Imre Nagy and his comrades had been asking the Hungarian Government for permission to leave the territory of the Hungarian People's Republic and to go to another Socialist country. Permission to go there having been granted by the government of the Romanian People's Republic, Imre Nagy and his comrades left November 23 for that country.

None believed it. The Yugoslav Note made public what most people already felt,

> The Yugoslav Government is entirely unable to accept the account that Mr Nagy and the other Hungarian personalities left for Romania of their own free will. The Yugoslav Government was aware that they wished to remain in their own country; it also knew that while they were in the Yugoslav embassy at Budapest they had rejected the proposal that they should go to Romania.

The abduction had of course been masterminded by Andropov, and three days later Kadar spoke on the radio in a naïve attempt to cover up. The action against Nagy, he said, had been taken for his own safety, for 'we had reason to believe that counter-revolutionary elements still at large might resort to provocation, killing Nagy or one of his collaborators'.

To Pal Ignotus, listening in, 'there had never been a premier in such a pathetic position – compelled so conspicuously to spit in his own face'.

For more than eighteen months the ordinary Hungarian had no idea where Nagy was living, or even if he were dead. Nagy and his group had in fact gone to Romania after all – or, to be more precise, had been taken there against their will by Soviet troops. Once in Bucharest they were placed under house arrest in a villa standing in its own grounds (which they were at liberty to use) on the outskirts of the capital.

Yet the shabby episode had had such sinister overtones that none believed the official announcements, even when the Romanian foreign minister, Grigore Preoteosa, told the United Nations in December that Nagy was in his country 'as a temporary measure' enjoying 'the benefits of all the rights of political asylum'.

So many Communists had told so many bare-faced lies to the UN delegates that few people could rid their minds of the suspicion that this was yet another lie. And people were hardly reassured by Preoteosa's final, fatuous remark, 'I can also state to the Assembly that the attitude of Imre Nagy and his group is characterised by good humour and understanding.'

There were many other rumours. According to one report, the group had been jailed in the Romanian dungeons at Doftna. A released prisoner swore he had met Nagy briefly in the corridor of a Budapest jail on his way to interrogation. Another report insisted that the group was living in luxury in Sinaia, in the former summer palace of the Romanian kings.

Nothing was confirmed until the night of 16–17 June 1958. Then came the horrifying climax to the months of silence, broken to an anguished Hungarian nation in a chilling announcement on Radio Budapest and Radio Moscow. Imre Nagy had been executed.

According to the communiqué, eight others had been brought to trial with him. They were Pal Maleter, Ferenc Donath, Miklos

Gimes, Zoltan Tildy, Sandor Kopacsi, Ferenc Janosi, Jozsef Szilagyi and Miklos Vasarhelyi. In addition to Nagy, Maleter, Gimes, Szilagyi were executed. Kopacsi was jailed for life, Donath for twelve years, Janosi for eight, Vasarhelyi for five, Zoltan Tildy for six. Hungarians were aghast to learn that the patriot Tildy was in jail, for his arrest had never been announced. It became public only with the news of his sentence.

The communiqué also announced that Geza Losonczy had 'meanwhile died of an illness'. The nature of the ailment was never specified – understandably, for Losonczy, who suffered from severe pulmonary trouble, was killed 'by mistake' while on a hunger strike, after a clumsy doctor, trying to force a tube down his throat, had pierced his remaining lung.

The final words of the communiqué were, 'The sentences are final, with no right of appeal. The death sentences have been executed.'

The communiqué made no mention of the name of the prosecutor, the counsel for defence, the witnesses called. Nor did it make any mention of the fate of the women and children. (Not until December was it announced that they had been allowed to return to Hungary.) Apart from the absurd nature of the charges (Nagy, for instance, was accused of having made a secret pact with Mindszenty) the communiqué brazenly ignored the manner in which international law had been violated.

Communists in Western countries were shocked beyond belief. In Italy Pietro Neni publicly renounced his Stalin Prize. 'The executions', he cried, 'have re-opened old wounds and poured into them the salt of hate.' In France the Communist Henri Lefebvre wrote, 'A great man has just been killed, coldly and at a moment calculated in advance to serve as a warning to the world.' In London, that ardent Communist leader Arthur Horner of the Mineworkers' Union said, 'I can keep silent no longer. The fact that Imre Nagy and his companions have been assassinated is horrible and absurd.'

But, as Tibor Meray, his old friend, felt, 'Neither the anger nor the indignation, neither the protests nor the anguish, could do anything more for Imre Nagy. He was dead. He had to die, not because the accusations against him were true.... It was the price – terribly high but fully sublime – of a revolution that was victorious in itself. He had to die because, in a system that would not tolerate them, he wanted to give his people liberty and independence. He wanted to give to the workers of Hungary more bread and help them to live like human beings.'

Few details are known of the trial, which lasted twelve days in early June, but Gyula Hay, whose daring articles had so fired the enthusiasm of Hungarian youth, was also in the new secret police headquarters in Fo Street and saw part of it.

One day his cell door was opened and he was led to the courtroom to testify on behalf of Zoltan Tildy. Nagy was in court, but at first Hay could hardly make out any faces for, as he remembered later, 'I was in full light and around me a wall of light surrounded me like a cube.' Hay was not a witness at Nagy's trial, but after his testimony the judge asked Nagy if he wanted to question him. Nagy stood up, walked towards Hay, looked long at him, and 'with hardly a noticeable smile' said simply, 'Thank you. I have nothing to ask.'

Slowly the trial dragged on to its predetermined end, a sordid, shabby epilogue to a revolution in which thousands of young Hungarians – figures vary from 4000 to Nehru's estimate of 25,000 – were killed, and tens of thousands deported to Soviet labour camps.

When the judge turned to Nagy and pronounced the death sentence, the elderly, jovial-looking man with flowing moustaches, a dedicated Communist for forty years, stood up, and in his last words gave his verdict on the cause and country he loved with equal passion. With the quiet dignity he had maintained throughout the trial, he said:

I have twice tried to save the honour and image of Communism in the Danubian valley, once in 1953 and again in 1956. Rakosi and the Russians prevented me from doing so. If my life is needed to prove that not all Communists are enemies of the people, I gladly make the sacrifice. I know there will one day be another Nagy trial, which will rehabilitate me. I also know I will have a reburial. I only fear that the funeral oration will be delivered by those who betrayed me.

Then the college professor – and ardent soccer fan – who had become 'a flaming revolutionary' almost by accident, almost against his wishes, carefully adjusted his *pince nez* and quietly sat down.

Eighteen years later Hungary is still a Soviet state and Janos Kadar is still its puppet ruler. But the uprising was not in vain. For a few glorious days it gave notice to the free world that the Hungarian pen was mightier than the Soviet sword. And it proved something else: that even when the youth of a country is indoctrinated for years, when it is handpicked almost from birth to be trained as tomorrow's Communist élite, no alien master can obliterate the desire for freedom that lies in everyone. It needed only a spark – provided by the writers – to send the youngsters of Hungary in their thousands to man the barricades, to fight and often to die in an uprising of youth triumphant.

Appendices

Bibliography

Index

APPENDIX I

The Students' Sixteen-point Demand

1. We demand the immediate evacuation of all Soviet troops, in conformity with the provisions of the Treaty of Peace.

2. We demand the election by secret ballot of all Party members from top to bottom, and of new officers for the lower, middle, and upper echelons of the Hungarian Workers' Party. These officers shall convoke a Party Congress as early as possible in order to elect a Central Committee.

3. A new Government must be constituted under the direction of Comrade Imre Nagy; all the criminal leaders of the Stalin–Rakosi era must be immediately relieved of their duties.

4. We demand a public enquiry into the criminal activities of Milhaly Farkhas and his accomplices. Matyas Rakosi, who is the person most responsible for all the crimes of the recent past, as well as for the ruin of our country, must be brought back to Hungary for trial before a people's tribunal.

5. We demand that general elections, by universal, secret ballot, be held throughout the country to elect a new National Assembly, with all political parties participating. We demand that the right of the workers to strike be recognised.

6. We demand revision and readjustment of Hungarian–Soviet and Hungarian–Yugoslav relations in the fields of politics, economics, and cultural affairs, on a basis of complete political and economic equality and of non-interference in the internal affairs of one by the other.

7. We demand the complete reorganisation of Hungary's economic life under the direction of specialists. The entire economic system, based on a system of planning, must be re-

examined in the light of conditions in Hungary and in the vital interests of the Hungarian people.

8. Our foreign trade agreements and the exact total of reparations that can never be paid must be made public. We demand precise and exact information on the uranium deposits in our country, on their exploitation, and on the concessions accorded the Russians in this area. We demand that Hungary have the right to sell her uranium freely at world market prices to obtain hard currency.

9. We demand complete revision of the norms in effect in industry and an immediate and radical adjustment of salaries in accordance with the just requirements of workers and intellectuals. We demand that a minimum living wage be fixed for workers.

10. We demand that the system of distribution be organised on a new basis and that agricultural products be utilised in a rational manner. We demand equality of treatment for individual farms.

11. We demand reviews by independent tribunals of all political and economic trials as well as the release and rehabilitation of the innocent. We demand the immediate repatriation of prisoners of war and of civilian deportees in the Soviet Union, including prisoners sentenced outside Hungary.

12. We demand complete recognition of freedom of opinion and of expression, of freedom of the press and of radio, as well as the creation of a new daily newspaper for the MEFESZ Organisation [Hungarian Federation of University and College Students' Associations].

13. We demand that the statue of Stalin, symbol of Stalinist tyranny and political oppression, be removed as quickly as possible and be replaced by a monument to the memory of the martyred fighters for freedom of 1848–9.

14. We demand the replacement of the emblems that are foreign to the Hungarian people by the old Hungarian arms of Kossuth. We demand for the Hungarian army new uniforms conforming to our national traditions. We demand that the fifteenth of March be declared a national holiday and that the sixth of October be a day of national mourning on which schools will be closed.

15. The students of the Technological University of Budapest declare unanimously their solidarity with the workers and students of Warsaw and Poland in their movement towards national independence.

16. The students of the Technological University of Budapest will organise as rapidly as possible local branches of the MEFESZ, and they have decided to convoke at Budapest, on Saturday, October 27, a Youth Parliament at which all the nation's youth will be represented by their delegates.

APPENDIX II

Nagy's 'Cease Fighting' Speech, 24 October

People of Budapest, I announce that all those who cease fighting before 14.00 today, and lay down their arms in the interest of avoiding further bloodshed, will be exempted from martial law. At the same time I state that, as soon as possible and by all the means at our disposal, we shall realise, on the basis of the June 1953 Government programme which I expounded in Parliament at that time, the systematic democratisation of our country in every sphere of Party, State, political and economic life. Heed our appeal! Cease fighting, and secure the restoration of calm and order in the interest of the future of our people and nation. Return to peaceful and creative work!

Hungarians, comrades, my friends! I speak to you in a moment filled with responsibility. As you know, on the basis of the confidence of the Central Committee of the Hungarian Workers' Party and the Presidential Council, I have taken over the leadership of the Government as Chairman of the Council of Ministers. Every possibility exists for the Government to realise my political programme by relying on the Hungarian people under the leadership of the Communists. The essence of this programme, as you know, is the far-reaching democratisation of Hungarian public life, the realisation of a Hungarian road to socialism in accord with our own national characteristics, and the realisation of our lofty national aim: the radical improvement of the workers' living conditions.

However, in order to begin this work – together with you – the first necessity is to establish order, discipline and calm. The hostile elements that joined the ranks of peacefully demonstrating Hungarian youth, misled many well-meaning workers and turned against the people's democracy, against the power of the people. The paramount task facing everyone now is the urgent consolidation of our position. Afterwards, we shall be able to discuss every question, since the Government and the majority of the Hungarian people want the same thing. In referring to our great common responsibility for our national existence, I appeal to you, to every man, woman, youth, worker, peasant, and intellectual to stand fast and keep calm; resist provocation, help restore order, and assist our forces in maintaining order. Together we must prevent bloodshed, and we must not let this sacred national programme be soiled by blood.

The Hungarian Government is preparing for peaceful and creative work. The Government is determined not to allow itself to be diverted from the road of democratisation, from realising a programme corresponding with the interests of the Hungarian people and discussed with the broad masses of the people. We do not want to pursue a policy of revenge but of reconciliation. For this reason the Government has decided that all those who voluntarily and immediately lay down arms and cease fighting will not be subjected to summary prosecution, as is the case with groups which have so far surrendered.

Workers! Defend the factories and machines. This is your own treasure. He who destroys or loots harms the entire nation. Order, calm, discipline – these are now the slogans; they come before everything else.

Friends! Hungarians! I will soon announce in detail the programme of the Government, and it will be debated in the National Assembly which will meet soon. Our future is at stake. Before us lies the great road of raising our national standards. Line up behind the Government. Ensure peace, the continuation of peaceful and creative labour, so that every worker of our country can work undisturbed for his own and his family's future. Stand behind the Party, stand behind the Government! Trust that we have learned from the mistakes of the past, and that we shall find the correct road for the prosperity of our country.

APPENDIX III

The Soviet '30 October Declaration'

The unchangeable foundation of Soviet foreign relations has been and remains a policy of peaceful coexistence, of friendship, and of collaboration with all other states.

The most profound and the clearest expression of this policy is to be found in the relations between the socialist countries. Linked together by the common goal of building a socialist society and by the principles of proletariat internationalism, the countries of the great community of socialist nations can base their relations only on the principles of complete equality of rights, of respect for territorial integrity, of political independence and sovereignty, and of non-interference in the internal affairs of one state by the other. This does not preclude, but on the contrary assumes, a close fraternal collaboration and a mutual assistance between the countries of the socialist community in economic, political, and cultural matters.

It was on this foundation that, after World War II and the collapse of fascism, the democratic people's regime leaped ahead. It was on this foundation that the regime was strengthened and that it was enabled to demonstrate its vitality throughout numerous European and Asian countries.

In the course of establishing the new regime and in the course of establishing deep revolutionary changes in socialist relations, there have come to light several difficulties, several unsolved problems, and several downright mistakes, including mistakes in the relations among socialist states. These violations and these mistakes have demeaned the principle of equal rights in socialist interstate relationships.

The Twentieth Congress of the Communist Party of the Soviet Union strongly condemned these violations and errors and decided that the Soviet Union would base its relations with the other socialist countries on the strict Lenin principles of equal rights for the people. The Congress proclaimed the need for taking into account the history and the individual peculiarities of each country on its way towards building a new life.

The Soviet Government has systematically applied the historic decisions of the Twentieth Congress in creating the conditions for strengthening the amity and the co-operation between socialist countries. It has based its application of these decisions on the firm foundation of complete respect for the sovereignty of each socialist state.

As recent events have shown, it is apparently necessary to declare the position of the Soviet Union concerning its relations with the other socialist countries, and, above all, concerning its economic and military relations with such countries.

The Soviet Government is prepared to examine, along with the governments of the other socialist states, the measures that will make possible the further development and reinforcement of economic ties between the socialist countries, in order to remove any possibility of interference with the principles of national sovereignty, of reciprocal interest, and of equality of rights in economic agreements.

This principle must also be extended to cover the question of advisors. It is well known that during the period just past, when the new socialist regime was being formed, the Soviet Union, at the request of the governments of the people's democracies has sent into these countries many specialists, many engineers, and many agronomists and scientists and military advisors. Recently, the Soviet Government has frequently proposed to the socialist states the question of withdrawing those advisors.

Inasmuch as the people's democracies have trained their own personnel, who are now qualified to handle all economic and military matters, the Soviet Government believes that it is necessary to reconsider, together with the other socialist states, the question of whether it is still advantageous to maintain these advisors of the USSR in these countries.

As far as the military domain is concerned, an important basis for relations between the USSR and the people's democracies has been provided by the Warsaw Pact, under which the signatories have made political and military commitments with each other. They have committed themselves, in particular, to take 'those concerted measures which are deemed necessary for the reinforcement of their capabilities for protecting the peaceful employment of their people, for guaranteeing the integrity of their frontiers and their territories, and for assuring their defence against any aggression.'

It is well known that, under the Warsaw Pact and under agreements between the governments, Soviet troops are stationed in the republics of Hungary and Romania. In the republic of Poland, Soviet troops are stationed under the terms of the Potsdam Agreement with the other great powers, as well as under the terms of the Warsaw Pact. There are no Soviet troops in the other people's democracies.

In order to insure the mutual security of the socialist countries, the Soviet Government is prepared to review with the other socialist countries signing the Warsaw Pact the question of Soviet troops stationed on the territory of the above-mentioned countries.

In doing so, the Soviet Government proceeds from the principle that the stationing of troops of one member state of the Warsaw Pact on the territory of another state shall be by agreement of all the member states and only with the consent of the state on the territory of which, and on the demand of which, these troops are to be stationed.

The Soviet Government believes it is essential to make a declaration regarding the recent events in Hungary. Their development has shown that the workers of Hungary have, after achieving great progress on the basis of the people's democratic order, justifiably raised the questions of the need for eliminating the serious inadequacies of the economic system, of the need for further improving the material well-being of the people, and of the need for furthering the battle against bureaucratic excesses in the state apparatus. However, the forces of reaction and of counter-revolution have quickly joined in this just and progressive movement of the workers, with the aim of using the discontent of the workers to undermine the foundations of the people's democratic system in Hungary and to restore to power the landlords and the capitalists.

The Soviet Government and all the Soviet people deeply regret that these events in Hungary have led to bloodshed.

At the request of the People's Government of Hungary, the Soviet Government agreed to send Soviet military units into Budapest to help the Hungarian People's Army and the Hungarian Government to re-establish order in that city.

Being of the opinion that the continued presence of Soviet units in Hungary could be used as a pretext for further aggravating the situation, the Soviet Government has now given instructions to its military commanders to withdraw their troops from the city of Budapest as soon as the Hungarian Government feels that they can be dispensed with.

At the same time, the Soviet Government is prepared to engage in negotiations with the Hungarian People's Government and the other signatories of the Warsaw Pact regarding the question of the presence of Soviet troops elsewhere on the territory of Hungary.

The defence of socialist gains in the Hungarian People's Government is at the moment the primary and sacred task of the workers, the peasants, the intellectuals, and all the working people of Hungary.

The Soviet Government expresses its conviction that the people of the socialist countries will not allow reactionary forces, whether foreign or domestic, to undermine those foundations of the democratic People's Government which have been won and strengthened by the struggle and sacrifice and work of the people of this country. These people will, it believes, employ all their efforts to eliminate any obstacles in the way of strengthening the democratic foundations, the independence, and the sovereignty of their country. Such actions will, in turn, strengthen the socialist foundations of the economy and the culture of each country and will continue to increase the material well-being and the cultural level of all the workers. The Hungarian people will strengthen the brotherhood and the mutual cause of the socialist countries in order to consolidate the great and peaceful aims of socialism.

APPENDIX IV

The Revolution's Four Governments

Government constituted on 27 October:

President of the Council: Imre Nagy (Communist)

Deputy Presidents: Antal Apro (Communist), Jozsef Bognar (former member, Smallholders' Party), Ferenc Erdei (former member, National Peasant Party)

Minister of State Control: Never designated

Minister of State Farms: Miklos Ribianszky (former member, Smallholders' Party)

Minister of State: Zoltan Tildy (former member, Smallholders' Party; former President of the Republic)

Minister of Mining and Power: Sandor Czottner (Communist)

Minister of Ingathering: Antal Gyenes (Communist)

Minister of Internal Trade: Sandor Tausz (Communist)

Minister of Interior: Ferenc Munnich (Communist)

Minister of Health: Antal Babits (Univ. Prof., Communist)

Minister of Food: Rezso Nyers (former Soc. Dem. Party, Communist)

Minister of Construction: Antal Apro (Communist)

Minister of Agriculture: Bela Kovacs (former member, Smallholders' Party)

Minister of Defence: Karoly Janza (Communist)

Minister of Justice: Eric Molnar (Communist)

Minister of Metallurgy and Machine Industry: Janos Csergo (Communist)

Minister of Light Industry: Mrs Jozsef Nagy (Communist)

Minister of Communications and Post: Lajos Bebrits (Communist)

Foreign Minister: Imre Horvath (Communist)
Minister of Foreign Trade: Jozsef Bognar (former member, Smallholders' Party)
Minister of People's Culture: Gyorgy Lukacs (Univ. Prof., Communist)
Minister of Education: Albert Konya (Communist)
Minister of Finance: Istvan Kossa (Communist)
Minister of Urban and Rural Development: Ferenc Nezval (Communist)
Minister of Chemical Industry: Gergely Szabo (Communist)
Minister of Central Planning Board: Arpad Kiss (Communist)

Government constituted on 30 October:
Premier and Foreign Minister: Imre Nagy (Communist)
Ministers of State: Janos Kadar (Communist), Geza Losonczy (Communist), Bela Kovacs (Smallholder), Zoltan Tildy (Smallholder), Ferenc Erdei (Peasant Party)

Government constituted on 3 November:
Premier and Foreign Minister: Imre Nagy (Communist)
Ministers of State: Zoltan Tildy (Smallholder), Bela Kovacs (Smallholder), Istvan B. Szabo (Smallholder), Anna Kethly (Social Democrat), Gyula Keleman (Social Democrat), Jozsef Fischer (Social Democrat), Istvan Bibo (Petofi Peasant), Ferenc Farkhas (Petofi Peasant), Geza Losonczy (Communist) Janos Kadar (Communist)
Minister of Defence: Pal Maleter (Independent)

Government constituted on 4 November:
Premier: Janos Kadar (Communist)
Deputy Premier and Minister of Armed Forces and Public Security: Ferenc Munnich (Communist)
Minister of State: Gyorgy Marosan (Communist)
Minister of Finance: Istvan Kossa (Communist)
Foreign Minister: Imre Horvath (Communist)
Minister of Industry: Antal Apro (Communist)
Minister of Agriculture: Imre Dogei (Communist)
Minister of Commerce: Sandor Ronai (Communist)

APPENDIX V

Nagy's Note to Hammarskjöld on 1 November

Reliable reports have reached the Government of the Hungarian People's Republic that further Soviet units are entering into Hungary. [The Prime Minister] summoned M. Andropov, the Soviet Ambassador, and expressed his strongest protest against the entry of further Soviet troops into Hungary. He demanded the instant and immediate withdrawal of these Soviet forces.

He informed the Soviet Ambassador that the Hungarian Government immediately repudiates the Warsaw Treaty, and, at the same time, declares Hungary's neutrality, turns to the United Nations, and requests the help of the great powers in defending the country's neutrality.

Therefore I request Your Excellency promptly to put on the agenda of the forthcoming General Assembly of the United Nations the question of Hungary's neutrality and the defence of this neutrality by the four great powers. . . .

It was signed: 'Imre Nagy, President of the Council of Ministers of the Hungarian People's Republic, designated Minister of Foreign Affairs.'

APPENDIX VI

Inside the Yugoslav Embassy

In addition to Nagy, those who sought refuge in the Yugoslav embassy were: Geza Losonczy, Ferenc Donath, Gyorgy Tanczos (general secretary of the Petofi Circle), Sandor Haratzi (president of the Hungarian journalists' union and a former prisoner under Rakosi), Ferenc Janosi, Gyorgy Fazekas, journalist, Jozsef Szilagyi, Peter Erdos, journalist, Mme Rajk, General Ferenc Nador (commander of the Air Force), Szilard Ujhelyi (former Communist leader, and prisoner under Rakosi, president of the Cinema Office), Miklos Vasarhelyi, and members of their families totalling fifteen women and seventeen children. There were also three non-political personalities: the philosopher Gyorgy Lukacs, the former ambassador Zoltan Szanto, and Zoltan Vas (former fellow prisoner with Rakosi under Horthy, appointed by the insurrectionary government to take charge of food supplies). These three, together with Erdos and General Ferenc Nador, later left the embassy of their own accord.

APPENDIX VII

What Happened to Them

TAMAS ACZEL now lives in the United States.

LESLIE BAIN died of a heart attack in the early seventies.

LAZLO BEKE, his wife Eva, and their son now live in Canada.

VALERIA BENKE was re-instated after the revolution as Director of Radio Budapest.

ISTVAN BIBO was never arrested, but he was 'isolated' and finally given a small post as a librarian.

CAPTAIN LAJOS CSIBA, the man who warned Maleter, now lives in Switzerland.

JOAN FISH was transferred from Hungary to a post in the United States by the Foreign Office because she had been so deeply involved. There she met and married an American, and now lives in Tennessee.

SEYMOUR FREIDEN is at the time of writing the London correspondent of the Hearst Newspapers of America.

Leslie Fry, the British Minister, had a distinguished career as ambassador, is now Sir Leslie, and lives in retirement near Petworth, in Sussex.

Anna Gabor now lives in London.

Erno Gero, who fled to the Soviet Union, later returned to Hungary. When his wife died, Gero married her sister. Latest reports say that he is now totally blind.

Miklos Gimes was sentenced to death in the Nagy trial.

Peter Gosztony, who fought in the Kilian Barracks, now lives in Switzerland.

Gyula Hay stayed in Hungary, was arrested in February 1957, and jailed for six years.

Andras Hegedus, the Prime Minister under Gero, fled to the Soviet Union, but returned to Hungary in 1958, to become a sociologist.

Gyorgy Heltai is now a professor at the University of Charleston, South Carolina.

John Horvath, head of the Office of Church Affairs, who tried to move Cardinal Mindszenty, was intercepted when returning on orders to Budapest. He has never been seen or heard of since.

Marton Horvath, head of the editorial board of *Szabad Nep*, is now director of the Petofi Museum in Budapest.

Ferenc Janosi, Nagy's son-in-law, was jailed for eight years at the Nagy trial.

Sandor Kopacsi was jailed for life.

Geza Losonczy, who was kidnapped with Nagy after leaving the Yugoslav embassy, died in prison. After going on a hunger strike, guards attempted to force feed him through the throat and one of the pipes penetrated a lung.

Pal Maleter was executed with Nagy.

Tibor Meray and his wife, who escaped into Yugoslavia with Tamas Aczel, now live in Paris.

Mark Molnar, after escaping from Hungary, settled in London.

Miklos Molnar, senior editor of the *Literary Gazette*, now lives in Switzerland.

Gyula Obersovszky, editor of *Truth*, was sentenced to death, but the sentence was later commuted to life imprisonment.

MAJOR ANTAL PALINKAS, who rescued Cardinal Mindszenty, was executed.

LAZLO PIROS, Minister of the Interior, was granted asylum as a 'political refugee' in Russia.

JULIA RAJK, who was kidnapped with Nagy when leaving the Yugoslav embassy, was released at the end of 1958, and now lives in some poverty in Budapest.

MATYAS RAKOSI, tried to return to Hungary, but as soon as Kadar heard that he was telephoning his old political friends he was sent back to Russia. When he died his ashes were sent to Budapest, and an inconspicuous plaque, surrounded by hundreds of others, is his only memorial in a Budapest cemetery.

JOZSEF REVAI remained in Budapest after the revolution. He died in July 1959.

DORA SCARLETT now runs a clinic in southern India.

THOMAS SZABO escaped to the West, wrote his book in Paris, and is believed to have emigrated to the United States.

BELA SZASZ now lives in London.

ATTILA SZIGETTI was arrested after the revolution, and committed suicide in jail.

JOZSEF SZILAGYI, Nagy's personal secretary, was executed with Nagy.

ZOLTAN TILDY was jailed for six years at the Nagy trial and was granted amnesty in April 1959.

ZOLTAN VAS, who organised the food supplies at the end of the first week of the revolution, remained in Hungary, was kidnapped with Nagy but later freed, and is living as a pensioner in Budapest.

MIKLOS VASARHELYI, Nagy's Minister of Information, was jailed for five years.

ZOLTAN ZELK stayed in Hungary, was arrested in February 1957, but released from prison in September 1958.

Notes on Further Reading

Most of the books written about the Hungarian uprising fall into three categories: those written by eye-witnesses of the fighting at the barricades, who saw all the action but little of the reaction; those concerned with the political struggle; those explaining the root causes leading up to the revolution.

Many books in my bibliography are useful only for reference, but for general reading I would recommend several titles. Tibor Meray's *Thirteen Days that Shook the Kremlin* brilliantly describes the political struggle. As a close friend of Nagy's, Meray was privy to many secrets, and his book is filled with exciting and intimate detail. Meray later joined forces with Tamas Aczel to write *The Revolt of the Mind*, a brilliant analysis of the tortured consciences of Hungarian Communist writers.

The late Leslie Bain saw a great deal of the fighting, but he was also a political animal who knew many of the Hungarian leaders and his book *The Reluctant Satellites* is eminently readable. So is *The Hungarian Revolution* by David Pryce-Jones, which tells the story of the uprising day by day, together with excellent chapters on the causes and effects. I also found *Revolution in Hungary* by Paul Zinner invaluable. In it Professor Zinner has distilled much of the two-year research project on the uprising undertaken by Columbia University, and his book contains shrewd judgments of the extraordinary political decisions taken not only in Hungary, but in the Kremlin and in Washington.

Many Hungarian writers have written of the despair they encountered while rotting in Avo jails. Among the best of these is *Volunteers for the Gallows* by Bela Szasz, a distinguished scholar whose very moderation makes his personal story all the more horrifying. He takes one right into the torture chamber.

Bibliography

ACZEL, TAMAS, and MERAY, TIBOR. *The Revolt of the Mind.* London: Thames & Hudson, 1960.

———*Ten Years After.* London, MacGibbon & Kee, 1966.

ANDERSON, ANDY. *Hungary '56.* London: Solidarity Books, 1964.

APHEKER, H. *The Truth About Hungary.* New York: Mainstream Books, 1957.

ARENDT, HANNAH. *Die Ungarische Revolution und der totilare Imperialismus.* Munich: Piper Verlag, 1958.

BAIN, LESLIE. *The Reluctant Satellites.* New York: Macmillan, 1960.

BALINT, IMRE. *Hungaria no Muere.* Florida: Soc. Pablo, 1956.

BARATH, TIBOR. *La crie de la Hongrie.* Montreal: Le Monde Hongrois, 1957.

BARLAY, S., and SASDY. *Four Black Cars.* London: Putnam, 1958.

BEKE, LASZLO. *A Student's Diary, Budapest October 16—November 1.* London: Hutchinson, 1957.

BELOKEN, A., and TOLSTIKOV, V. *The Truth about Hungary; Facts and Eyewitness Accounts.* Moscow: Foreign Languages Publishing House, 1957.

Bibliography of the Hungarian Revolution. New York: Free Europe Press, 1957.

BONE, EDITH. *Seven Years Solitary.* London: Hamish Hamilton, 1957.

BURSTEN, MARTIN A. *Escape from Fear.* New York: Greenwood Press, 1973.

Captive Hungary, an Unsolved Problem of Soviet Aggression. New York: Hungarian Freedom Fighters Assn., 1960.

DELANY, R. F., *This is Communist Hungary.* Chicago: Regnery, 1958.

DEWAR, HUGO, and NORMAN, D. *Revolution and Counter Revolution in Hungary*. London: Socialist Union of Central Eastern Europe, 1957.

EDEN, SIR ANTHONY. *Full Circle*. London: Cassell, 1960.

EISENHOWER, DWIGHT D. *The White House Years*. 2 vols., limited ed. Vol. I, *Mandate for Change, 1953–1956*, Garden City: Doubleday, 1963. *Waging Peace, 1956–1961*. Garden City: Doubleday, 1965.

FEJTO, FRANÇOIS. *Behind the Rape of Hungary*. New York: David McKay, 1957.

FLORIS, GEORGE. *Hungary Behind the Headlines*. Calcutta: New Horizon, 1959.

FRYER, PETER. *The Hungarian Tragedy*. London: Dennis Dobson, 1956.

GOSTSZTONYI, PETER VON. *Die Ungarische Revolution von 1956*. Frankfurt: Bernard & Graefe Verlag, 1963.

HORVATH, GYORGY PALOCZI. *The Undefeated*. Boston: Little, Brown, 1959.

IGNOTUS, PAL. *Political Prisoner*. London: Kegan Paul, 1959.

———*Hungary*. New York: Frederick A. Praeger, 1972.

JUHASZ, DR. WILLIAM, and ROTHBERG, ABRAHAM. *Flashes in the Night*. New York: Random House, 1957.

JUHASZ, DR. WILLIAM. *Hungarian Social Science Reader 1954–63*. New York: Columbia University Press, 1965.

KADAR, JANOS. *The Hungarian White Book*. 5 vols. Budapest: Hungarian Government Press, 1957.

KECSKEMETI, PAUL. *The Unexpected Revolution: Social Forces in the Hungarian Uprising*. Stanford: Stanford University Press, 1961.

KIRKPATRICK, E. M. *Years of Crisis, Communist Propaganda Activities in 1956*. New York: Macmillan, 1957.

KOVACS, IMRE. *Facts about Hungary*. New York: Hungarian Committee, 1959.

KOVACS, IMRE, ed. *The Fight for Freedom*. New York: Hungarian Committee, 1966.

KOVAGO, JOZSEF. *You Are All Alone*. New York: Frederick A. Praeger, 1959.

KOVRIG, B. *National Communism in Hungary*. Milwaukee: Marquette University Press, 1958.

————*The Rebellion of '56, A Phase of Hungary's 20th Century Revolution.* Milwaukee: Marquette University Press, 1963.

LASKY, MELVIN J., ed. *The Hungarian Revolution: A White Book.* New York: Praeger, 1957. Facsimile ed. (Select Bibliographies Reprint Series.) Freeport, N.Y.: Books for Libraries, 1970.

LETTIS, R., and MORRIS, W. E. *The Hungarian Revolt.* New York: Scribner, 1961.

MERAY, TIBOR. *Thirteen Days that Shook the Kremlin.* New York: Frederick A. Praeger, 1959.

MICHENER, JAMES A. *The Bridge at Andau.* New York: Fawcett World Library, 1972.

MIKES, GEORGE. *The Hungarian Revolution.* London: André Deutsch, 1957.

————*A Study in Infamy.* London: André Deutsch, 1957.

MINDSZENTY, CARDINAL JOZSEF. *The World's Most Orphaned Nation.* New York: Book Milere, Inc., 1962.

MOLNAR, MIKLOS. *Budapest 1956: A History of the Hungarian Revolution.* New York: Crane Russak, 1971.

MURPHY, ROBERT. *Diplomat Among Warriors.* New York: Doubleday, 1964.

NAGY, B. *Journal d'un insurge hongrois.* Paris: Edition de la Pensée Moderne, 1956.

NAGY, FERENC. *The Struggle Behind the Iron Curtain.* New York: Macmillan, 1948.

NAGY, IMRE. *On Communism.* London: Thames and Hudson, 1957.

NEMES, JOSEPH. *Signs in the Storm.* London: Hodder and Stoughton, 1956.

PALOCZI-HORVATH, GEORGE. *The Undefeated.* London: Secker and Warburg, 1959.

PFEIFFER, E. *Child of Communism.* London: Weidenfeld and Nicolson, 1958.

PRYCE-JONES, DAVID. *The Hungarian Revolution.* London: Ernest Benn, 1969.

ROMAN, ERIC. *The Best Shall Die.* Englewood Cliffs, N.J., Prentice Hall, 1961.

SANDERSON, JAMES DEAN. *The Boy with a Gun.* New York: Henry Holt, 1958.

SCARLETT, DORA. *Window onto Hungary.* Bradford: Broadacre Books, 1958.

SCHRAMM, W. L. *One Day in the World's Press.* Stanford: Stanford University Press, 1959.

SCHUSTER, G. N. *In Silence I Speak.* New York: Farrar, Straus and Cudahy, 1956.

SEBESTYN, GYORGY. *The Doors Are Closing.* London: Angus and Robertson, 1956.

SETON-WATSON, HUGH. *The East European Revolution.* New York: Frederick A. Pі ϲ ꬲger, 1956.

SINOR, DENNIS. *History of Hungary.* London: Allen and Unwin, 1959.

STIL, ANDRÉ. *Je reviens de Budapest.* Paris: Maison des Metallurgistes, 1959.

STILLMAN, EDMUND. *Bitter Harvest.* New York: Frederick A. Praeger, 1959.

SURVEY, eds. *Hungary Today.* New York: Frederick A. Praeger, 1962.

SZABO, TAMAS. *Boy on the Rooftop.* David Hughes, trans. Gloucester, Mass.: Peter Smith.

SZASZ, BELA. *Volunteers for the Gallows.* New York: W. W. Norton, 1972.

SZTARAY, ZOLTAN. *Books on the Hungarian Revolution.* Brussels: Imre Nagy Institute for Political Research, 1960.

URBAN, GEORGE. *The Nineteen Days.* London: Heinemann, 1957.

URQUHART, MACGREGOR. *Hungary Fights.* London: Digit Books, 1957.

VALI, FERENC A. *Rift and Revolt in Hungary.* Cambridge: Harvard University Press, 1961.

VENN, MARY ELEANOR. *Refugee Hero: A Hungarian Boy in America.* New York: Hastings House, 1951.

VOLKES, EDWIN ARNET. *Aufstand de Freiheit: Documente zur Erhebung des ungarischen.* Zurich: Artemis Verlag, 1957.

WAGNER, FRANCIS S., ed. *The Hungarian Revolution in Perspective.* Elmsford, N.Y.: British Book Centre, 1967.

ZINNER, PAUL E. *Revolution in Hungary.* New York: Columbia University Press, 1957. Facsimile ed. (Select Bibliographies Reprint Series.) Freeport, N.Y.: Books for Libraries, 1972.

ZINNER, PAUL E., ed. *National Communism and Popular Revolt in Eastern Europe; A Selection of Documents on Events in Poland and Hungary, February–November 1956.* New York: Columbia University Press, 1956.

ZINNER, PAUL E. *Revolution in Hungary: Reflections on the Vicissitudes of a Totalitarian System.* New York: Journal of Politics, 1959.

Documents

FRYER, PETER. "Hungary and the Communist Party." London: privately published, 1957.

GALAY, N. "Lessons of the Hungarian Uprising." Munich: *Bulletin for the Study of the USSR,* Vol. IV, No. 2, February 1957.

GLEITMAN, HENRY. "Youth in Revolt." New York: Free Europe Press, 1957.

JUHASZ, WILLIAM. "The Hungarian Revolution: The People's Demands." New York: Free Europe Press, 1957.

KALLAI, GYULA. "The Hungarian Revolution in the Light of Marxism-Leninism." Budapest: Kossuth, 1957.

KOVAGO, JOZSEF. "Have They Died in Vain?" London: privately published, 1956.

KUZNETSOV, V. V. "Documents on Hungary." London: *Soviet News,* 1956.

LENNOV, V. "The Events in Hungary." New York: Foreign Languages Publishing House, 1957.

MIKLOS, SZABO. "Je rentre dans mon pays. Mémoires d'un émigré désabusé." Budapest: Kossuth, 1957.

NADANYI, P. "The Revolt that Rocked the Kremlin." Washington: Hungarian Reform Federation of America, 1963.

Documents not attributed to authors

"Aftermath of the Hungarian Revolution." *World Today Magazine,* November 1957.

"Anatomy of Revolution." Washington: Public Affairs Press, 1957.

"The Case for Hungary." Editorials in *Globe and Mail,* Toronto, October–December 1956.

"Ce qu'l faut savoir sur la Hongrie." Budapest: *Revue Hongroise*, 1958.

"Contribution de la révolution à la pensée socialiste." Brussels: Institut Imre Nagy de Sciences Politiques, 1960.

"Criminal Justice in Hungary after the Revolt." New York: Hungarian Freedom Fighters Federation, 1959.

"Current Problems of the Dictatorship of the Proletariat in Hungary." Budapest: Kossuth, 1957.

"Documents on Hungary; Speeches at UNO." London: *Soviet News*, 1956.

"Emergency Relief for Hungarians in Austria, U.S. Treaties." Washington: Government Printing Office, 1957.

"The Exodus from Hungary." New York: *United Nations Review*, 1957.

"Facts on Hungary." London: Communist Party of Great Britain, 1956.

"Far Eastern Reaction to Hungarian and Polish Upheavals." Washington: U.S. Information Agency, 1956.

"Four Days of Freedom, the Uprising in Hungary and the Free Unions of the World." Brussels: International Confederation of Free Trade Unions, 1957.

"Hongrie après la drame." Paris: Democratic Nouvelle, 1957.

"How Russian Treachery Throttled Revolt." *Life* Magazine, February 18, 1957.

"Hungarian Listeners to Western Broadcasts." Munich: Radio Free Europe Audience Analysis Section, October 1957.

"Hungarian Refugee Students and United States Colleges and Universities, a progress report." New York, 1957.

"The Hungarian Revolution and Struggle for Freedom as Reflected in Domestic Radio Broadcasts October 23–November 9, 1956." New York: Free Europe Press, 1956.

"The Hungarian Revolution of October 1956." New York: Columbia University Men's Faculty Club, 1958.

"The Hungarian Revolution." London: *World Today*, Royal Institute for International Affairs, January 1957.

"The Hungarian Situation and the Rule of Law." The Hague: International Commission of Jurists, April 1957, plus supplement June 1957.

"Hungarian Workers' Revolution." London: *Direct Action*, 1958.

"Hungaricus." A secret pamphlet circulated in Hungary, December 1956, and reissued by the Imre Nagy Institute for Political Research, Brussels, 1959.

"Hungary under Soviet Rule." New York: American Friends of Captive Nations, 1957.

"Hungary and the 1956 Uprising." New York: International Research Associates, 1957.

"Hungary and the World." Speeches commemorating the third anniversary of the revolution. London: Hungarian Writers' Association Abroad, 1958.

"Hungary's Fight for Freedom." New York: *Life* Magazine, special issue, 1956.

"The Ideology of Revolution: The People's Demands in Hungary, October–November, 1956." New York: Free Europe Press, 1957.

"International Communism: Revolt in the Satellites." Washington: U.S. Congress, 1957.

"Jeunesse d'octobre. Témoins et combattants de la révolution Hongroise." Paris: La Table Ronde, 1957.

"The Murder of an Idea. The Execution of Imre Nagy." New York: Intercontinental Press Service, 1958.

"Report on Hungary." Brussels: International Confederation of Free Trade Unions, 1957.

Reports of the Special Committee on the Problem of Hungary. New York: United Nations, 1957.

"Revolt in Hungary: a documentary chronology of events." New York: Free Europe Press, 1956.

"Revolt in Hungary: internal broadcasts October 23–November 4." New York: Free Europe Committee, 1956.

"Revolt in Hungary." New York: Free Europe Committee, 1957

"La Révolte de la Hongrie." Paris: special issues of *Les Temps Modernes,* 1956–7.

"Le Révolte du peuple hongrois," issued by L'aide Suisse aux victimes du communisme. Lausanne, 1957.

"Revolution for the Privilege to Tell the Truth." Manila: *Comment,* 1958.

"Role of the Hungarian People's Army in the Revolution." New York: Free Europe Press, 1956.

"The Story behind Hungary's Revolt." *Life* Magazine, February 18, 1957.

"The Truth about Hungary: Facts and Eyewitness Accounts." Ottawa: Press Office, USSR Embassy, 1957.

"The Truth about the Nagy Affair." Published for the Congress for Cultural Freedom, London, 1958.

U.S. President's Committee for Hungarian Refugee Relief: Report to the President. Washington: Government Printing Office, 1957.

"Verettes sur la Hongrie." Paris: French Communist Party, 1956.

"What Really Happened in Hungary." London: Davidson, 1957.

"Why? The History of a Mass Revolt in Search of Freedom." Vienna: International Union of Socialist Youth, 1957.

Index